ENCHANTED PLACES

Recent Title in
Contributions to the Study of American Literature

The Short Fiction of Kurt Vonnegut
Peter J. Reed

ENCHANTED PLACES

The Use of Setting in
F. Scott Fitzgerald's Fiction

AIPING ZHANG

Contributions to the Study of American Literature,
Number 2

GREENWOOD PRESS
Westport, Connecticut • London

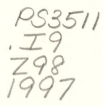

PS3511
.I9
Z98
1997

Library of Congress Cataloging-in-Publication Data

Zhang, Aiping, 1955–
    Enchanted places : the use of setting in F. Scott Fitzgerald's
fiction / Aiping Zhang.
        p.   cm.—(Contributions to the study of American literature,
    ISSN 1092–6356 ; no. 2)
    Includes bibliographical references and index.
    ISBN 0–313–30238–3 (alk. paper)
    1. Fitzgerald, F. Scott (Francis Scott), 1896–1940—Settings.
    2. Setting (Literature) I. Title. II. Series.
    PS3511.I9Z98   1997
    813′.52—dc21   97–9379

British Library Cataloguing in Publication Data is available.

Library of Congress Catalog Card Number: 97–9379
ISBN: 0–313–30238–3
ISSN: 1092–6356

First published in 1997

Greenwood Press, 88 Post Road West, Westport, CT 06881
An imprint of Greenwood Publishing Group, Inc.

Printed in the United States of America

The paper used in this book complies with the
Permanent Paper Standard issued by the National
Information Standards Organization (Z39.48–1984).

10 9 8 7 6 5 4 3 2 1

Copyright Acknowledgments

The author and publisher gratefully acknowledge permission to reprint from the following sources:

Excerpts reprinted with permission of Scribner, a Division of Simon & Schuster and Harold Ober Associates, Inc., *The Beautiful and Damned* by F. Scott Fitzgerald. Copyright 1922 Charles Scribner's Sons. Copyright renewed 1950 by Frances Scott Fitzgerald Lanahan.

Excerpts reprinted with permission of Scribner, a Division of Simon & Schuster and Harold Ober Associates, Inc., from *The Great Gatsby* by F. Scott Fitzgerald. Copyright 1925 Charles Scribner's Sons. Copyright renewed 1953 by Frances Scott Fitzgerald Lanahan.

Excerpts reprinted with permission of Scribner, a Division of Simon & Schuster and Harold Ober Associates Inc., from *The Short Stories of F. Scott Fitzgerald*, edited by Matthew J. Bruccoli. Copyright 1922 by Metropolitan Publications, Inc. Copyright 1925, 1926 by Consolidated Magazines Corp. Copyright 1930, 1931 by The Curtis Publishing Company. Copyrights renewed 1950, 1953, 1954, 1958, 1959 by Frances Scott Fitzgerald Lanahan.

Brief scattered quotes and excerpts are also used with permission:

This Side of Paradise by F. Scott Fitzgerald (New York: Charles Scribner's Sons, 1920).

Tender Is the Night by F. Scott Fitzgerald (New York: Charles Scribner's Sons, 1933).

Taps at Reveille by F. Scott Fitzgerald (New York: Charles Scribner's Sons, 1935).

The Pat Hobby Stories and *The Vegetable* by F. Scott Fitzgerald (New York: Charles Scribner's Sons, 1923).

The Last Tycoon by F. Scott Fitzgerald (New York: Charles Scribner's Sons, 1941).

Afternoon of an Author by F. Scott Fitzgerald. Intro. and Notes by Arthur Mizener (New York: Charles Scribner's Sons, 1957).

The Letters of F. Scott Fitzgerald, edited by Andrew Turnbull (New York: Charles Scribner's Sons, 1963).

Excerpts from *The Crack-Up* by F. Scott Fitzgerald, copyright 1945 by New Directions Publishing Corp. Reprinted by permission of New Directions. *The Crack-Up* by F. Scott Fitzgerald, edited by Edmund Wilson (New Directions, 1956).

For

Sally, Jimmy, and Melanie

CONTENTS

Acknowledgments   xi

Abbreviations Used in the Text   xiii

1. Introduction   1

2. Home: A Showcase of Human Experience   15

3. Bars: Windows of Society   49

4. Schools: Cradles of the Elite   79

5. City: A Land of Glamour and Despair   111

6. Hollywood: A World of Art, Business, and Rivalry   147

Selected Bibliography   173

Index   183

ACKNOWLEDGMENTS

Many, many people helped in various ways with this project. My professors and friends at the English Department of Harvard University have been unstinting in their kindness and assistance to me over the years. My deepest debt of gratitude goes to Philip Fisher and Sacvan Bercovitch, who have virtually taught me how to read, interpret, and teach American literature and have inspired me to study this subject. Without their great and indefatigable guidance, assistance, and encouragement, this project would not be possible. I also thank Warner Berthoff, Robert Kiely, and Alan Heimert, who have read and commented on part of my early draft. I benefited tremendously from their wisdom and advice.

I wish to thank the following institutions for their assistance in researching and writing the book. The Widener Library, Harvard University, offered me all the materials and assistance I requested during the early stage of my project. The Firestone Library, Princeton University, graciously showed me some of their Fitzgerald collections and answered my inquiries. The Inter-Library Loan Office of the Meriam Library, California State University, Chico, literally put all the best libraries within my reach.

I have been very fortunate to work with Nina Pearlstein and Liz Leiba, whose great patience and professional guidance made my work much easier. I thank them and others at Greenwood Press who assisted in making the publication of the book possible.

Special thanks is also given to my friends and colleagues, Ernst Scheon-Rene, Robert Burton, and Roger Kaye, who helped me improve my writing greatly with their insights and suggestions, thereby preventing me from embarrassing myself completely.

Finally, my greatest gratitude goes to my wife, Sally, whose support, understanding, and advice encouraged me through all difficulties.

ABBREVIATIONS
USED IN THE TEXT

The following abbreviations are used to indicate the source of each quote from the original texts:

AA	*Afternoon of an Author*
BD	*The Beautiful and Damned*
CU	*The Crack-Up*
GG	*The Great Gatsby*
TSP	*This Side of Paradise*
TAR	*Taps at Reveille*
TIN	*Tender Is the Night*
LT	*The Last Tycoon*
V	*The Vegetable*
PHS	*The Pat Hobby Stories*

1

INTRODUCTION

As a traditional form in literature, the presentation of setting is as old as literature itself. The use of setting is not only a crucial contributing part of a story's success but also a primary indicator of its author's artistry. Back in 1973, Alexander Gelley claimed in his article "Setting and a Sense of World in the Novel" that setting is "a relatively neglected aspect of the aesthetics of the novel."[1] Twenty-three years later, Gelley's remark may still be applicable. And it seems more so in the study of F. Scott Fitzgerald's fiction. The contention of this book, therefore, is to fill up such a void by presenting a close study of the use of domestic and urban settings in Fitzgerald's fiction.

The use of setting represents an extraordinary achievement in Fitzgerald's fiction-writing career. Through his powerful visions and descriptive skills, settings in his fiction are always featured as what I would call "enchanted places," charming but elusive, heavily weighted with symbolic connotations. They help him dramatize his perspectives of life. His novels and scores of his short stories may start as a romance of love or a fantasy of extravagant glamour set in various places, but as we read them through carefully, we soon discover a parabolic quality in them. Each scene seems like a parable, functioning as suggestively as a microcosm of the whole American society. I use the term "parable" in the sense that reading Fitzgerald's fiction is often like reading a parable, in which setting is no longer just a locale, or a site for a story's action, but a sophisticated device and an integral part of the story designed to convey a unique vision of life in a profound way. Such a parabolic quality gives Fitzgerald's fiction enormous possibilities of temporal span and multiple situations, as well as a microcosmic capacity for containing the complexities of reality, creating and reinforcing the strongest possible impression upon them and giving his fiction the power of a symbolic and penetrating display.

Very few writers showed as much explicit concern for the connection between the inner world of the characters and the domestic and social world in which the characters live as Fitzgerald did. Fitzgerald believed that setting could be used as a rich source of imagery to objectify the social trend and individual desire at a certain time and to turn a story into a parable. In other words, what he does in his fiction is to structure his work as a series of dramatic scenes that function as an exteriorization of world within. Each scene is marked, at every critical point of the whole creative process, by the popular qualities of parables and charged with meaning by a style that is, despite the sharpness of its realistic detail, alive with poetic force. Specifically, with the aid of a well-structured central setting, such as a house or a city, Fitzgerald is able to inscribe a highly concentrated, at times ironically parabolic and forcefully microcosmic, narrative into the very place where his story takes place, to challenge his reader's wayward assumption and generalization, and to shield himself from the public's dispute and potential attacks that would have resulted from its displeasure with the nonpleasing, even cynical, tone in his narrative. This parabolic strategy, when it works, offers Fitzgerald two advantages: It provides the more observant reader of his story the means to a deeper and broader understanding, and it instills a greater subtlety into the composition of his story. However, one thing that has made Fitzgerald's parabolic settings all the more remarkable and interesting is that one can hardly tell to what degree they are deliberately contrived. They are not awkward or overstretched; at least they do not appear so. Nevertheless they are, to borrow Mikhail Bakhtin's words, "far more remote from abstract symbolism and schematism."[2] Central to Fitzgerald's use of settings is a dramatic representation of the real world, a representation that takes on the verisimilitude of his personal experience and consciousness. In many ways, the parabolic imagery resembles the same kind of richness Bakhtin discovered in Rabelais's work: "Beyond the images that may appear fantastic we find real events, living persons, and the author's own rich experience and sharp observation."[3] Fitzgerald's constant and creative attempt at transforming his fiction from a parable-like story into a microcosmic reflection of his world clearly indicated his equal emphasis on the truthfulness of vision and the effectiveness of artistry.

Fitzgerald's novels and stories, as Malcolm Cowley has observed, "are in some ways the best record of the 1920s and 1930s."[4] The publication of his first novel, *This Side of Paradise*, almost instantly turned Fitzgerald into the "Laureate of the Jazz Age"[5] and "a kind of king of our American youth."[6] His name has been inseparable from the 1920s and 1930s. From the very beginning of his career, he showed a keen awareness of the qualities of the time in which he lived and the places he went and the people he met, the kind of awareness that understands people and events, not in abstract but in concrete terms. Virtually all his novels and stories are carefully grounded in a particular time and place, full of substance, more thoroughly American than any fiction written by his contemporaries. There is no doubt that as Benjamin Spencer has suggested, Fitzgerald's novels and stories "bear an American stamp to a unique degree. In choice of characterization and scene, in temper and theme, and even in the recklessness of his own literary career, he reflects comprehensively his national origin."[7] As a voice and exemplar of the postwar generation, Fitzgerald used his pen to evoke the rhythms of the Jazz Age and the Depression, to capture the public mind, and to convey its fantasies and frustrations. Most, if not all, of his novels and stories attempt to celebrate the spirit of his time and to draw a picture of America. Two years before *This Side of Paradise* was accepted for publication, Fitzgerald wrote a letter to Edmund Wilson, saying, "I really believe that no one else could have written so searchingly the story of the youth of our generation."[8] It is true, as Gertrude Stein suggests in *The Autobiography of Alice B. Toklas,* that Fitzgerald has "really created for the public the new generation."[9] Few people would dispute that Fitzgerald not only invented the Jazz Age in America but also lived it and depicted it. Not surprisingly, one of the obituaries ran shortly after his death with such a line on its head, "Lost Generation Loses Its Prophet."

The important question to ask of Fitzgerald's fiction is how its parabolic representation of a character's inner world and his experience in life turns into a microcosmic perception of the great world of America, not so much in its superficial aspects as in its pitch and beat. The answer is simple. It is Fitzgerald's commitment to combining a concern for artistic form with a social vision that has made it possible. As a writer who always worked consciously toward the perfection of his artistry, Fitzgerald has received high praises for his novelistic techniques, for his observer-narrator, composite characterization, psychosymbolic landscapes, striking imagery, delicate modulations of mood, temporal juxtaposition, archetypal figures, and clear diction; yet it is his masterful exploitation of setting that ultimately enabled Fitzgerald to score thematic richness, amplitude of meaning, and the aesthetic triumph that mark his work.

To understand how Fitzgerald constantly explores the potential of setting for innovation, and how he successfully re-creates and reinvents a form that helps him to present his visions with accuracy and intensity, it is essential to redefine, briefly, the function of setting in fiction. The function of setting differs in different contexts. Setting in fiction can be defined as a place presented by fixed descriptions, or by indirect references in the narrative or in the speeches of characters, a place that serves as the site (a given locale), as the necessary showplace for a sequence of actions or for an evolving pattern of human relations. To a great novelist, setting is not merely a place, or a locale for action; it accounts for the formal perfection and the novelty of fiction. Stephen Gray suggests, "It assumes great importance"; it "percolate[s] through a work, conditioning plot, characters, actions, etc."; and "it affects every other element in fiction."[10] Clearly, one major task for a novelist, even before he creates a character or a plot, is to establish a place, or a series of places, as setting, a seemingly self-contained world in which characters react over a long period of time and plot develops. The chosen setting does not have to body forth the places and individuals in all their concrete particularity; rather, the settings reveal a certain social vision, proportion, and understanding. In other words, it is crucial for the novelist to reveal his setting not merely as a physical entity but as a set of social and/or moral indices of a specific kind. More than simply a locale, even in realistic novels and stories, setting must have dimensions and depth; there must be open spaces and hidden places, and more importantly, as Lennard J. Davis has argued, "there must be a thickness and interiority to the mental constructions that constitute the novel's space."[11] Sometimes even though a novel or a story is set in an actual locale, the descriptions may well be rendered romantically or imaginatively. The writer selects, for his own purpose, visual details that enable the reader to construct the physical environment and figure out its potentialities as a charged figure in a given novel. Despite its common enough definition, therefore, a setting may operate in ways far more complex than we would think: A single image in a setting may serve as a symbol; an entire setting may also operate symbolically, or even several settings may work together to reinforce a major theme of a novel. Besides, as settings recur in different contexts, they acquire a meaning beyond themselves, a ménage that deepens with each repetition, a meaning frequently more important than the literal one; settings may combine to show a consistent concern and endeavor of a novelist and allow him to present a message with greater subtlety and greater impact.

In its simplest form, setting operates as a background against which the action of a narrative takes place. But a sense of place, and what it implies, is central to a novel. In the tradition of fictional writing, it is easy to find many of the earliest works of fiction, especially the picaresque tales of the early eighteenth century, tales such as Daniel Defoe's *Robinson Crusoe* and *Moll Flanders,* using settings like landscapes, houses, gardens, and even interiors to create an occasion and situate a character in both a physical and symbolic way. These settings, by the nature of their physical structure, denote time and suggest a mood, such as terror, gaiety, or serenity; and it is this suggestion that intensifies the atmosphere for a particular thematic purpose.

Since the nineteenth century, novelists on both sides of the Atlantic have become more and more preoccupied with setting as a means of effective artistic expression. Novelists such as Sir Walter Scott, Charlotte Brontë, Charles Dickens, Nathaniel Hawthorne, Herman Melville, H. G. Wells, Mark Twain, James Joyce, and F. Scott Fitzgerald found that setting could function in ways other than merely to evoke atmosphere. They set their novels in actual locales but artistically rendered their descriptions in imaginative or romantic ways. If we read *The Great Gatsby* carefully, we can see a telling example of how a setting can make an essential contribution to the work's mood, and we will hardly miss the point that as a crucial factor in the creation of atmosphere, a given scene plays a major part in raising, developing, sustaining, and repeating emotions in fiction. Calling a sense of place "the whole foundation" on which her fiction rests, Eudora Welty stresses the connection between the place in fiction and the emotion it evokes: "Place in fiction is the named, identified, concrete, exact, and exacting, and therefore credible, gathering spot of all that has been felt, is about to be experienced, in the novel's progress. Location pertains to feeling, feeling profoundly pertains to place; place in history partakes of feeling, as feeling about history partakes of place."[12]

We know that literature is the product of perception, for it is both a source of new insights and a testing ground for hypothesis. Setting, then, is visionary. It is the space that the novelist creates for himself to see things better. With all the details necessary to contribute a trope of vision, setting comes to designate perspective. In this sense, setting can be exploited for differentiated imaginative purposes. As a stance or a set of values, the metaphysical power of setting seems to be a primary advantage that would enable the novelist to be in the right place, to see particular things in a particular way, totally free from various constraints that usually govern these things and our vision of them, and more importantly, to reflect whatever the novelist *thinks* about the things he sees. And what he "thinks" is what Bakhtin defined as "a confirmed and full-valued authorial idea," and this idea "as a principle of representation becomes one with the form. It determines all the formal accents and all the ideological assessments which constitute the formal unity of artistic style and the unified tone of the work."[13] As a matter of fact, in novels written by the above-mentioned novelists, *The Great Gatsby* in particular, theme and setting, a major "formal accent," are inextricably interwoven. We could not imagine *The Great Gatsby* set in any other time but the 1920s, with its social context of wealth, power, movement, and exclusion.

As a site of action, setting serves as a mirror, a reflection of character. It does not imply paragraphs of flat description or assertion about the place where characters appear. A superbly structured and depicted setting always appears to be impregnated with the feelings and experiences of the novel's representative hero, who is in search of himself and the world. There are two age-old methods of revealing character through setting. The first is to use some specific, sometimes even shifting, features of the setting to underline the hero's mood and personality, as well as his cultural and moral background; the second and more effective method is the character's constant confrontation with the setting in the novel, namely, the places in the world, whether they are the allegorical places of romance, the geographical places in real life, or the places filtered through the tangled consciousness of the modern hero, as in Joyce's *Ulysses*. In his essay "Character," Ralph Waldo Emerson speaks of the central man, who takes the world "as a material basis for his character, and a theater for action."[14] What Emerson stresses is the importance of nature, that is, the place and the world, in one's life. In a similar sense, Wallace Stevens once remarked, "Life is an affair of people, not places. But for me life is an affair of places and that is the trouble."[15] Obviously, Stevens is quite aware of the intricate relationship between man's life and his living environment, be it a city or a house. Just like Emerson's central man, however, the hero of a novel will often set out on a long journey of discovery, wandering from one place to another. The places he journeyed through would become symbolic markers of his personal growth and the universal human experience. As Catherine A. Middleton insists, "a person who is 'rooted in some spot of a native land' is rooted not only in a geographical landscape, but also in a social landscape (in a community), in an emotional landscape (in a family or in intimate relationships with a few individuals) and in an intellectual landscape (in the knowledge and ideas which he has acquired). An individual is also located in a temporal landscape; his life in a particular place has been lived at a particular time."[16] The impact of setting (places in the novel) on man's life (the hero's) is incontestable and, therefore, inescapable. In many great novels, setting is so fully realized that it dominates the whole novel. The prairie in James Fenimore Cooper's *Leatherstocking Tales*, America in John Dos Passos's *U.S.A,* Dublin in James Joyce's *Ulysses*, Yoknapatawpha County in William Faulkner's fiction, and Hollywood in Fitzgerald's *The Last Tycoon* convey more than just the locations of the events; they have long been recognized as "real" characters within the novels.

Setting also contributes to the aesthetic aspect of fiction. The juxtaposition of settings within a single work supplies structural coherence and creates a unified wholeness. This is a major defining trait of Fitzgerald's *The Great Gatsby* and *The Beautiful and Damned*. He shares with the best the use of setting to enforce theme, to unite structure, and to give verisimilitude. Through the evocation of setting and the character's perception of the setting, rather than the author's own assertion, Fitzgerald orients the reader to a narrative so as to make the reader hear, feel, and before all, see as the action is gradually unfolded.

What is so unique about Fitzgerald's portrayal of place, from domestic scenes to urban locations, then? To answer this question, a brief comparison between the strategies adopted by Fitzgerald and his predecessors might be necessary. In the nineteenth century, the trend was to delineate the locale in minute details, thus adding a social and scientific aspect to it. In *The Political Unconscious,* Frederic Jameson cites a good example for us from Balzac's novels. "The Balzacian dwelling," he says, "invites the awakening of a longing for possession, of the mild and warming fantasy of landed property as the tangible figure of a Utopian wish-fulfillment."[17] The crucial point to be made here is that the description in Balzac's novel is associated not simply with the object but with the social system's interest in objects. Many writers, including Scott, Dickens, and Joseph Conrad, either set their novels in urban and domestic scenes or extended their description to objects and places that had seldom, if ever, been regarded as serious constituents of setting. As to the twentieth century, the most important change in the exploitation of setting is the departure from the naturalistic extreme of the nineteenth century. Writers now introduce a greater variety of locales and objects as settings, cultivating the indirect presentation of settings through dialogue and the consciousness of characters and charging settings with multiple, but subtle, meanings through the interplay between settings and characters.

The use of setting in American literature has been marked by freshness and innovativeness because of our country's unique historical and geographical characteristics. Of course, writers in America learned from and matured on the diverse and rich lessons left by their European predecessors. As an unspoiled New World, a new paradise on the earth, the landscape of America is endowed with a unique symbolic significance. Writers in America closely associated the places they portrayed with the hopes and dreams for which they were anxiously searching. For example, the wild West, the free natural world of the frontier as defined by Henry N. Smith in his book *Virgin Land,* represents the ideal of freedom and the possibility of transcendence, but "this vast free space" also turns into a kind of "test site" for anyone who wants to cross the frontier in an attempt to fulfill his dreams. In a lecture called "The Young American," Emerson said that he saw "the nervous, rocky West . . . as a commanding and increasing power on the citizen," a decisive factor in the formation of American character.

On the most basic level, as many critics have already noted, the West is as essential for Cooper's Natty Bumppo as the forest is for Hawthorne's Hester Prynne, the sea for Melville's Ishmael, and the big River for Twain's Huck Finn. For Hester, who is torn between Puritan rigidity and her own thirst for love and freedom, the forest seems to be the only place where she can taste the flavor of freedom and happiness. For Ishmael, who is utterly bored by his dull life and sees no worldly prospects on shore, the sea opens up a new and vast world,, full of excitement and promises. It is interesting to recall that Charles Olson once began his book on Melville with such a declaration: "I take SPACE to be the central fact to man born in America."[18] For Huck, who is too young and too rebellious to endure the abuse of his drunkard father and the restrictions of society, the Mississippi River symbolizes a spacious world, a long adventurous path leading him to freedom and maturity.

By the time Fitzgerald's writing career took off, the use of setting had already shifted away from stereotypes established in the past. Natural landscape, which used to dominate the exploitation of setting in fiction all the time, gradually gave way to urban locales and domestic interiors. Motivated by curiosity about and enthusiasm for practical industrial processes, social structures, and new patterns of urban life, writers in America found a purely modern environment for their characters. Among them, Fitzgerald is arguably the most versatile modern landscapist. Of all the locales in his fiction and stories, the majority come from the urban and domestic categories. Furthermore, it is difficult, if not impossible, to find someone who can rival him in depicting almost every kind of setting, especially house, bar, school, city, and even Hollywood, a spectacular place in modern American life, or surpass him in exploring these settings for thematic purposes without compromising a high degree of aesthetic finesse.

Fitzgerald's brilliant use of setting belongs to a tradition in the most favorable sense: It is not obviously derivative. In fact, it is highly original, yet it does reflect a deep interest in the work of some of his European and American predecessors. This is not something surprising at all because, as T. S. Eliot pointed out in his famous comment on this issue, "No poet, no artist of any art, had his complete meaning alone. His significance, his appreciation is the appreciation of relation to the dead poets and artists. You can not value him alone; you must set him, for contrast and comparison, among the dead. I mean this as a principle of aesthetic, not merely historical, criticism."[19] As we shall see later on, Fitzgerald worked conscientiously and thoroughly with different physical backgrounds with which he was familiar, but in his attitude to the art of fiction, his approach to his themes and his patterns of using settings, he is remarkably tied to his predecessors. There is plenty of evidence to show that in one way or another, writers like H. G. Wells, Compton Mackenzie, and Booth Tarkington affected Fitzgerald's early work and that later Henry James, Henry Adams, Edith Wharton, James Joyce, T. S. Eliot, and, most importantly, Joseph Conrad figured prominently in the evolution of Fitzgerald's concept of fiction writing. His awareness of, his keen interest in, and his admiration for these writers have been observed by his various biographers and proved by references in his letters. He even had personal contact with some of them. He met Henry Adams several times through Monsignor Fay. He was once invited to a dinner at Andrew Turnbull's house in honor of Eliot, and was asked to read Eliot's lengthy poem *The Waste Land*.

To examine the originality in Fitzgerald's settings, one has to start by taking a close look at his sense of time. Coleridge once pointed out that the idea of time is "always blended with the idea of space."[20] For Fitzgerald, any particular place chosen as a setting for a story would, consciously or unconsciously, bear the mark of the particular period of time in which the story takes place. He never doubted that sensitivity to place and time was vital in the creative life of a writer. In his discussion of the literary use of geography in Marcel Proust, James Joyce, and William Faulkner, Leonard Kriegel emphasizes that "the creation of place was among the writer's primary obligations," and that these writers "brought to their novels and stories not only a daring capacity for invention but an insistence on the importance of fictional landscape that was exclusively the writer's own." What is remarkable about these writers' use of setting, Kriegel further suggests, is that "the uniqueness of place, as much as the demands of time, dominates the way each of them sees the world."[21] In this regard, it appears, Fitzgerald's name could well be placed among these writers. It would be more accurate to say that Fitzgerald experienced the time and observed the place intensely, and he presented them more honestly and vividly than most of the writers during his time. He knew that a setting should be selected and exploited in a manner suitable to the writer's purpose, and that through his innovative literary power, the writer should present his purpose with a scene, a designated world that is philosophically adequate and aesthetically satisfying. With the utmost exercise of his vision and artistry, Fitzgerald succeeded in applying this principle to his own writing and established three remarkable features in his aesthetics of settings.

First, each setting is rendered as a material entity always associated with a social implication, embodying a certain part of the entire social landscape and forming, symbolically, a microcosm of the American society. More than any other writer of his time (except, perhaps, Dreiser whom he greatly admired), Fitzgerald had the sense to remain in the mainstream of society. From the very beginning of his career, he tried to catch the color of the place and time. In doing so, he resorted to every possible means. On the one hand, his settings, which are so meticulously composed and depicted, comprise more than buildings, streets, and locations in the background. The ambiance he tried to create establishes itself on well-selected details. For example, he introduced a distinctive slang of a certain group in a particular locale, the popular dance steps among certain groups of people, the heroes of the sports fans, the suitable clothes and the right emotional expressions for his characters. None of these details is accidental. These minute details are so real and telling that each setting takes on a unique character and strikes the reader with a feeling of familiarity and intimacy.

Undoubtedly, such a masterful skill enables his contemporary readers to realize that they are not only shown the things and emotions they know and share but also subtly immersed in the excitements and disillusions of their time. On the other hand, he interwove his personal experience with the experiences of his generation and his country. Long before Fitzgerald, as Mark Schorer observed, "there are novelists who find their material almost entirely outside themselves, and there are others who find it almost entirely within themselves. Scott Fitzgerald's talent lay in an unusual combination of these two modes. The basis of his work was self-scrutiny, but the actual product was an eloquent comment on the world."[22] In his introduction to *F. Scott Fitzgerald: A Life in Letters*, a new collection of Fitzgerald's letters, Matthew J. Bruccoli insists, "Everything F. Scott Fitzgerald wrote was a form of autobiography. His fiction is transmuted autobiography."[23] Fitzgerald had a strong instinct, if not a compulsion, to base his novels and stories on his personal experience, and he continually made use of real episodes in which he had participated. According to his biographers, Fitzgerald more than once received complaints from his friends and colleagues for cross-examining them and writing them into his fiction. Many of his settings are the very places he visited or lived for some time, places like Princeton in *This Side of Paradise*, the streets and bars of New York in *The Beautiful and Damned,* suburban Long Island in *The Great Gatsby,* the French Riviera in *Tender Is the Night,* and the film world of Hollywood in *The Last Tycoon.* He felt that his own life was not merely typical but, rather, representative of a new generation. In a sense, he was writing about himself and his generation simultaneously by writing about a Fitzgerald-like character in the third person. Once he told a visitor late at night that he did not know whether he was real or whether he was a character in one of his own novels. It is this fusion of himself and his characters that helped him to write his first novel, *This Side of Paradise*. The setting in this novel shifts from one place to another, each embodying a phase of a young American's life in the years preceding and following World War I. From the campus of Princeton to the streets of New York, Fitzgerald used perfect settings to express the turbulent emotions and restless groping of his class and generation, and to catch the rich but authentic color of Jazz Age America. The setting is accurate and, to borrow John O'Hara's words, "the people were right, the talk was right, the clothes, the cars were real."[24]

Second, each setting is not just a place, but a state of mind. It is selected and depicted for the purpose of reflecting the personality and mentality of the characters. In a symbolic sense, therefore, each setting serves as a part of the human landscape, a microcosm of the psychological landscape in America. In his review of William Carlos Williams's *In the American Grain,* D. H. Lawrence pointed out that "all creative art must rise out of a specific soil and flicker with a spirit of place."[25] Perhaps there is no way to tell whether Fitzgerald was aware of this well-known dictum, but there is no denial about the specificity of the "soil" and its rich emblematic suggestiveness of a certain "spirit" in his fiction. Fitzgerald always firmly located his work in a specific place, which often proved to be the most suitable setting for staging the narrative action and evoking the state of mind of the character. What is distinctive in Fitzgerald's work is not the attribution of a character to a kind of "soil," an environment in which he lives, but the intensified (repeated) transformation of the "soil" as a reflection of the soul of the character. Fitzgerald tried to figure out the constant reciprocation between the outer world of nature and, to use M. H. Abrams's words, "the life and soul of man the observer."[26] Once his characters are so sensitive and tied to their surroundings, setting ultimately assumes a designated role in characterization. Therefore, settings in Fitzgerald's fiction, either social or domestic, may be viewed as metonymic, or metaphoric, expressions of the inner world of a character. If it is a social setting, such as New York City or Hollywood, it may be a projection of the character's will, the will to survive and succeed; if it is a domestic setting, such as a villa, a house, or a room, it may be an extension of the character himself, namely, his social status, his financial situations, and his psychological nuance.

Third, each setting is chosen and exploited in such a way as to ensure the verisimilitude of his fiction. In his preface to *Roderick Hudson,* Henry James warns that "to name a place in fiction, is to pretend in some degree to represent it."[27] Obviously, what James implies here is that representation of places in fiction must be based on faithful rendering of particular locations in order to increase the credibility of the story. With unfailing literary instinct, Fitzgerald knew that even in fiction having a high degree of verisimilitude settings must only seem to be modeled on actual places, otherwise the writer's freedom is impaired, and that place used as a setting, as with all elements in fiction, has a literal and symbolic value, a function serving both geographical and metaphorical ends. In his work, almost every setting corresponds to an actual geographical site. In fact, he is fond of employing real place names—except for a few fictionalized but easily identifiable names like "East Egg" and "West Egg" in *The Great Gatsby*—to lend authenticity to his settings. Even if these real place names are rooted in reality in terms of their descriptiveness, they are used for symbolic purposes. Occasionally, one might get the impression that Fitzgerald is writing, as it were, something historical, but the fact is that Fitzgerald never intends to do just that. He never attempts to take on the role of a historian, describing historical events as they actually took place.

A more appropriate way to look at his fiction is to compare his presentation of living actuality to a superb painting of a real historical event by a great artist, a painting that, despite its concrete presentation, leaves room for an individual interpretation. Nevertheless, it would be a mistake to assume that Fitzgerald set his story only in places that exist in the actual world. He did explore fictional ones that seem as complex as real-life places and contain their own physical and psychological features. What sets him apart from other writers in this respect is that he was effortlessly able to turn each of his settings, real or fictional, into a kind of encoded figure or implicit signifier, which not only contains a specific meaning but also contributes to the thematic significance of the entire work, thus conveying what Michael Orlofsky defined as "a sense of the historical present as well as the past—even the future."[28] Usually it seems unnecessary for Fitzgerald to describe his setting explicitly; a brief suggestion through the use of appropriate image is enough, for the reader can complete the scene and sense the meaning in his imagination. Whatever the setting, a house, a bar, New York, Princeton or Hollywood, Fitzgerald sticks to his own way of creating images familiar to his contemporaries by animating either the interior essence of a place or the physical surroundings, so that he can elicit the desired response from the reader. In analyzing Dickens's use of settings, Martin Price comments that "Dickens's world is alive with things that snatch, lurch, teeter, thrust, leer."[29] To a certain extent, Price's comments can also be applied to Fitzgerald's work, in which the house, bar, school, city, and Hollywood have been endowed with a sort of personality, charged with social and human content, and transmuted as an image of voice. The scenes that Fitzgerald revives are much like those of Dickens's. The difference is that Dickens's scenes tell us about his London and England, whereas Fitzgerald's tell us about New York and America.

Telling and articulate as Fitzgerald's place symbols and setting images are, one should nevertheless remember that they are not exact and true all the time. Yet all of them are tied up with an ideological, that is, thematic, system of presupposition. It is not so easy to arrive at the meanings with which these inanimate aesthetic objects are endowed. To understand Fitzgerald's art, therefore, one must be cognizant of the technical and thematic patterns that pervade Fitzgerald's use of settings; one must also look into the contexts within which his setting is established—and this does not just mean its geographical location or physical being; personal and social factors are equally important. To my knowledge, these patterns and contexts are terrains that have not been covered in the study of Fitzgerald. At least they have not been adequately recognized. Apart from some random remarks and Eugen Huonder's interesting but sketchy book *The Functional Significance of Setting in the Novels of Francis Scott Fitzgerald* (1974), in which only a few settings are analyzed, no critics have given us a full-dress analysis of Fitzgerald's use of setting, especially his use of domestic and urban settings. Given that Fitzgerald is one of the first, and perhaps the best, of the twentieth-century American writers who created their fictional world primarily on modern homestead and cityscape, it is wrong to let his use of domestic and urban settings remain virgin territory. The single greatest need in Fitzgerald studies has long been for a thorough study of his treatment of setting as a major part of his artistry, and this study is thus an attempt to break new ground in this area.

Because scores of books and hundreds of articles have been written about Fitzgerald's life and writing career, this book will not delve into biography, except to make passing references when necessary. In order to trace the consistent pattern in Fitzgerald's exploitation of domestic and urban settings, I will explore examples from his novels and stories and look into his nonfiction writings for an insight or a clue to his talent. My examination will not be an exhaustive study; instead, it will be focused mainly on what I perceive as the five most frequently adopted and most essential settings in Fitzgerald's fiction. Each chapter will discuss one setting: home in Chapter 2, bars in Chapter 3, schools in Chapter 4, city in Chapter 5, and Hollywood in Chapter 6. My choices have been made not only in keeping with my personal preferences but also with an aim to draw more attention to and appreciation for Fitzgerald's brilliant treatment of domestic and urban settings. To overlook Fitzgerald's achievement in this respect is to disregard an essential part of the artistry in his fiction. While I can claim that my book is the first major attempt in many years to prevent that from happening, much more effort still needs to be made.

NOTES

1. Alexander Gelley, "Setting and a Sense of World in the Novel," *Yale Review* 62 (winter 1973): 186.

2. Mikhail Bakhtin, *Rabelais and His World,* trans. Helene Iswolsky (Cambridge, Mass.: MIT Press, 1968), 438.

3. Ibid.

4. Malcolm Cowley, *Exile's Return: A Literary Odyssey of the 1920s* (New York: Penguin, 1976), 243.

5. Arthur Mizener, "The Poet of Borrowed Time," in *The Lives of Eighteen from Princeton*, ed. William Thorp (Princeton, N.J.: Princeton University Press, 1946), 333.

6. Glenway Wescott, "The Moral of F. Scott Fitzgerald," in *F. Scott Fitzgerald: The Man and His Work*, ed. Alfred Kazin (New York: Collier Books, 1951), 115.

7. Benjamin Spencer, "Fitzgerald and the American Ambivalence," *The South Atlantic Quarterly* 66, no. 3 (summer 1967): 367.

8. F. Scott Fitzgerald, *The Letters of F. Scott Fitzgerald*, ed. Andrew Turnbull (New York: Charles Scribner's Sons, 1963), 323.

9. Gertrude Stein, *The Autobiography of Alice B. Toklas* (New York: Harcourt Brace Jovanovich, 1933), 268.

10. Stephen Gray, "Sense of Place in the New Literatures in English, Particularly South Africa," in *A Sense of Place in the New Literatures in English*, ed. Peggy Nightingale (St. Lucia, N.Y.: University of Queensland Press, 1986), 7.

11. Lennard J. Davis, *Resisting Novels* (New York: Methuen, 1987), 53.

12. Eudora Welty, *The Eye of the Story: Selected Essays and Reviews* (New York: Random House, 1978), 122.

13. Mikhail Bakhtin, *Problems of Dostoevsky's Poetics*, trans. R. W. Rotsel (Ann Arbor, Mich.: Ardis, 1973), 67.

14. Ralph Waldo Emerson, *Emerson: Essays and Lectures*, ed. Joe Porte (New York: Viking Press, 1983), 498.

15. Wallace Stevens, *Opus Posthumous*, ed. Samuel French Morse (New York: Knopf, 1957), 158.

16. Catherine A. Middleton, "Roots and Rootlessness: An Exploration of the Concept in the Life and Novels of George Eliot," in *Humanistic Geography and Literature*, ed. Douglas C. D. Pocok (New York: Barnes and Noble, 1981), 101.

17. Frederic Jameson, *The Political Unconscious* (Ithaca, N.Y.: Cornell University Press, 1981), 157.

18. Charles Olson, *Call Me Ishmael* (San Francisco: City Lights Books, 1947), 11.

19. T. S. Eliot, "Tradition and the Individual Talent," in *Selected Prose of T. S. Eliot*, ed. Frank Kermode (New York: Farrar, Straus and Giroux, 1975), 38.

20. Samuel Coleridge, *Biographia Literaria*, ed. John Shawcross (London: Oxford University Press, 1907), 87.

21. Leonard Kriegel, "Geography Lessons," *Sewanee Review* 102, no. 4 (autumn 1994): 606.

22. Mark Schorer, "Fitzgerald's Tragic Sense," in *F. Scott Fitzgerald: The Man and His Work*, ed. Alfred Kazin (New York: Collier Books, 1951), 170.

23. Matthew J. Bruccoli, ed., *F. Scott Fitzgerald: A Life in Letters* (New York: Charles Scribner's Sons, 1994), xv.

24. Quoted from Arthur Mizener, *The Far Side of Paradise: A Biography of F. Scott Fitzgerald* (Boston: Houghton Mifflin, 1951), 100.

25. D. H. Lawrence, *Phoenix*, ed. Edward D. McDonald (London: Heinemann, 1961), 334.

26. M. H. Abrams, *The Mirror and the Lamp* (New York: Norton, 1958), 64.

27. Henry James, Preface to *Roderick Hudson* (Boston: Houghton Mifflin, 1917), x.

28. Michael Orlofsky, "The Power of Place," *Writer's Digest* 74, no. 10 (October 1994): 37.

29. Martin Price, ed., *Dickens: A Collection of Critical Essays* (Englewood Cliffs, N.J.: Prentice-Hall, 1967), 2.

2

HOME: A SHOWCASE OF HUMAN EXPERIENCE

Home is the most recurrent setting in fiction, though used in different ways by different writers. In his Foreword to *Home by the River*, an autobiography of Archibald Rutledge, Frances P. Keyes writes that Rutledge, the former poet laureate of South Carolina, is "a man who not only knows how to use correctly one of the most beautiful words in the English language, the word 'home,' but who understands and reverences its full meaning."[1] This comment seems to be quite appropriate for Fitzgerald. The term "sense of home," as Walter Pater called it, is not something that can be easily defined; it is open to interpretation. Henry James told us, "Objects and places, coherently grouped, disposed for human use and addressed to it, must have a sense of their own, a mystic meaning proper to themselves, to give out."[2] Every writer defines the value and meaning of home in his own way. Even within the same context, different homes carry different meanings. Writers never give up their attempts to interpret the concept of home, however, because they know that home is the most natural symbolic container of values and meanings, and that, as Earl H. Rovit put it well, it is "one of the major structuring forces of the human psyche, basic not only to the individual's search for and sense of identity, but fundamental, as well, to the group's collective attempt to achieve a cohesive image of itself."[3]

HOME AS A UNIT IN SPACE AND TIME

The word home is a familiar term, but it is not an easy one to define. *Webster's Third International Dictionary* gives it three definitions: first, "family's place of residence"; second, "social unity formed by a family living together"; third, "a congenial environment." What we see here is a reference to the physical establishment of a family and the innate role for this most basic functioning unity in society. In a specific sense, home could suggest intimacy, relationship, and communion. There are a lot of novels in which family activities and parties of some sort—tea parties, cocktail parties, dinner parties, and weekend parties held in someone's house, like Gatsby's mansion—are essential to the plot and theme. Evidently, through these functions, the house becomes the center of community, or communion, among people. Also, home is a launching site from which one may start a pursuit of ambitions and ideals; it is a place to which one may always come back for consolation and support. Allan Gurgannus speaks fondly of what he likes about the word home in his afterword for *Home: American Writers Remember Rooms of Their Own*: "I love the way its stately gate of an 'H' swings open onto the shielded domesticity of roundness, the way Home's little 'e' stands, back-looking, bye-saying, like the household's child sent out to wave company safe into the night."[4] In his poem "The Death of the Hired Man," Robert Frost offers his definition of home through the words of the wife in the dialogue: "Home is the place where, when you have to go there, they have to take you in."[5] What Frost means is that home is one's final refuge, and all one has to do is search hard enough to discover it. However, home is not always associated with congenial values. Home could suggest introversion, separateness, and isolation, too. There have been numerous examples in early novels, revealing figuratively characters confined in cell-like houses or rooms, such as Mr. Osborne's forbidden study in William Thackeray's *Vanity Fair*, the sterile bedroom of Joyce's Mr. Duffy, Hawthorne's house of seven gables, and Edgar Allan Poe's House of Usher. What these examples show to us is that home could be an unpleasant and disappointing place, where one may be victimized by endless confusion, distress, abuse, and psychological bewilderment.

In a larger sense, home is a concept always associated with the history, possibilities, aspirations, and frustrations of humankind. According to sociologists, it is the place where family functions as part of society. But it is more than a stage for the drama of domesticity; it becomes a stage where all conflicts among people get laid out. Hawthorne seems to strike on the same cord in his description of his famous House of the Seven Gables: "So much of mankind's varied experience had passed there—so much had been suffered, and something, too, enjoyed—that the very timbers were oozy, as with the moisture of a heart. It was itself like a great human heart with a life of its own, and full of rich and somber reminiscences."[6]

Observant readers will quickly discern this prominence that the house setting has in Fitzgerald's fiction. For Fitzgerald, the chief value of home as a setting in fiction is more than the identity of an individual; he sees home as a unit in space and time. His assertion is that one's identity is not formed solely on the basis of one's home, but on one's experience as well. Characters in his fiction make their home in mansions, houses, or rented apartments. Some of them have managed to keep their homes, whereas others do not have such luck and are forced to wander from one place to another. A difference in living places usually shows differences in characters and, in some cases, the difference in various stages of one character's life. Fitzgerald exemplifies this difference in fiction as the evidence of his conclusion that the sense of home is the embodiment of one's social, psychological, and personal sense of life.

It may seem unbelievable, though, that a writer of Fitzgerald's stature never had a place he could call a stable and secure home at any time in his life. When he was only a year-and-a-half old, his family had to go East and moved between Buffalo and Syracuse and back to St. Paul again and again. Even in St. Paul, his family moved from one street to another every year before they finally settled on Summit Avenue. Up to this time, Fitzgerald never found a world into which he could fit, because he was not able to live in a single neighborhood long enough to mingle with other youngsters. By the time his family settled down in the best residential area in St. Paul, Fitzgerald had gone East to boarding school and Princeton. With such a background, it seems inevitable that as Henry Dan Piper has observed in his brilliant biography, "Fitzgerald's memories of early childhood were haunted by a series of hotels, flats, and semidetached houses."[7] It is not difficult to imagine that such frequent moves in and out of unfamiliar places had a psychological effect on the young Fitzgerald.

Even after his wedding, Fitzgerald took Zelda to live in New York's Biltmore Hotel. Home was still nothing but an illusion to him. D. H. Lawrence spent his life searching for a place where he could fulfill himself as a person as well as a writer, to "establish a living relationship with his surroundings," but "after he had left his home village, he never found a permanent home and was condemned to be an exile for ever."[8] Apparently, Fitzgerald followed suit. He and Zelda floated from one hotel to another, renting a series of villas, houses, and apartments in place after place. Zelda stayed in a succession of asylums in Europe and America, while Fitzgerald sent his daughter away to his friends for care, and he drifted from one place to another. Seldom, if ever, did the three members of the family spent time together. They did not even maintain a decent residence of their own for a relatively long period of time. More unbelievable is that even though Fitzgerald had earned more than $400,000 by 1934, according to his wife's estimate, they never owned a house. They were always broke and in debt. During the later years of his life, when he returned to Hollywood in late 1930s for a new start of his writing career, Fitzgerald lived in rented apartments, struggling to support his family with his pen. It is sadly fitting that Fitzgerald died in an apartment rented by his lover, Sheilah Graham, while his own family was far away.

One has to ask what impact such a life of transience had on his treatment of home as setting in his fiction. Not surprisingly, the memories of his early years with his family and the chaos in his marriage later made him dubious about the traditional sense of home and in his mind generated an obsessive sense of insecurity. As revealed in letters to his family and friends, he was acutely aware that in his life, home meant more isolation and uncertainty than intimacy and security. All his doubts and negative memories surrounding the concept of home did not deter him from confronting the issue head on. Home became one of his major themes and figures prominently in his fiction. Home, depicted either as the grand nest in a mansion or a house, or a shabby den in rented apartments, is a major setting and a paramount symbol—indeed, in *The Beautiful and Damned* and *The Great Gatsby*, it is the hub of the plot and theme. Many of his stories also deal with the American scene, or "Americans traveling in an English or European" scene with some symbolic reference to the concept of home. In his fiction, homes that are intended as motifs for romance, sentimentality, and stability in family life are constantly coupled with homes described as sources of conflicts, frustration, and flawed lives. Such a dual employment of home reminds us of the similar depiction of the dual role of English country house as the true house and "the other house" in the novels of Ann Radcliffe, William Thackeray, Jane Austen, and George Eliot. The country house always functions, to borrow Richard Gill's words, "as a symbolic paradise or symbolic prison."[9] Although not many of Fitzgerald's characters made their home in a country house, their mansions, villas, and rented apartments are frequently presented in the same way as the English country house, as either a "paradise" or a "prison." The significance of their dwellings goes beyond expressing a character's understanding of his own place and value in life. They are deployed for three thematic purposes: First, they are emblematic of social process, portraying the character's role and experience in society and simultaneously reflecting his time and his world; second, they are symbolic of the character's mood and desire, mirroring the inner workings of his mind; third, they contain specific but well-designed details exemplifying various aspects of the character's personality.

HOME AS A METAPHOR OF ONE'S FALL

In *The Beautiful and Damned,* home appears to be a central image or even *the* central image in which Fitzgerald brings to perfection the contrapuntal device of employing houses and apartments. His depiction of a series of Anthony Patch's residences constitutes an essential part of the long novel. In spite of the visual precision he gives the interior, the appearance, and the environment of Anthony's houses, Fitzgerald is not primarily interested in the potential aesthetic beauty they might contribute to the novel. What is more important to him is their functional role in the structural and thematic scheme of the novel. In other words, what matters is not what these houses look like, but what they could possibly suggest and whether they could serve as the places that define his characters, reflect them, and mold them. They are put forward as pivotal scenes around which the whole narrative is centered and from which the action of each episode unfolds; they are turned into milestones of Anthony's quest for life. Houses are the most visible signs of one's fortune, success, and social status; thus Anthony's move from his initial, large gorgeous house to his final crummy apartment in a rough neighborhood delineates his gradual decline toward his ultimate degeneration.

Anthony's metamorphosis from a young man obsessed with "Beautiful" illusions to a "Damned" wreck is symbolically suggested by the title of the novel. As the grandson of Adam J. Patch, a multimillionaire, Anthony is an out-and-out offspring of what Fitzgerald refers to as an "aristocracy founded sheerly on money" (*BD*, 4). At the age of eleven, Anthony lost his parents. It is his grandfather who gave him all the social security he needed and guaranteed his future with the prospect of a large inheritance. Although handsome and witty, Anthony "had lived almost entirely within himself, an inarticulate boy, thoroughly un-American and politely bewildered by his contemporaries" (*BD*, 7). He was shy enough to have spent his time reading many books in bed, or collecting and playing with various colorful stamps. He went to Harvard with the belief that Harvard "would open doors, it would be a tremendous tonic, it would give him innumerable self-sacrificing and devoted friends" (*BD*, 7). He graduated from Harvard with the reputation of being "a rather romantic figure, a scholar, a recluse, a tower of erudition" (*BD*, 8). Nevertheless, Anthony is constantly disturbed by his conflicting attitudes and unresolved aspirations. At first he pursued his interest in architecture and painting; he tried to perfect his writing by composing "some ghastly Italian sonnet" (*BD*, 8); and he now plans to write a history of the Middle Ages some day. The problem for Anthony is that he is not committed to anything whole-heartedly. It might not be inaccurate to say that he is knowingly committing the sin of "sloth" because he never sees any need for hard work and nothing prompts him into action. Anthony's ambition to be a social success through his own endeavors gives way to complacency in the established security in his life. Richard D. Lehan has pointed out, "He is completely uncertain about what to do with himself, and not sure that there is anything worth doing."[10] With the prospect of inheriting a big fortune, Anthony asserts that it is unnecessary to commit himself to anything else but dreaming about all the luxury and pleasure his grandfather's money will bring him.

When we first see him in a gallant apartment on Fifty-second Street in New York, which he took after "a prolonged search" (*BD*, 9), Anthony has just returned to America because of his grandfather's sudden illness. To his dismay, his anxious hope for gaining the family money is postponed by the old man's miraculous recovery, but the thought of the possibility that the transfer of his family fortune could take place at any time due to his grandfather's old age and poor health is always tantalizing enough to put him in a chivalrous mood. In the meantime, a life of leisure seems just fine to him. With an income of "slightly under seven thousand a year, the interest on money inherited from his mother" (*BD*, 12) and a "five-hundred-dollar bond," a Christmas gift from his grandfather every year, Anthony is rich enough to set up a cozy apartment uptown. To him, it is a decent place. "Here, after all, life began. Here he slept, breakfast, read and entertained" (*BD*, 10). For a time, at least ostensibly, his life seems to be graceful and exciting. Each morning he is awakened by an English servant, who "arrived with the mail and breakfast" (*BD*, 12); he arises to dress and arrange his immaculate hair; he meets his broker in the mornings; he visits, hastily and unwillingly, his grandfather; he hangs out with two friends. Taking a closer look at what he does every day, however, one would find that Anthony is not really a carefree dandy; he is constantly torn between his aspirations, hopes, illusions, and worries. Fitzgerald's meticulous description of Anthony's apartment is deliberately designed to reveal his emotional upheavals and the innate weaknesses in his personality.

Using a newsreel-like technique, Fitzgerald begins his description of Anthony's apartment from the outside, first the street where it is located, and then the interior of the apartment. His description of the front room, written in first-rate prose, is filled with specific details, giving the reader a clear view of its location and a sense of its structure, space, and condition, both physically and symbolically: its "stuffiness, bareness, and decadence" (*BD*, 10). Then his description freezes on a piece of furniture in the room, a "deep lounge." What is intriguing about it is that the lounge is presented as having "somnolence drift about it like a haze" (*BD*, 10). This image is worth noting in that it turns out to be prophetic about the listless life Anthony will lead in New York. From the front room, Fitzgerald leads the reader through the long hall into the immense bedroom and bathroom, which he calls "the heart and core of the apartment" (*BD*, 11). Here it is quite obvious that Fitzgerald wants the reader to pay close attention to the unusually huge space in Anthony's apartment. His reference to high ceilings, large windows, and the big bedroom is meant to hint at Anthony's emotional emptiness and morbid loneliness. In a similar manner, his description of the atmosphere of "somnolence" becomes a vivid metaphoric expression of Anthony's physical lethargy.

If the front room and bedroom are depicted for the purpose of revealing Anthony's state of mind, the bathroom is almost like a kaleidoscope of Anthony's personality:

His bathroom, in contrast to the rather portentous character of his bedroom, was gay, bright, extremely habitable and even faintly facetious. Framed around the walls were photographs of four celebrated thespian beauties of the day: Julia Sanderson as "The Sunshine Girl," Ina Claire as "The Quaker Girl," Billie Burke as "The Mind-the-Paint-Girl," and Hazel Dawn as "The Pink Lady." (*BD*, 11)

What we see here is by no means an ordinary bathroom, and what Anthony does in this bathroom is more than one could even imagine—in fact, he "did everything but sleep and eat there" (*BD*, 11). The "extremely habitable" and "faintly facetious" quality of it adequately manifests a touch of eccentricity and even a Narcissistic trait in the personality of a rich idler like Anthony, while the pictures of actresses around the walls represent his personal taste and his yearning for beauty and fame far more than the vogue of the time. As to the other items in the bathroom, Fitzgerald does not describe them one by one as Balzac does in his nine-page opening description of Madame Vauquer's boarding house in *Le Père Goriot*. Instead, he only highlights some of the key things, including the bathtub equipped with an ingenious book-holder, the wall wardrobe, the neckties and the rich rug, as suggestive decor of their owner. By comparisons with the descriptions of homes made by some of his predecessors,

Fitzgerald's treatment of the bathroom interior strikes one as so much different, so much more focused. The description of every object appears to be characterization-oriented. Thus, Anthony's indulgence in sumptuousness is virtually exposed; his image as an indolent "would-be" *nouveau riche* is roundly established; the direction in which his life is going to sail is clearly mapped out.

A commonality in most, if not all, indulgent dreamers like Anthony, is that a vital part of their fantasy world is their obsessive and, sometimes, pathetic perception of what Fitzgerald described as the "golden girl," who has an aura of all the "virtues" a woman could have. With the hefty Patch family fortune in close sight, the only mission Anthony needs to accomplish is to find his golden girl, the concluding part of his pursuit for perfection as a man. At this point in Anthony's life, a charming and radiant girl, Gloria Gilbert, comes into his world, but she fails to bring along with her any "golden" virtues. Critics have assumed that Gloria was modeled on Fitzgerald's wife, Zelda, but that is not entirely true. As a matter of fact, Gloria combines the personalities of two important women in Fitzgerald's life: Ginevra King, his first serious lover, and Zelda. Perhaps it may be far-fetched to say that Anthony's marriage resembles Fitzgerald's own, yet there is no doubt that he deliberately portrays Gloria in such a way as to make her seem very much like Zelda; many of Zelda's features are interwoven into the character of Gloria; even the relationship between the Patches is as abrasive from the beginning as that between the Fitzgeralds. Born and brought up in surroundings of inescapable vulgarity, Gloria has never been as lucky as Ginevra King or Zelda who enjoy all the advantages of well-to-do society. Fitzgerald gives her a touch of elusive loveliness, a suggestion of the kind of invisible seductive power that drives the young men around her wild. It is this power that causes Anthony to believe that "she moved him as he had never been moved before." In Anthony's eyes, "She was a sun, radiant, growing, gathering light and storing it—then after an eternity pouring it forth in a glance, the fragment of sentence, to that part of him that cherished all beauty and all illusion" (*BD*, 73). Besides, she has a romantic guise that makes her seem more accessible to Anthony than the money of the Patch family. With her almost magic ability to tease and control, Gloria can easily dominate Anthony. In many ways, she reminds us of John Keats's "Belle Dame Sans Merci." Gloria decides to marry Anthony not because she is in love with him, but because she sees him as a wealthy man who might be content to play the "temporary passionate lover" to her. "She was beautiful—but especially she was merciless." Fitzgerald describes her as a girl who "had been so spoiled—in a rather complete and unusual way" (*BD*, 79) and who "has no sense of responsibility" (*BD*, 39). On more than one occasion, Gloria appears to be egocentric, impractical, indiscreet, and even unpredictable.

Nevertheless, "because Anthony and Gloria are compatible in their joint desire for graceful idleness, they are able to ignore, for a time, their essential differences."[11] Blinded by his romanticized notions of beauty and charm, Anthony deludes himself to Gloria's glowing popularity and sensuality. Only after he decides to marry Gloria does he reveal a deeply hidden, eerie feeling about the unpredictable consequence of his choice. Again, that feeling is forcefully conveyed, with a very disheartening irony, in Fitzgerald's description of Anthony's apartment on the eve of their wedding. In this particular scene, Fitzgerald focuses his description on an "evanescent and Summery" sound that comes through the wide-open windows into Anthony's high-walled bedroom, and he then turns his attention to the vast world outside Anthony's room, elevating that sound into something romantic that could be shared by young lovers like Anthony and Gloria. From Harlem to the Bronx, the sound is traveling all over the city in this "blue summer dark" (*BD*, 149). At this point, Fitzgerald seems to let imagination take over his figurative description: people in the city are "playing" with this sound and fantasize that "life would be beautiful as a story, promising happiness," and that it would give love "hope in its own survival" (*BD*, 149). No matter how wonderful, the sound is purely contrived as a forewarning of peril to the soon-to-be bridegroom, for it is immediately subdued by a woman's hysterical laughter outside Anthony's window. Sensing that the tranquillity of the romantic night is shattered, Anthony instantly finds himself "upset and shaken" (*BD*, 149); he feels a return of "his old aversion and horror toward all the business of life," and even his room seems to have grown "smothery" (*BD*, 150). What flashes in his mind at this moment is no longer the rosy picture of his marriage to a golden girl but the horrifying thought of paying for Gloria's meals, jewels, and the huge expenses for their upcoming honeymoon trip.

Although shocking, such an ominous inkling does not linger long in the mind of Anthony. He is too immersed in his illusions to realize that he and Gloria are slipping into the trap of a meaningless life they have fixed for themselves because they "opt for romance, not life."[12] Both of them have a naive hope that their youth will last forever and their future might just be as ideal and exciting as their six-week honeymoon. That they mistake the illusory for the real good remains totally unheeded. Fitzgerald cites a salient example in his representation of the couple's home after they returned from their honeymoon trip. This scene not only pictures the chaotic start of their life together but foreshadows their unavoidable degeneration in the near future. Their apartment is a mess, and "in a stifled atmosphere of open trunks" and "laundry bags," they spend their day impatiently" (*BD*, 170). Judging from words like "trunk," "callers," and "bags" in Fitzgerald's detail-packed description, one gets a vivid image of Anthony's new life, a life that has already been marred by disorder, distraction, and disorientation. The word that captures the real nature of this couple's discontent with their life at this point is "impatiently." Having described their long and exciting honeymoon in great detail, Fitzgerald now shifts his tone and satirically calls attention to the reality that Anthony and Gloria have to face: There is no way to tell when they will get the Patch family fortune. Before Gloria, Anthony's life has been one of thoughtless self-gratification. Although he is keenly aware of what he has to offer to his golden girl, he never doubts that the moment he takes over the control of the Patch family fortunes he will be free of all worries. Such thinking divulges Anthony's self-indulgent callousness and parasitic pitifulness. Nearly two months into their marriage, nothing has happened. Anthony and Gloria are still not anywhere closer to the money they have been dreaming about. What irks them more is their knowledge that there is not much they can do about it. No matter how "impatient" they are, Anthony and Gloria do nothing more than shallowly evaluate their situation, and the conclusions they draw illustrate their shortsightedness: they will continue to wait.

Up to this point, Anthony's immense apartment on Fifty-second Street has been employed as a major setting for the first phase of the couple's fantasylike life. However, it is their lease of the old house in the country that marks the beginning of their destined degeneration. Fitzgerald presents a lengthy and detailed account of their days in the gray house. He uses the space to examine, with great lucidity and sharp insight, Anthony and Gloria's obsession with the prospect of the Patch family fortune and their indulgence in a hedonistic way of life. One thing to note about the gray house is that Anthony and Gloria discovered it totally by coincidence. They saw the for lease sign because their car broke down after running into a fire hydrant. Fitzgerald presents the house as something closely related to history: "Colonial it defiantly remained" (*BD*, 178). To begin with, Fitzgerald shows us that the gray house is a fitting place for Anthony to work on his history project. Fitzgerald, then, ridicules his character by implying that Anthony's ulterior motive was not to fulfill his intellectual plan at all but to ingratiate himself with his rigid and cynical grandfather for the prospect of inheritance, so he and Gloria would be able to embark on the pastoral life they had fantasized about at the Marietta Inn on the evening they signed the lease for the gray house.

Eventually, however, nothing of what they hope for comes true. Instead, they are beguiled by the insubstantiality of their own illusion. Their life in the gray house is a purposeless and monotonous one. "As a sort of change," they either invite people over to the house, or loiter through endless parties somewhere else. This becomes "their chief source of entertainment" (*BD*, 227), without which life will be intolerable, because "staying home in the evening palled on them" (*BD*, 227). The sense of expectation, which has been so far a spiritual pillar in their life, has become the sense of uncertainty, and the euphoria, with which they have intoxicated themselves all along, is gradually giving way to a worrisome and intense atmosphere in the house. They live so passively that their daily life has gradually lost the glamour and vigor they tried so hard to maintain; it turns empty and gloomy just like the gray color of the house. Inside the house it is a scene of disorder, a perfect reflection of their tawdry life: The front room is filled with "the dank staleness of wine and cigarettes" (*BD*, 225); the floor is littered with "broken glass" (*BD*, 225); the fabric of the chairs and sofas is stained. What is worse is that they are gnawed by poverty from time to time because of their careless spending. Sometimes they have to borrow money on bonds. With their financial resources draining away and their energies wasted, each day, as Fitzgerald implies, is "taking relentlessly its modicum of youth" (*BD*, 195). The heavy smoking and excessive drinking, the heated arguments between the couple, all start to take a toll not only on their mood but on their health. Tensions flare up so often that the house becomes a battleground instead of a love nest. The "impatience" Anthony and Gloria have been putting up with is more agonizing than ever. One night Gloria is almost driven crazy by the chaotic party in the gray house. All of a sudden she feels an unbearable weight pressed on her bosom, and she wants desperately to flee from the house. When she hears Anthony's steps on the lower stair, she is completely paranoid, fearing that Anthony is "part of this weight, part of this evil house and the somber darkness that was growing up about it" (*BD*, 244). She felt an unnamable but imminent danger. Intuitively she pushed Anthony aside and burst through the front door into the street. Stunned and bewildered, Anthony swiftly regained his wits and ran after her. The whole incident ended with a violent argument at the railway platform. This highly dramatized episode is, in effect, part of Fitzgerald's well-concerted attempt to demonstrate both the disarray that resulted from Anthony's naive illusions and to peel away Gloria's disguising aura of a golden girl.

What captures our attention here is this first association of something evil with the gray house, with Fitzgerald using a term like "the somber darkness" to define the life inside the house. Interestingly, Fitzgerald adds more to the misfortune of the gray house, as if he believes that he needs more examples to make his point. Something much worse happens on the fateful night when Anthony's grandfather, Adam Patch, and his secretary, Edward Shuttleworth, unexpectedly walk into the gray house amid the drunken spree.

Once again, Fitzgerald shows his unique artistry in employing the strategy of refraction, rather than direct presentation. While unfolding this dramatic scene, Fitzgerald stresses the "messiness" in the room, the "artificiality" of the things inside, and the "staleness" of the air, and he implies, with a touch of irony, that something dreadful is bound to happen. As soon as Adam Patch realizes what is going on in his grandson's house, he turns around and leaves in a fury before Anthony has a chance to say a word. The sudden appearance and swift departure of Anthony's grandfather instantly sends the whole house into a silent freeze, unable to recover from the tremendous shock and fear. Anthony's face is "the color of chalk," and Gloria's is "tense and frightened" (*BD*, 275). The dramatic turn of events in this scene is essential, for it gives us a few glimpses of the distinctive character of Anthony and his grandfather by staging the old man's swiftness to act against the backdrop of Anthony's lack of action. As an important measure to secure his inheritance, Anthony has tried hard to please his grandfather. He thought that he had given his grandfather an impeccable impression of his potential and conduct by visiting him frequently and convincing him that he had been working on a book of history. Knowing well that his grandfather will never forgive him, Anthony does not even have the courage to go to see him, not because he feels guilty or shameful but because he is afraid of the serious consequences of his encounter with Adam Patch, who is known to be a staunch moralist and ardent supporter of Prohibition. When he does go to see him, "in trepidation and vainly," Anthony is not allowed to meet him, and his letter to him is not answered (*BD*, 280). After that, Anthony and Gloria spent their days in great fear; everything in their life is "slipping perceptibly" (*BD*, 278). Indeed, Anthony's fear of being disowned by his grandfather is increasing day by day.

As a desperate attempt to clinch the money they have been waiting for for two years, Anthony and Gloria decide to show their repentance by moving out of the gray house. To them, the move is their last resort to regain the grandfather's favor. To the reader, however, the move symbolizes another phase in the couple's ongoing degeneration. This unmistakable implication can be seen in Fitzgerald's brilliant description of the inside view of the gray house at the time of their departure:

They left the gray house, which had seen the flower of their love. Four trunks and three monstrous crates were piled in the dismantled room where, two years before, they had sprawled lazily, thinking in terms of dreams, remote, languorous, content. The room echoed with emptiness.

Gloria shook her fist defiantly at the four walls.

"I'm so glad to go!" she cried, "So glad. Oh, my God, how I hate this house!" (*BD*, 280-81)

The description is direct and economic, but the meaning is profoundly metaphorical. We are immediately made aware that the "flower" of their love, as indicated by Fitzgerald's use of the past perfect tense, is now withered and gone, and that the "dismantled room" is the embodiment of the big turmoil in their minds. With the wonderful dreams they had brought along when they first moved into the gray house entirely shattered, Anthony and Gloria are leaving with nothing but unspeakable disappointment.

On their return to New York, they move into a small one-bedroom apartment on Fifty-seventh Street, rented for $150 a month. Their ominous inference is finally confirmed. Anthony's grandfather, who dies soon after his visit to the gray house, disinherits Anthony and gives his money to charity and reform societies. Anthony and Gloria decide to contest the will, even though they know that it will be years before the legal battles are over. They still naively believe that it is better to cling to their slim hopes for the inheritance than to take control of their own lives. This is, without doubt, Fitzgerald's way of dissecting the incurable flaw in their character and the deepening impetus of their irreversible degeneration.

As the legal battle drags on, life for Anthony and Gloria is going from bad to worse. In presenting a truthful image of their current predicament, Fitzgerald's skill of exploiting the house setting works at its best. Contrary to the conventional strategy in characterization, Fitzgerald lines up the physical features of the setting to reflect his characters' mentality. In his description of this apartment, one striking detail is that "the rooms were too small to display Anthony's best furniture" (*BD*, 288). Such a seemingly simple detail is more than a revelation of their financial trouble; it is also a sarcastic swipe at their inability to maintain the vanity that they care about so much. Such an illuminating detail is further reinforced by a much longer representation of their apartment, the third home in their marriage. Fitzgerald tells us that both Anthony and Gloria "smoked incessantly," and therefore everything in their apartment has the odor of tobacco, including their clothes, blankets, curtains, and the ash-littered carpets. Besides, Anthony's "best furniture is littered with dirty items, or even ringed with glass circles." It seems that this disorderly physical condition mirrors the human condition in the apartment: "There had been many parties—people broke things; people became sick in Gloria's bathroom; people spilled wine; people made unbelievable messes of the kitchenette" (*BD*, 296). This is the routine of their new life or, in Fitzgerald's words, "a regular part of their existence" (*BD*, 296). They used to live recklessly on the sure prospect of inheritance; now, one step backward, they still place their naive hopes on the victory of the challenge to the will.

Nothing in the condition of their residence, the company they keep, and the things they do carries any sign of repentance. Why so? The reason remains the same: They are blinded by a distorted idea of success and happiness in life. Anthony does make some abortive attempts at writing fiction, but he soon gives it up as he realizes that it is not the best way out. As to Gloria, she believes that "life is not purposeful, it was, at any rate, essentially romantic!" (*BD*, 305). She does not care to go on a wild spree even at the cost of all the money they have. Even when Anthony is sent away to an army training camp in the South, he is, in a sense, not entirely separate from his life in the small apartment back in New York. In fact, as part of their plan, Gloria remains in New York to "use the apartment" and "to watch the progress of the case" (*BD*, 308); thus Anthony can be well informed, by letters and phone calls, of anything that happens in the lawsuit. To their distress, their life is made more miserable by their interminable wait as the lawsuit drags on and on and they are down to their last few bonds. Despite these insurmountable odds, Anthony and Gloria continue to hang on to the hope that their long wait will be rewarded. Fitzgerald's insistent implication of this couple's mentality needs no further explication as a direct reflection of the hedonist yearning for the fantasy world of glamour, luxury, and fame among the young "flappers and philosophers" during his time.

The legal case is not the only source of agony for Anthony and Gloria. Heavy drinking and violent quarrels become usual occurrences in their life. Both in and outside their apartment, Anthony seems to have turned into a "confused specter" (*BD*, 388), no longer a man who is anxiously expecting the reversal of a will that will turn his messy life around. To him, the hope is now too remote to be true. In the meantime, as Fitzgerald's increasingly satirical narrative implies, Gloria is more and more like a "conscious flower" (*BD*, 393), vulnerable but desperately trying to prolong its beauty. For the first time, she decides to fall into "the old lure of the screen" in the hope that she is still young enough to launch her career. To her dismay, however, she is turned down because of her age. A scene of Gloria in the apartment, reading the dreadful letter she has just picked up from "the dirty tiles of the hall," shows how deeply devastated she is by the disappointing news. Her eyes are instantly filled with tears, unable to see anything on the opposite wall. With the letter "crinkled" in her hand, Gloria goes into the bedroom, sinking "down upon her knees before the mirror on the wardrobe floor." She realizes, "This was her twenty-ninth birthday, and the world was melting away before her eye" (*BD*, 403). Shifting his focus between the letter and the character reading the letter, Fitzgerald shows the psychological disintegration of Gloria right in front of his reader's eyes, allowing no confusion about why Gloria wanted an acting job. Her failed attempt does not mean that she has come to see the futility in their dreams of the Patch family fortune, or that she has started to do something to turn their life around. Her sole purpose is to satisfy her own ego by proving to others as well as herself that she still has what she considers her own self-worth: youth and beauty.

The clear visual image of Gloria "sinking" upon her knees expresses one of Fitzgerald's evolving conclusions about the couple's dilemma: They are helpless. Just as Anthony and Gloria cannot do anything about the prolonged legal case, neither can they take any actual steps to prevent themselves from slipping down the road to ruin. A new phase of their downfall is equally well delineated by their move into another apartment on Claremont Avenue, at $80 a month. Unlike his treatment of this couple's previous three abodes, Fitzgerald does not give much detailed description about the physical condition of this apartment. His brief mention of its low rent is enough to suggest that this one is much worse in terms of facilities and location. Fitzgerald focuses his observation on the couple, rather than on the couple's new dwelling. By describing the things they do, the things they worry about, and the things they need, Fitzgerald exposes the disorderly and deteriorating state of the couple's mind.

At the age of thirty-two, Anthony is jobless yet still does not want a job. Unable to pay the dues, he has resigned from his last club, a club that his grandfather and his father used to join. In many ways, his resignation is extremely revealing; symbolically, he severs his connection with aristocratic society. Anthony no longer cares about the potential privilege and opportunity the club offers him, for now he has more immediate ends to meet. Grimly, Gloria sadly and rightly reveals their immediate concern, which is to figure out what to do after Sunday because a loaf of bread, a half-pound of bacon, and two eggs are the only food left in the house. After spending the last small change in his pocket, all Anthony can do is to walk around the streets looking for an acquaintance from whom to borrow money; but he is snubbed by everyone. Anthony is hurt and angry, and his mind has become "a bleak and disordered wreck" (*BD*, 400). Gloria is no better than her poor husband. Without "the great gift of money," she has to forget the way she used to live and has to learn to pass the days and nights without receiving invitations to social gatherings. In Fitzgerald's words, "she was being bent by her environment into a grotesque similitude of a house wife" (*BD*, 424), sitting in the dark room or leaning on the window sill to look out at the street and the children. Remembering her days on the Fifth Avenue, the sight of 125th Street, the people, and the neighborhood, gives her a sad and nostalgic feeling; the silence in the room escalates her unbearable loneliness and *ennui*. At this stage of her life, "she was miserable," keenly aware that "this existence, without hope, without happiness, oppressed her" (*BD*, 414).

The legal battle with Adam Patch's secretary, Shuttleworth, has turned into a cruel siege for Anthony and Gloria, for it has been extremely expensive and frustrating. All they have gotten from it are huge costs and mental distress. So intense is the atmosphere in the apartment that a day never passes without bickering between the couple. As a retribution for their illusion and greed, Gloria's youth is wasted and her beauty is lost forever; Anthony, who is thirty-three, but "looked forty" (*BD*, 444), has suffered a nervous breakdown. By the time they win the legal battle and are granted $30 million, he has been reduced to a pitiful invalid who is in no shape to think about, let alone enjoy, the fantasylike life that the fortune can bring about. At the end of the novel, Anthony and Gloria are about to sail for Europe, but they are still deep in reminiscences of the "hardship" and the "retribution" they have suffered. The scene draws an ironic comparison between Anthony and a general who might look back on a successful campaign to analyze his victory. Since we know that Anthony has done nothing to deserve the honor accorded a victor, none of us can miss the real portrait of Anthony that Fitzgerald has been painting throughout the novel: Anthony is a naive dreamer and a pathetic loser who is mercilessly ridiculed and punished for "his very craving for romance" (*BD*, 448-49).

Philippa Tristram insists, "Every newly built house or freshly furnished room is a fiction of the life intended to be lived there. Every inhabited building or interior tells a different story of how life is or was."[13] From Anthony's old but magnificent apartment to the gray house, to the two small apartments they rent afterward, the novel charts a symbolic metamorphosis exemplifying the degeneration of this couple. Every "move" Anthony and Gloria have made brings them closer to their final downfall. One thing Fitzgerald does effectively in presenting home imagery as a metaphor of his characters' lives and world is to delineate the inseparable connection and the reciprocal reflection between the physical features of a home and the mental developments of its inhabitants. In piling up minute details about his characters' homes, Fitzgerald does more than evoke the disarray of their lives; he implicates money, or rather the worship of money in the whole society, in Anthony and Gloria's failings and miseries; he discloses the pervasive breakdown of moral values with a powerful literalness. More importantly, he wants readers to understand that although Anthony's "small world" is fictive in nature and built on a distorted perception of life, it is by no means an isolated domain of an unfortunate soul. In one way or another, it is intricately entangled with the "large world," defined against it, and at the same time used to mirror the ethos of the time. In this sense, the dismal story in a "small world" like Anthony's is not uncommon because it is part of the universal disillusionment experienced by countless people caught up but then soon lost in the hedonistic waves of the Jazz Age.

Some readers and critics tend to dismiss *The Beautiful and Damned* as the least interesting among Fitzgerald's novels mainly because they believe that it is too sentimental and its ending too inconsistent. Nevertheless, if we read the novel within the context of Jazz Age America and the conventions of novel writing at the time, we will discover that the theme of the novel is more profound and its structure is more coherent than it appears. At least, a reading of this parablelike story can help a recent generation to learn its lessons about those years of American life, and an examination of Fitzgerald's use of image patterns in describing Anthony's dwellings will reward us with a new perspective of Fitzgerald's great skill in exploiting home settings.

HOME AS A MIRROR OF ONE'S INNER WORLD

In depicting the houses and apartments in Anthony's life, as we have seen, Fitzgerald relies on concrete details to reflect the physical and mundane world beyond home. It would be wrong, however, to assume that Fitzgerald's sense of home responds exclusively to events and changes in the outer world. Houses in his fiction are heavily weighted with social and psychological implications, thus providing readers with a paradigm of the interactions between individual subjectivities and social realities. For him, the sense of home is closely interconnected with the inner world, the world of one's consciousness. The metaphysical dimension of home setting is also a key effect that Fitzgerald kept trying to build into his fiction. This he did by exploring the rich symbolic meanings of the architecture and interior decoration of home settings.

Sigmund Freud once said, "The only typical, that is to say, regularly occurring representation of the human form as a whole is that of the house."[14] A similar point seems to be underscored in a complaint made by Margaret Schlegel in E. M. Forster's *Howards End* when she says, "Houses are alive."[15] To a certain extent, home can become an alter ego of its owners. It is the owners' self-designated domain, private and secure, where they can enjoy the freedom of being themselves. The physical character they maintain for their home, the things with which they fill their home, and the events they allow to happen at home inevitably bear witness not only to their taste but to their character and consciousness. As Ralph Waldo Emerson says in his essay "Nature," "Every spirit builds itself a house, and beyond its house a world, and beyond its world a heaven."[16] Fitzgerald's treatment of house setting, especially in his depiction of Gatsby's mansion in *The Great Gatsby*, adheres to this Emersonian concept and gives his character's home an autonomous being. This autonomy lies in a unique personality of its own, one that originates from and, in turn, mirrors the subconscious of the character who lives in that home. Even though Fitzgerald's description of Gatsby's mansion may not strike one as specific as Defoe's well-known description of Robinson Crusoe's cave on the island, it contains nothing irrelevant; the significant details about the mansion are carefully selected for the purpose of analyzing what they can tell us about the thoughts, anxieties, or obsessions deeply hidden in Gatsby's mind. The whole mansion serves as an index to the different aspects of Gatsby's imagination and as an external picture guide to his vision of paradise; indeed everything about it adds up to a full representation of Gatsby's inner world.

Of course, it is not easy to lay out the inside workings of a character like Gatsby, who is portrayed with a quality of vagueness. We do not see him until half way through Chapter 3. Even when he does appear on the scene, most of the time he remains evasive and does not mingle with the guests coming to the parties in his house. By the beginning of Chapter 8, he has completely disappeared from the story, becoming a mystery to everyone around him. This vagueness is by no means a wayward or indiscreet mistake, however. Instead, it is a deliberate scheme in Fitzgerald's characterization of Gatsby. Maxwell Perkins, Fitzgerald's longtime editor and friend, once wrote to tell him that this vagueness "may be somewhat of an artistic intention," but in his view, "it is mistaken."[17] In his reply, Fitzgerald does not seem surprised by Perkins's criticism; on the contrary, he shows his confidence to "repair" Gatsby's vagueness and to "make him clear."[18] Yet as we can see from the novel, Gatsby's vagueness is retained. His role as the central hero is established, but his true nature is gradually demystified in the course of action.

If Gatsby is a myth in the novel, his mansion is a big part of that myth. At least, Fitzgerald wants readers to see it that way. To say that all attempts to demystify Gatsby should start with a careful look at his house may not be an exaggeration. The pivotal role of Gatsby's house is twofold in the novel. Structurally, the house is a scene to which the novel constantly returns, thus serving as a major arena of action throughout the story. Thematically, it not only stands as the most dominant symbol of Gatsby's success and wealth but also functions as the chief accomplice in his scheme to lure back his "golden girl," Daisy, whom he lost years ago, and to "repeat" the past that he has cherished for so long. The history and present condition of the house are introduced to us long before we see the mansion's proprietor in person. From the very beginning, Fitzgerald tries to establish and explore the correlation between Gatsby and his mansion to carve the portrait of Gatsby in relief. The grandeur of the mansion, for instance, is not necessarily a mere manifestation of Gatsby's abundant wealth; rather, it ought to be conceived as a symbolic expression of Gatsby's mind, which, as Frederick Hoffman observed, provides various clues to his morality and emotion.[19] In his comments on the correlation between Gatsby and his mansion, Eugen Huonder suggests that Gatsby is "an extension of his house."[20] In my view, however, the appropriate assessment should be just the opposite: Gatsby's mansion is an extension of his character. The simple reason is that the physicality of the mansion is not really Fitzgerald's primary concern. His purpose in presenting all these details about the mansion is to show how its physical order is closely intertwined with the moral order of its owner. In other words, the transformation of the house from a building of glamour to a building of desolation parallels Gatsby's tragic fall. Fitzgerald uses this "interconnection" metaphorically as a psychological spectrum for Gatsby's inner world.

Fitzgerald's strategy for depicting this parallel "decline" is to depend on an ingenious pattern, which divides the whole metamorphosis into three phases: First, we see the glamour of the mansion before Daisy's visit; then, we tour the mansion with Daisy, who is visiting; finally, we see the empty mansion left in deadly horror after Daisy disappears in order to escape her responsibility for the tragic deaths of Myrtle and, indirectly, Gatsby, deaths initially caused by her reckless driving. Fitzgerald begins his depiction of the mansion by calling it "a colossal affair by any standards" (*GG*, 8). The word "colossal" sounds a bit shocking but is perfectly appropriate, as Fitzgerald moves on to prove it with a more specific reference to its feature as "a factual imitation of some *hôtel de ville* in Normandy" (*GG*, 8-9). This succinct and graphic passage is suggestive enough to help us imagine the spectacular kind of magnificence a mansion like this imposes. Each detail projects one particular feature of the mansion: the "Hotel de Ville" indicates the spacious size of the house and its intended appeal to public gatherings; the tower reminds one of the glories of the past; the marble swimming pool represents modern luxury; the vastness of the lawn and garden symbolizes the abundant wealth of the owner, a mysterious member of the *nouveau riche* in the eyes of the community. However, not everything about this house is perfect. the tower, which according to Nick's description is "spanking new," shows hardly any dignity of tradition, for the "ivy" is "thin" and "raw." Besides, as Bryan R. Washington points out, one gets a feeling that Gatsby's house "is 'unnatural,' not simply because of the way it imposes itself on the landscape or because of who is invited there, but also because of its interior, which lacks an organizing logic beneath the labyrinth of exhibits."[21] The imitative nature of the mansion's architecture and the arbitrary fusion of old and new in the overall arrangement of the residence reflect Gatsby's impulsive desire to find what he used to cherish the most in the past and transform it into a present reality. Unfortunately, all the gorgeous features of antiquity displayed in the mansion are phony. Unlike the inheritance of history, they are nothing but cheap fabrications of authentic traditions that can be made with new, and probably "hot," money. Many critics insist, as does A. Robert Lee, that "Gatsby's house belongs to near historical fantasyworld, a 'present' as Nick sees it fashioned—distorted—from an European past."[22]

When we read the same description more carefully, we see that something ominous is implied beneath the seemingly wonderful images of the mansion. Later in the novel, we are also told that Gatsby's house was built before World

War II by a brewer, who used to be a *parvenu* just like Gatsby. To fulfill his ambition to "found a family" and leave a venerable mansion, something his descendants could show off in the community, the brewer offered to pay five years' taxes on all the cottages in the neighborhood if their owners would agree to thatch their roofs with "straw." With his offer rejected, the brewer's health deteriorated shortly afterward, and his mansion was sold by his children days after his funeral. By stressing the false glittering quality of the mansion and, particularly, telling us what has happened to the brewer, Fitzgerald scores two points. On the one hand, he penetrates the glaze of antiquity, the glamour of luxury, and the haze of romance of Gatsby's mansion to expose the inner world of Gatsby permeated with great anxieties and aspirations; on the other hand, he foreshadows Gatsby's failure in achieving his goal of restoring the illusions of the past and his ultimately tragic demise.

Gatsby's mansion is a work of imitation, but his character is absolutely not. What is his character, then? How could his true character be embodied by his imitative house? In his comments on the concept of character in fiction, William H. Gass suggests, "Gatsby is not an imitation, for there is nothing he imitates. Actually, if he were a copy, an illusion, sort of shade or shadow, he would not be called a character at all. He must be unique, entirely himself as if he had a self to be."[23] Deep in his mind, Gatsby knows what he wants to be in his life and what it takes to be what he wants to be. He never doubts the possibility or, rather, his own ability to fulfill his long-cherished hope of recapturing his past with Daisy. For him, this has become a sacred mission, with which he is so obsessed that he does not have the slightest idea of that the pursuit of his illusion is doomed from the very beginning. Perhaps he simply does not want to believe the futility of his mission, or face it. The reunion with Daisy years after their separation seems to be the only motivating force in his life. Almost every reader wants to know what "magical charm" Daisy possesses to make a man like Gatsby willingly sacrifice everything he has in order to relive the time they had spent together as youngsters. The simple answer is that Daisy is not just a "sweetheart"; she is Gatsby's "golden girl," without whom his success as a man can never be complete. She, or what she symbolizes, is the central pillar of Gatsby's inner world, without which it will instantly fall apart. If it is in Dan Cody that Gatsby sees the glorious image of a wealthy and successful man, then it is in Daisy that he discovers a perfect woman, one who embodies all the glamour of wealth and the wonder of romantic possibilities. When he kissed her for the first time, he knew that he would "forever wed his unutterable visions to her perishable breath" (*GG*, 141). Daisy has become the symbol of his illusion and the incarnation of his dreams. Nick says of Gatsby while listening to the story of his past, "Some idea of himself perhaps had gone into loving Daisy" (*GG*, 140). Gatsby's life has been "confused and disordered" (*GG*, 140) since then; the love for Daisy has become part of himself; all his heightened sensitivity is focused on Daisy. With an unyielding fervor, he worships and pursues Daisy, not merely as a particular woman, but more as a mystical union with the most promising life embodied in Daisy. "To Gatsby," as Miles Donald says, "the dream of Daisy is worth taking blame for, suffering for and ultimately dying for."[24] She "is the green light that signals him into the heart of his ultimate vision."[25]

To understand Gatsby's perception of what Daisy stands for, one first needs to find out who he is. According to the brief biographical recollection given by Nick, Gatsby used to be an extremely lonely child, who, like his creator, Fitzgerald, did not have a decent and secure home. "His parents were shiftless and unsuccessful farm people—his imagination had never really accepted them as his parents at all" (*GG*, 124). For young James Gatz, it was almost his destiny to "be about his father's business," which turns out to be "the service of a vast, vulgar, and meretricious beauty" (*GG*, 124). To change such a course of life, he needs to create a new self for himself. At the age of seventeen, Gatz abandoned his own mediocre father, "beating his way along the south shore of Lake Superior as a clam digger and a salmon fisher or in any other capacity that brought him food and bed" (*GG*, 25), struggling with "a constant, turbulent riot" in his mind, a riot between his "grotesque and fantastic conceits" and "fancies" (*GG*, 125). Like the Horatio Alger hero, though, Gatz knew that the attempt to accomplish what one envisions must, as an absolute premise, involve acquiring a big fortune. It is at this moment that he was led by "an instinct toward his future glory" (*GG*, 125) to a meeting with Dan Cody, who in a certain sense, as Richard D. Lehan observes, "takes on godlike proportions, and his business— the exploitation of America—becomes Gatsby's business as well, even to the extent that Gatsby creates the kind of self necessary for such a pursuit."[26] Gatsby made the first step, a successful one, in his lifelong pursuit of his visions. Nevertheless, Gatsby's new fortune was lost in a battle for money, and his girl was snatched away from him by the irresistible charm of money before he came back from the war. When he returned, he was nothing but a poor and miserable soldier wandering in New York. Before long, however, Gatsby regained his ground by working with Meyer Wolfshiem, who became Gatsby's second father figure after Dan Cody and introduced him to the illegal but profitable underworld. It is then that Gatsby made a big fortune and turned into a millionaire himself. In addition to the grand mansion, Gatsby has his own private beach, his own hydroplane, and several fancy automobiles.

Although Gatsby seems to have accomplished all he can in business, his romantic visions are still far from being realized. To him, no success in the material world can make up for his sacred, but now lost, love for Daisy, who in his mind symbolizes the ideal of the ultimate self-perfection a person can achieve. Money can do nothing but provide him with a great resource of power, with which he may try to make his dream come true, the dream to restore the love between Daisy and himself and to regain the pride and dignity he had lost in losing Daisy five years before. Evidently, it is for this purpose that Gatsby comes to West Egg, establishing an immense mansion as a base where he can do everything at will, such as putting on a glamorous show of extravagance to lure back his old idol. "It wasn't a coincidence at all," as Jordan argues with Nick about Gatsby's intention, "Gatsby bought that house so that Daisy would be just across the bay" (*GG*, 100). The more pragmatic goal is to throw grand parties in the hope of meeting her among the uninvited guests. Gatsby sees it as the best chance to find his way into Daisy's world and relive the wonderful moment of his past with Daisy, even if for a limited time.

Gatsby's dream is still alive, but it has been tinged with the extravagant glamour of wealth and the glow of romance. Gatsby makes a great effort to present a glamorous way of life right under Daisy's nose. After he bought the estate, he spent a lot of money to refurbish it, equip it, decorate it, and turn it into a kind of dream castle, bright with lights, noisy with music and laughter, and crowded with dignitaries and celebrities. In a figurative sense, the garden is the launching pad for Gatsby's campaign to regain what he has lost. Every weekend, a big party takes place and drags on deep into the night. One thing worth noticing is that Fitzgerald does not give much detail about the physical feature of the garden itself; he is more concerned with the faces and events in the garden. Nonetheless, it is easy to draw a conclusion based on the number of guests and the variety of activities that the garden is a beautiful and huge place. Its significance as part of the home setting lies in its dual role as "a world of dream" and "a world of festival." These two worlds are inseparable, since the latter is designed for the perfection of the former. We know from Gatsby's confession to Nick that he is not a "good" host, and he does not like to mingle with his guests. The "world of dream" is a domain for Gatsby only when there is no party in the garden. It is usually in this domain that we see the real person of Gatsby. A perfect example can be drawn from the first glimpse of Gatsby described by Nick, the narrator, near the end of Chapter 1:

The silhouette of a moving cat wavered across the moonlight, and turning my head to watch it, I saw that I was not alone—fifty feet away a figure had emerged from the shadows of my neighbor's mansion and was standing with his hands in his pockets regarding the silver pepper of the stars. Something in his leisurely movements and the secure position of his feet upon the lawn suggested that it was Mr. Gatsby himself, come out to determine what share was his of our local heavens. (*GG*, 28)

This scene of the garden is set at night under the moonlight. There is no one else around, except for Gatsby and Nick, and Gatsby may not even know that Nick is watching him. The moonlight, the stars, and the tranquillity of the night combine to give the garden a strong touch of romance and sentimentality. In addition, the image of Gatsby walking out of the mansion gives us an impression that he has just come out of the shadow of the past. Then, however, there is a discernible shift of tone in Nick's description of Gatsby. He declares that Gatsby "was content to be alone" (*GG*, 29), and he presents another scene in which Gatsby "stretched out his arms toward the dark water in a curious way" (*GG*, 29); and he was trembling, too. Again, this is a symbolic image placed in sharp contrast to the previous leisurely movements, and "the secure position" of his feet, because the "arm-stretching" gesture is a common expression of one's longing; the "dark water" is clearly symbolic of something gloomy and unknown; the 'body-trembling" gesture is an indication of a flurry of feelings in Gatsby's mind, such as anxiety, regret, and fear. To put it in a simpler way, what we see in this scene is a place as elusive as a dreamland. It is private and tranquil, romantic and mysterious. As the scenic change and dramatic development run parallel in the novel, the imagery of the garden as a world of dream is further elaborated. In the last chapter, the garden is again set at night under the moonlight. The mansion is deserted; Gatsby is no longer in sight; Gatsby's world of dream has turned into his world of death.

The garden as "a world of festival" is often presented at night under the moonlight, but it is strung with colored lights and is the scene of a "spectroscopic gaiety" (*GG*, 57). The combination of moonlight and the electric light embodies as a peculiar fusion of romantic ideal and harsh reality. Unlike the "world of dream," the "world of festival" is bright and glamorous, but noisy and wild. Each of the three parties depicted "looks like the World's Fair" (*GG*, 103). One of them is depicted as still going in full swing at two o'clock, "the whole corner of the peninsula was blazing with light." "Gatsby's house," Nick tells us, is lit from tower to cellar (*GG*, 103). To demonstrate the glamour of a "world of festival," Nick gives us scrupulous information about the quests and all kinds of preparations as well. "People were not invited—they went" (*GG*, 53). Gatsby sends his station wagon to meet all trains, and uses his Rolls-Royce as an omnibus for passengers on weekends. The number of servants, gardens, and caterers, as well as the amount of food consumed every Friday, shows the huge number of guests gathered at this festival. As to the preparations for the festival, Fitzgerald, through his narrator, presents two kinds of sharply focused images: One is the fancy food on the buffet tables and the drinks at the bar; the other is the orchestra, which is, unlike the small band one would normally expect to see, "a whole pitful of oboes and trombones and saxophones and viols and cornets and piccolos, and low and high drums" (*GG*, 51). Besides, to create a romantic haze for the festival, Nick presents a series of passing but impressive scenes. First, we see Gatsby's quests, "diving from the tower of his raft, or taking the sun on the hot sand of his beach" (*GG*, 50); we see more of them coming from New York: "The halls and salons and verandas are gaudy with primary colors, and hair bobbed with in strange new ways, and shawls beyond the dreams of Castile" (*GG*, 51). Then, we see that "the bar with a real brass rail" in the main hall is in full swing (*GG*, 51); "the air is alive with chatter and laughter" (*GG*, 51), while "the orchestra is playing yellow cocktail music" (*GG*, 52); the girls maneuver their way in the center of the crowd; gypsies dance out on the canvas platform. At this moment, "the party has begun" (*GG*, 52), but Nick, though amazed by what is going on in front of his eyes, is still an observer on the side.

Before long Nick begins to feel that there is something indescribable and abnormal underneath the extravagant glamour and romantic haze of such a festival-like party. Two things seem puzzling to him. First, on the first night he visited Gatsby's house he found out that he "was one of the few guests who had actually been invited" (*GG*, 52), whereas the others swiftly "came and went like moths among the whisperings and the champagne and the stars" (*GG*, 50). "They conducted themselves according to the rules of behavior associated with an amusement park" (*GG*, 53), greeting each other enthusiastically but never bothering to know each other's names, making casual innuendoes and introductions forgotten on the spot. They got drunk by the time the parties broke up; "women fought with men said to be their husbands" (*GG*, 66), and men talked to other women "with curious intensity" (*GG*, 66). Most of them did not even care whether they would get the chance to meet their host, Gatsby, because what interested them was not the man himself but how he made his fortune. Second, during the most part of these parties, Gatsby remained out of sight. He was never part of any event at the party. Even when Nick stumbled upon Gatsby, their conversation was often interrupted by some mysterious calls. Having noticed not only the shallowness and insincerity in the guests' character and the disgrace and vulgarity in their behavior but also the aloofness of the host, Nick is still too confused to figure out the real meaning of these random gatherings, let alone understand that they are well planned by Gatsby to provide "pastime and grazing because he hopes Daisy will someday mosey in like the others."[27]

To Gatsby's disappointment, nevertheless, no matter how swanky these parties are, Daisy is never lured to cross the bay to attend one of them. Gatsby has to ask Nick to entice Daisy to a tea in Nick's house. There have been many speculations about Gatsby's, or rather Fitzgerald's, objective in using Nick's house, instead of Gatsby's mansion, as the trysting place. Although it may be true that such a choice gives Gatsby the benefit of surprise and privacy, Fitzgerald uses this arrangement to make two additional points about how Gatsby feels about this long-awaited reunion with Daisy. First, having waited so long for this moment, Gatsby is not so sure he can handle it properly by himself. An afternoon tea in an ordinary but well-maintained house, with plenty of homemade lemon cakes, has a natural and homey atmosphere that no big mansion or fancy restaurant can offer. A setting as ideal as this can help ease their initial shock and awkwardness (Nick does reveal that it took some time for Gatsby to overcome his "embarrassment and unreasoning joy" [*GG*, 116]). Second, the next-door location of Nick's house guarantees Gatsby a chance to impress Daisy with his own magnificent mansion. Gatsby knows clearly that the meeting is far from enough to regain Daisy; a guided tour of his mansion may be the quickest self-introduction he can give to Daisy. This is because Gatsby has this lifelong conviction that a man's accomplishment is always measured by his residence. His reverence for house is evidenced by a series of details in the novel: His memory of a visit to Daisy's beautiful home at Louisville never fades; he bought his mansion at West Egg and opened it to strangers; he proudly sent a picture of his mansion to his parents; he even bought a house for his parents. Assuming that Daisy is the same woman who yearns for glamour and romance, Gatsby's forlorn hope at this moment of their reunion is to convince Daisy that he has obtained the kind of wealth and status she wished him to have years ago. As Hilton Anderson has said, "Gatsby wants to show her that he is now worthy of her love, that he has now arrived in the Buchanan's world."[28]

Gatsby's hope looks quite promising when we see Daisy's stunning reaction upon her first sight of the house: "'That huge place there?' she cried pointing" (*GG*, 114-15). For a moment, Daisy keeps murmuring while looking around the house. Obviously, she admires everything she sees. Daisy's admiration is exactly what Gatsby had hoped for, and that is why he leads her into the house through the "big postern" instead of the short cut along the Sound. First he takes Daisy and Nick through the "Marie Antoinette music rooms," "the Restoration Salons," and "the Merton College Library, . . . a high Gothic Library, paneled with carved English oak" (*GG*, 58), in which the nameless owl-eyed drunken man was astonished to find out that those books are "absolutely real." Up on the second floor, Gatsby leads them through period bedrooms, dressing rooms, poolrooms and bathrooms with sunken baths before stopping in his own "apartment, a bedroom, a bath, and an Adam Study" (*GG*, 116). Except for "a toilet set of pure dull gold on the dresser" (*GG*, 116), nothing is as fancy or showy as other parts inside the mansion. There is no doubt that this virtue of simplicity is by no means a "glitch" in the decor of Gatsby's house. Conversely, it is a smart arrangement designed to offer an extra glimpse of Gatsby's inner world. As Richard Cohen pointed out, "Gatsby is aware of the façade he has created and wishes to maintain some semblance of personal integrity."[29] But he does not want to reveal this "virtue" to anyone, especially to Daisy on this crucial occasion. Without much delay, Nick informs us, Gatsby opens two bulking patent cabinets full of suits, gowns, ties, and silk and flannel shirts in different colors, throwing a pile of shirts before Daisy and Nick. That these luxuries are meant to be Gatsby's "gestures," as Nick calls them, which would help him win back Daisy, is one thing, but how effective they are, or how deeply Daisy is touched, is another. She cries uncontrollably over the shirts simply because she has "never seen such—such beautiful shirts before" (*GG*, 117). Daisy's tearful reaction to Gatsby's clothing, or more accurately, his wealth, has incurred various assessments. To say that she is overwhelmed by what she sees in Gatsby's bedroom and his mansion is definitely a half-truth at best. Given her own social and financial status as Mrs. Buchanan, Gatsby's display of wealth is nothing more than a fabulous show. Daisy is not Myrtle; she does not have much concern or craving for materialistic things. Her fascination with what is shown to her comes, in part, from her astonishment that her formerly destitute suitor has reappeared in front of her eyes with such immeasurable wealth. Her sense of tradition and elegance, which has been instilled into her upbringing, does not allow her to embrace the rawness and repulsiveness embedded in Gatsby's estate and West Egg. After all, what Gatsby has displayed to her is not the same kind of magnificence or power maintained by the circle of the

Buchanans. That seems to be the reason why Daisy, when she is prompted for an answer by the anxious and overconfident Gatsby, declares that she is not willing to leave her husband.

Sadly, for the same reason that he is unable to see the difference between the two Eggs, Gatsby never fully understands Daisy's ambivalent feeling toward his return; he never realizes that his dream of Daisy is an absurd and impossible illusion. After the final showdown between Daisy, Tom, and himself, he still cannot face the stark reality that Daisy does not want to leave Tom for him. He builds his entire hope upon Daisy's unhappiness with her marriage and life, but what he does not know is that Tom's society, into which Daisy is married, has already changed and corrupted her with its wealth and expectations. In recounting their stormy love affair of years ago, Nick provides us with a sharp insight into Gatsby's doomed pursuit of his illusion. In his view, Gatsby fervently believes that Daisy is "extraordinary," but he has no idea about how "extraordinary" Daisy actually is. He cannot accept that Daisy has changed and has her own life. He is still kept darkling with "nothing" (*GG*, 187). Nick's observation predicts what is to happen to Gatsby eventually. Daisy not only invalidates Gatsby's endless struggle to accomplish his great vision but literally leads him to his demise after the car accident.

Symbolically, Gatsby's tragedy is implied by Nick's description of the mansion toward the end of the novel. After the fatal car accident, Nick comes to Gatsby's house and is astonished to find it permeated in a threnodic air: The house "had never seemed so enormous." As Gatsby and Nick search for cigarettes, they "felt over innumerable feet of dark wall for electric light switches"; the piano has taken on a "ghostly" look; there is "dust" everywhere and the rooms are "musty"; they have to smoke the "stale, dry cigarettes" in the darkness (*GG*, 184-85). Nick's brief but illustrative description of Gatsby's house on this particular night presents a horrifying picture in sharp contrast to what we have seen, both in and outside the house, before and during Daisy's visit. The "World Fair" is over; the garden is deserted and deadly quiet; the luxurious *decor* of the interior of the rooms has lost its glow and vanished into oblivion; the swimming pool, which the gardener (now the last and only servant in the house) wants to drain for the year but cannot because Gatsby wants to use it for the first time in the whole summer, turns out to be a place where Gatsby ends his life while waiting for a telephone call from Daisy, who has already run away with Tom and has decided never to return.

The final scene of Gatsby's house is deliberately depicted in a much sharper contrast to the "colossal affair" in the first chapter. The house is empty; the grass in the garden has grown as long as that on Nick's lawn, as if the house has not been occupied for years. Before heading back West, Nick pays his last visit to Gatsby's place, which he calls, quite accurately, "the huge incoherent failure of a house." He finds it empty, desolate; particularly, "there were hardly any lights" (*GG*, 227). Thus, by using the contrasting images in his depiction of Gatsby's house before, during, and after Daisy's visit, Fitzgerald has revealed a symbolic metamorphosis of Gatsby's inner world, degenerating from a place of glamour and illusion to a place of defeat and desolation. What is more important is that Gatsby's tragedy has a universal and timeless relevance in American life because such a metamorphosis could very well be seen as a compelling portrayal of the failure of the American dream, and because what Gatsby strives and dies for is a great dream that has actually existed, still exists, and probably will exist forever in the American imagination. As Robert G. Deamer has said, "This dream is, in the final analysis, the same Adamic waking dream that Cooper, Twain, Hemingway, Faulkner, and Thoreau imaged in Natty, Huck, Nick, Ike, and the 'I' of *Walden*: the dream of regaining and of freeing in time the intense, innocent, thoroughly affirmative life-existence of youth."[30] Gatsby's name might well be added to these famous dreamers of America because his dream is to repeat something he deemed not only the most precious in his past but also the most promising in his future. It is not a dream of success; rather, it is what Richard Chase calls "a transcendent ideal." If the collapse of Gatsby's inner world suggests anything, it is the impossibility of pursuing romantic dreams in an unromantic world.

HOME AS A MOTIF OF ONE'S PERSONALITY

Just as the title of one of his short stories says, each house in Fitzgerald's fiction is "More than Just a House." All the details about a house, from its appearance to its interior, are designed as motifs, rendering subtle supporting images to specific aspects of a character's personality. They may combine to embody the primary features of the character, his past, his taste, and his habits; they may bespeak his virtues and sensibilities. Allen Tate once praised Flaubert for developing "a technique of putting man wholly into his physical setting."[31] In Fitzgerald's fiction, such a technique seems to have been explored more widely and more effectively. What distinguishes Fitzgerald's achievement is his success in depicting the character' home as an expression and extension of the self-image a character wants to project to, or to be seen by, others.

As previously cited, Fitzgerald's depiction of domestic decoration is neither irrelevant nor wasteful; rather, it may be viewed as metonymic or metaphoric expressions of character.[32] House decoration has always been exploited as a device in characterization. Balzac, writes Percy Lubbock, "cannot think of his people without the homes they inhabit," and he cannot imagine them without imagining "certain furnished room."[33] Obviously, this is also true about Fitzgerald. He supplements characterization through the detailed specifications for the house which his character occupies. Usually Fitzgerald gives the reader only a small amount of information about a given character at any single moment. He utilizes the condition of home to reflect the nature of the character on the one hand, and on the other hand, allows the character to reveal himself in his attitudes toward the way in which he maintains his home, for as Leonard Lutwack has said, "A response to a place becomes material for characterization when it is individualized."[34] A reader knows Fitzgerald's character much better because of this polyphonic technique in his use of home setting. This close articulation of the character and his abode seems to have been Fitzgerald's favorite strategy to represent and develop different dimension of his characters. Although sometimes Fitzgerald stresses only one particular detail about the interiors or about the outlook of the house, this particular detail expresses one side of its occupant. Fitzgerald's selection of one or more details about the house is always carefully determined, depending upon his intention and theme or by the tone he sets for a certain story. This method of using selective details to portray the character works especially well when Fitzgerald wants to endow his character with distinctive features and beliefs, either as romantic or mysterious or eccentric. Just as Dickens in *Bleak House* describes Mr. Tulkinghorn's room as an extension of his character, Fitzgerald often uses a direct simile to build a parallel between the character and the house in which he lives. Even the adjectives used in his description may well be humanized and applied to the occupant of the house. Of course, Fitzgerald does not overtly tell the reader that these adjectives exactly suggest the character of the occupant, but what they have modified is analogous to the unique nature of the occupant; they may bespeak the illusion, the sentimentality, the misery, the hypocrisy, and the vanity of Fitzgerald's characters.

Examples of this type of motif in characterization are not difficult to find in his novels and stories. As a matter of fact, Fitzgerald used this motif more than once in his depiction of Anthony's deterioration and Gatsby's tragedy. In *Tender Is the Night,* it is through his polyphonic technique that Fitzgerald depicts the Villa Diana, the palatial home of the Divers, as motif, reflecting the personality of its occupants and of their guest, Rosemary. First, Fitzgerald gives a two-page-long but vivid description of the house "in the ancient hill village of Tarmes": "The villa and its ground were made out of a row of peasant dwellings that abutted on the cliff—five small houses had been combined to make the house and four destroyed to make the garden" (*TIN*, 26). Although the house and the "lovely grassless garden" (*TIN*, 25) 700 feet above the Mediterranean seem to present an image of the perfect residence, the name of the villa, Diana, just like Gatsby's mansion, or *hôtel de ville,* suggests its mysterious past and its owner's social status, while the garden, which focuses on a huge pine, serves as the romantic place where the Divers hold their parties. Taking a closer look at the scene, one can quickly see not only in the villa the signs of blight juxtaposed with those of affluence but also in the garden, "Nicole's garden," as Dick calls it, the evidence manifesting Nicole's madness and alienation from her husband and the lack of authentic intimacy between the couple. To put it straightforwardly, the "pastoral" setting of the garden is extremely deceiving. What Dick means by "Nicole's garden" is nothing but "an enclosed refuge that Dick established for his half-cured bride," where Nicole is spontaneously protected and confined.[35] As her husband and doctor, Dick keeps a tight control over Nicole's life. At the same time, Nicole is still not totally free from the relapses of her mental illness. In the portrayal of Nicole, Fitzgerald's use of flower metaphors, such as associating her with wild flowers and roses, poignantly underscores the nature of her personality as glamorous, but vulnerable, unstable, and even dangerous, gradually preparing readers for the drastic reversal of roles between the couple, with Nicole changing from the woman who used to be well cared for in the garden into a woman who now attends and rearranges the garden, not for her husband and protector, Nick, but for her new lover, Tommy.

The same scene of the Divers' villa, however, could convey an entirely opposite impression. To Rosemary, the young and promising Hollywood star, the Divers' villa is "the center of the world," a stage on which "some memorable thing was sure to happen" (*TIN*, 29). Shortly after their arrival, "under the spell of the climb on to Tarmes and the fresher air, she and her mother looked about appreciatively" (*TIN*, 28). She is fascinated by the "calculated perfection of Villa Diana" (*TIN*, 28). In her eyes, the setting is filled with a romantic haze: the party held out of doors in the garden, the trees dressed with lamps, the table set with fancy food, the summer night with a few fireflies "riding on the dark air," the ghostly wash of the sea far below the cliff, and the guests arriving with excitement. Here, it is not hard to sense Fitzgerald's deliberate emphasis on the Keatsian romantic atmosphere as suggested by the title of the novel, or to see how vividly Fitzgerald delineates Rosemary's personality by allowing her to reveal herself in her reflections upon the scene of the Divers' villa.

By comparison, however, this motif-creating strategy is explored more successfully in his short stories because the form of short story does not give the author much descriptive space for characterization, and the author has to resort to every other means available to him within the capacity of the form. One story in *Tales of the Jazz Age*, "The Jelly-Bean," is a telling example of Fitzgerald's expertise in illustrating the character's sentimentality through the depiction, not of the character himself, but of the home he inhabits and the way he perceives it as well. "Jim," the idler—as Fitzgerald defines his nickname the "Jelly-Bean"— "was born in a white house on a garden corner. It had four weather-beaten pillars in front and a great amount of lattice-work in the rear that made a cheerful criss-cross background for a flowery sun-drenched lawn."[36] What is poignantly sad or even ironic is the fact that all these rich and beautiful qualities embedded in this brief description belong only to the past and, therefore, have nothing to do with Jim. By the time we see him appear in the story, these qualities no longer exist; the once-powerful Powell family and the home in which Jim was born have been on the course of decline for a long time. The huge homestead has been sold, and Jim's home is now a tiny shabby room over someone's garage, "a cheerless square of a room, punctuated with a bed and a battered table."[37] Worse than the deterioration of the family estate is the physical condition of the family members, the thin and sick Jim and the crazy old lady, Aunt Mamie, by whom Jim was raised. Everyday the only thing Jim does is to roam all over town. His perception is "a sense of futility, a dull ache at the grayness of his life."[38] His life is simply fading out.

Apparently, the representation of a character's desolate sentimentality as symbolically reflected and reinforced in the decline of the family homestead, the setting of this story, is done in the same fashion as we see in Poe's "The Fall of the House of Usher," but Fitzgerald did it without resorting to any mysterious or supernatural charm; instead, he accomplished it with a realistic, but very articulate, approach. His "More than Just a House," published thirteen years later, picked up the same subject and adopted the same parallel pattern in depicting the decay of the old Maryland house and the decline of the Gunther family. In other stories, homes are depicted in sentimental terms but without using Poe's pattern. "The Lees of Happiness" is a typical example of this different approach. In the story, the Curtains, as Arthur Mizener has observed, resemble the Fitzgeralds in many ways.[39] Having lived in numerous luxurious hotels, the Curtains start to dream of settling down in a house with impressive decor that reflects their happy marriage. Unfortunately, what the story actually presents is that their dream turns from bliss to not merely an empty fantasy but, rather, a source of sentimental disillusionment. Fitzgerald's description of the Curtains' house is focused on the gradual decaying process: the white paint turning gray under the summer sunshine, the peeling strips of old paint, the streaky paint on the front pillars, the darkened green blinds until "it began to be a house that was avoided by the tender-mind." The male owner of the house has turned into a "living corpse."[40]

Another frequent motif in Fitzgerald's use of domestic settings is his treatment of home as a source of human misery. In stories like "Jemina" and "Mr. Icky," home, which is always supposed to be secure and happy, turns out to be what disrupts or even ruins the life of its occupant. "Jemina" is more shocking in that Fitzgerald blames the family and home as the source of the heroine's terminal miseries. As a result of the bloody feud between the Tantrum and the Doldrum families that has lasted for generations Jemina's home has lost its original function and turned into a place of violence. Finally, it is in her own home that Jemina is trapped and burned to death. Ironically, nevertheless, the home in "Mr. Icky," Fitzgerald's playlet, is rendered as a source or violence and death not by a feud between different families but by a feud, more or less, between the hero, Mr. Icky, and his children. His daughter leaves home to marry a rich man, while his son goes to sea. His other dozens of children abandon him simply because they do not want to rot with him; they want to live their own lives.[41] As a result, Mr. Icky is left alone to die without a home.

In a certain sense, the Hollywood producer in *The Last Tycoon,* Stahr, is also a miserable and homeless man. Although he is a giant figure in that kingdom of fantasy, money, and fame, a man who has everything in life, Stahr does not have a decent place he can call home. In the novel, we see him almost like "The Jelly-Bean," Jim, loafing around in Hollywood; sometimes he sleeps in his studio suite; sometimes he sleeps in a rented house; sometimes he sleeps in the roofless house he is building in Santa Monica. Each of the four trips he makes with Kathleen to the house on the beach carries a symbolic sense of the uncertain misery in his life. "The skeletal house," as Sergio Perosa argues, "suggestive of a movie set and somehow constituting a symbol of the desolation of Stahr's unstable life, is where their bodies are united. It is a breathless union—almost in the open, without any shelter—that will never turn into a harmonious life."[42] In terms of the effect of characterization, Stahr's lack of a steady home helps to bring out a frequently overlooked facade of this powerful and charismatic man's personality, making him more human and believable.

Perhaps Fitzgerald's most dynamic use of home settings can be found in his portrayal of Tom Buchanan and Myrtle Wilson. Everything he chose to place in the pictures of Tom's house and Myrtle's New York apartment spotlights on their hypocritical nature. The splendor of Tom's house as well as its surroundings serves as outward manifestation of its owner's true nature as a liar and a malicious bully. We see this house through the eyes of Nick, the narrator of *The Great Gatsby,* who is invited to a gathering there. It is significant to note that apart from Daisy, Tom, and their longtime friend, Jordan, Nick is the only one invited; in other words, he is one of the few people allowed in Tom's circle. One cannot help thinking that this is an implicit contrast to the open, wild, and nonstop parties of strangers at Gatsby's mansion. As soon as Nick gets out of his car and casts his eyes upon the house in front of him, he is taken by the indigenous architecture of the estate. It is "a cheerful red-and-white Georgian Colonial Mansion, over-looking the bay." The location and the design of the house are indicative of the wealth and status of its owner, who "in riding clothes was standing with his legs apart on the front porch" (*GG,* 10). Unlike his first description of Gatsby's mansion, in which a touch of disdain is apparently woven between the lines, Nick's discerning observation immediately gives us a sense of the quiet elegance and tasteful splendor of this large, old place. His initial impression is favorable as it nudges his old admiration for the traditional establishment of wealth and power in American society, but it does not linger for long. Instead, he claims, "Their house was even more elaborate than I expected" (*GG,* 10). The key word "elaborate" instantly calls into question the real intention behind the "elaborateness" of Tom's estate and entertains the conclusion that the Buchanans have devoted a great deal of effort and money to the graceful design of and decor of their house. This very "elaborateness" represented by the bay, the lawn, the beach, the walls, and the vines casts a veil over the place as well as over its inhabitants. Not many readers would quickly assert at this point of the novel that the image of Tom standing on the front porch fully embodies the Buchanans' arrogance toward the world; even his strong body, "capable of enormous leverage—a cruel body" (*GG,* 11), suggests his overwhelming dominance or menace over other people. Nor would readers readily see that his house resembles a confinement in which Daisy, the epitome of Gatsby's romantic dream, is detained and to which Gatsby cannot get access, but can only look at across the bay. The whole image of this gorgeous house is so deceitful that we will not be able to catch the suspenseful implication of what Tom and his house actually stand for unless we follow Nick's eyes closely and collect the clues he leaves behind.

The clues to the pretentious nature of Tom and his house are exposed as soon as Nick starts to describe what he sees inside the house. Nick finds himself standing in front of the flamboyant furnishings of the drawing-room. Instead of being amazed by such a display of wealth, he can literally feel the pomposity and hypocrisy of his hosts. Fitzgerald utilizes the color imagery, such as the white gleaming windows, the pale flaglike curtains and the two women in white, the "rosy-colored" space in the hallway, and the green grass (*GG*, 11-13), to create the false grandeur around the house. This time, however, it does not take too long before we see the subtle contrast between the ostentatious glitter of the place and the hypocrisy, snobbery, and cruelty hidden in the personality of these characters. Before the party is over, Tom's arrogant and aggressive nature, which has already been implied earlier by his standing posture on the porch, is now completely exposed in his words and actions; his gentle manner, in particular, is proved to be phony by the incident at the dinner table when Daisy shows a finger Tom has bruised and, later, by another incident when he breaks Myrtle's nose simply for mentioning Daisy's name. His lustful affair with Myrtle, especially his condescending and abusive attitude toward women, unmasks his true nature as a liar and a brute. Daisy, Gatsby's "golden girl" and, to use Leslie A. Fiedler's words, "Fair Maiden," "rich and elegant and clean and sweet-smelling," actually embodies "corruption and death."[43] Daisy's friend, Jordan, is not a fully developed character. The only thing we know about her is that tennis is the sole passion she has, but she cheats in the game.

Yes, indeed, a comparison will show that Fitzgerald seems to be more unsparing in his depiction of Myrtle's New York apartment. He does a much more effective job in delineating Myrtle's obsession with vanity, working to hit hard on her pathetic imitation of upper-class taste. It is an ordinary one-bedroom apartment, with limited space and facilities. The small living room, however, is "crowded to the doors with a set of tapestried furniture entirely too large for it, so that to move about was to stumble continually over scenes of ladies swinging in the gardens of Versailles" (*GG*, 37). Even though the description cannot be any simpler, its brevity belies its overtone of ridicule and contempt. Despite its limited space, Myrtle stuffs the rooms with all kinds of fancy things, from the tapestried furniture to portraits, old copies of *Town Tattle*, and small scandal magazines, all of which bespeak her ignorance and vanity. Evidently her purpose is to make a display of her "affluence" and lofty taste. Even the way she talks in the apartment appears to be another desperate means to hide her inferior background and her real station in the "valley of ashes." When the boy forgets to bring her ice, she raises her eyebrows, saying, "I told that boy about the ice, . . . these people! You have to keep after them all the time" (*GG*, 41). The most suggestive detail about her delusion is Fitzgerald's description of her swinging into the kitchen, as if "a dozen chefs awaited her orders there" (*GG*, 41). The relentless irony is that Fitzgerald makes Myrtle sound virtually like the hostess of a respectful household rather than a fleshy mistress summoned to this "trysting nest" procured by her lover, whom she ran into on the commuter train one day. The room is filled with her high-sounding orders and her "artificial laughter" (*GG*, 47) until Tom shuts her up with a "short and deft movement" (*GG*, 48), breaking her nose. We are made to realize that Myrtle's sense of insecurity is real, and her dream of transcending herself into Tom's world is literally smashed.

What exists, or happens, in this apartment epitomizes a world of pretense and obtrusive showiness, which, as Robert E. Long says, "evokes the idea of vacancy, as well as failure and casualty."[44] But it is by no means a world defining Myrtle alone. This obsession with vanity and insecurity is something that haunts all the people present in the apartment, especially the women guests, just as the disorderly objects in the apartment, the "innumerable pottery bracelets" jingling up and down the arms of Myrtle's sister, and the brag of Mrs. McKee about her former suitor, "a little kike," exemplify the instinct of selfishness and dishonesty among these people. Obviously, as Aerol Arnold has described, "this is lower middle class snobbery, not much different in kind from the snobbery of Gatsby and Tom."[45] Here again we have a compact example of Fitzgerald's artistry in turning a list of trivial objects in a home setting into an index of personality traits.

NOTES

1. Quoted from Frances P. Keyes's foreword to Archibald Rutledge's *Home by the River* (New York: Bobbs-Merrill, 1955), vii.

2. Quoted from Leon Edel's introduction to Henry James's *The Spoils of Poynton* (London: W. Heinemann, 1967), 23.

3. Earl H. Rovit, "The American Concept of Home," *The American Scholar* 29 (autumn 1960): 521-22.

4. Allan Gurgannus, afterword, in *Home: American Writers Remember Rooms of Their Own*, eds. Sharon Fiffer and Steve Fiffer (New York: Pantheon Books, 1995), 221.

5. Robert Frost, *The Poetry of Robert Frost* (New York: Holt, Rinehart and Winston, 1969), 38.

6. Nathaniel Hawthorne, *The House of the Seven Gables* (New York: Bantam Books, 1981), 18.

7. Henry Dan Piper, *F. Scott Fitzgerald: A Critical Portrait* (Holt, Rinehart and Winston, 1965), 7.

8. Claude M. Sinzelle, *The Geographical Background of the Early Works of D. H. Lawrence* (Paris: Etudes Anglaises, 1964), 46.

9. Richard Gill, *Happy Rural Seat* (New Haven, Conn.: Yale University Press, 1972), 252.

10. Richard D. Lehan, *F. Scott Fitzgerald and the Craft of Fiction* (Carbondale, Ill.: Southern Illinois University Press, 1969), 86.

11. Rose A. Gallo, *F. Scott Fitzgerald* (New York: Frederick Ungar Publishing, 1978), 26.

12. Dan Seiters, *Image Patterns in the Novels of F. Scott Fitzgerald* (Ann Arbor, Mich.: UMI Research Press, 1986), 33.

13. Philippa Tristram, *Living Space in Fact and Fiction* (London: Routledge, 1989), 1.

14. Sigmund Freud, *A General Introduction to Psychoanalysis* (New York: Pocket Books, 1971), 160.

15. E. M. Forster, *Howards End* (New York: Vintage Books, 1921), 155.

16. Ralph Waldo Emerson, "Nature," in *Selections from Ralph Waldo Emerson*, ed. Stephen E. Whicher (Boston: Houghton Mifflin, 1957), 56.

17. Maxwell Perkins, "Letter to Fitzgerald (November 20, 1924)," reprinted in *The Great Gatsby: A Study*, ed. Frederick Hoffman (New York: Charles Scribner's Sons, 1962), 174.

18. F. Scott Fitzgerald, in *The Letters of F. Scott Fitzgerald*, ed. Andrew Turnbull (New York: Charles Scribner's Sons, 1963), 170.

19. Frederick Hoffman, ed., *The Great Gatsby: A Study* (New York: Charles Scribner's Sons, 1962), 9.

20. Eugen Huonder, *The Functional Significance of Setting in the Novels of Francis Scott Fitzgerald* (Bern: Herbert Lang; Frankfurt/M.: Peter Lang, 1974), 65.

21. Bryan R. Washington, *The Politics of Exile: Ideology in Henry James, F. Scott Fitzgerald, and James Baldwin* (Boston: Northeastern University Press, 1995), 48.

22. A. Robert Lee, *Scott Fitzgerald: The Promises of Life* (New York: St. Martin's Press, 1989), 48-49.

23. William H. Gass, *Fiction and the Figures of Life* (Boston: Nonpareil Books, 1989), 48-49.

24. Miles Donald, *The American Novel in the Twentieth Century* (New York: Barnes and Noble, 1978), 19.

25. Marius Bewley, *The Eccentric Design* (New York: Columbia University Press, 1959), 278.

26. Richard D. Lehan, *The Great Gatsby: The Limits of Wonders* (Boston: Twayne, 1990), 35.

27. W. T. Lhamon, Jr., "The Essential Houses of *The Great Gatsby.*" *The Markham Review* 6 (spring 1977): 58.

28. Hilton Anderson, "From the Wasteland to East Egg: Houses in *The Great Gatsby*," *The University of Mississippi Studies in English*, no. 9 (1991): 114.

29. Richard Cohen, "The Inessential Houses of *The Great Gatsby*," *The Husson Review*, no. 2 (1968): 52.

30. Robert G. Deamer, *The Importance of Place in the American Literature of Hawthorne, Thoreau, Crane, Adams, and Faulkner* (Lewiston, N.Y.: The Edwin Mellen Press, 1990), 178.

31. Allen Tate, *On the Limits of Poetry* (New York: Swallow Press, 1948), 143.

32. Robert Scholes, *Approaches to the Novel: Material for a Poetics* (San Francisco: Chandler Publishing, 1966), 16.

33. Percy Lubbock, *The Craft of Fiction* (London: Jonathan Cape, 1954), 220.

34. Leonard Lutwack, *The Role of Place in Literature* (Syracuse, N.Y.: Syracuse University Press, 1984), 71.

35. Suzanne West, "Nicole's Gardens," in *Fitzgerald/Hemingway Annual 1978*, eds. Matthew J. Bruccoli and Richard Layman (Detroit: Gale Research, 1978), 86. West's article provides a detailed and insightful analysis of Fitzgerald's depiction of the two gardens in the novel.

36. F. Scott Fitzgerald, in *The Short Stories of F. Scott Fitzgerald: A New Collection*, ed. Matthew J. Bruccoli (New York: Charles Scribner's Sons, 1989), 143.

37. Ibid., 155.

38. Ibid., 156.

39. Arthur Mizener, *The Far Side of Paradise: A Biography of F. Scott Fitzgerald* (Boston: Houghton Mifflin, 1951), 147.

40. F. Scott Fitzgerald, *Six Tales of the Jazz Age and Other Stories* (New York: Charles Scribner's Sons, 1960), 134.

41. F. Scott Fitzgerald, *Tales of the Jazz Age* (New York: Charles Scribner's Sons, 1922), 310.

42. Sergio Perosa, *The Art of F. Scott Fitzgerald*, trans. Charles Matz and the author (Ann Arbor, Mich.: University of Michigan Press, 1968), 160.

43. Leslie A. Fiedler, *Love and Death in the American Novel* (New York: Dell Publishing, 1966), 315.

44. Robert E. Long, *The Achieving of The Great Gatsby* (Lewisberg, Pa.: Bucknell University Press, 1979), 126.

45. Aerol Arnold, "Picture, Scene, and Social Comment: *The Great Gatsby*," *The University Review* (Kansas City) 30 (1963): 117.

3

BARS: WINDOWS OF SOCIETY

To present a view of America in the early years of the century, one might create a story around a series of great historical events that shocked and remolded the entire society, or one might portray a typical character whose whole life is inseparable from and interwoven with these events, just as many of Fitzgerald's predecessors and contemporaries did in their fiction. What distinguishes Fitzgerald from them is his art in presenting an event or a character in a parabolic form, and transforming it into a microcosm of the society by exploring some common and even insignificant places as settings. Of course, Fitzgerald's achievement is not merely limited to the celebration and repudiation of home. His use of bar settings (though some of them are fictional, most of them are real and well known) constitutes a considerable portion of his work and displays a good variety of tactics. Although Fitzgerald was only one of many American writers who featured bars in their fiction, to this day no one has ever so articulately explored bars as major settings in the same way as Fitzgerald did. His superiority in terms of the selection, manipulation, and representation of the bar imagery is almost beyond match. Scenes of bars in his fiction are configured in such a visionary way that bars appear to be a series of "windows" that open onto the world of American society.

BARS IN FICTION AND IN THE JAZZ AGE

Bars existed long before Fitzgerald was born. The bar is somewhat like, and sometimes difficult to distinguish from, the café of France, the *bierstube* in Germany, the taverna of Greece, or the pub of England. Unlike the French café, or *le bistro* as the French usually call it, which turns outward in summer and inward in winter, the bar of America always accommodates its customers in secluded and dimly lit rooms. It is a lounging place, where one may have a drink or a bite of food, meet friends, or even socialize with strangers. Despite the difference in their names and the service they offer, these bars, cafés, *bierstubes*, tavernas, and pubs are thoroughly integrated into the cultures of these countries. According to Ray Oldenburg, a well-respected authority on the history and function of "public hangouts" like these, about three-fourths of the drinking done in England takes place in pubs or other public settings.[1] In defining the multiple roles of the Viennese café, Joseph Wechsberg suggests that it is a place where the common man can find "his haven and island of tranquillity, his reading room and gambling hall, his sounding board and grumbling hall. There at least he is safe from nagging wife and unruling children, monotonous radios and barking dogs, tough bosses and impatient creditors."[2] There is no similar assessment of bars in America, yet it is reasonable to say that bar visitation is a big part of many Americans' lives, because they seek the same kind of "escape," or "consolation" Wechsberg mentioned. H. L. Mencken used to describe the Biltmore bar of his day as "a quiet refuge" and "a hospital asylum from life and its care."[3] What Mencken did not mention in his description is the widely documented bond between bars and artists. Many a writer's life and work are associated with popular bars in cities the world over. Early in this century, it was very much a fashion among writers and artists to hang out in bars. Either they used the place as their study for reading and writing, or just thinking, or they got together for relief, companionship, and the joy of exchanging or debating their artistic aspirations. One anecdote worth noting says that Fitzgerald had his first meeting with his friend and rival Ernest Hemingway in the Dingo Bar on Rue Delambre, Paris, in late April 1925.

To be sure, bars have been an inspiring place for writers; they feature in literature, too. As settings, bars were frequent, though scattered subjects of exploration in the fiction of Charles Dickens, Emile Zola, Henry James, Stephen Crane, and Theodore Dreiser, whom Fitzgerald admired and to whom he owed a great deal. However, bars have seldom played a dominant role as a central stage of action in fiction. Mostly, they have either been chosen as a passing scene in a series of events or treated as isolated backdrops endowed with certain social and personal implications. It was only in Fitzgerald's time that the most significant use of bar settings occurred. The primary reason is the fast-growing importance of bars in modern life. Toward the end of the nineteenth century, bars flourished along the roads and around the street corners. After World War I, they mushroomed around towns and cities. The function of bars went beyond providing food and drink, and many of them turned into places of entertainment. Particularly, as the roaring twenties stimulated the bar business, the bar became an indispensable institution of life during the Jazz Age, an age of euphoria and hedonism. Its impact on the mode of urban life was so great that it became fashionable to frequent bars; bars began to feature prominently in literature. This chapter discusses the function of the bar as a social institution and examines its significance as setting in Fitzgerald's fiction.

For perceptive readers, it is not difficult to notice three facts in Fitzgerald's writing: First, most of Fitzgerald's novels and stories in which the bar functions as a central, or occasional, setting, were written during or shortly after the

1920s; second, the theme in these works is always related in one way or another to the life in the 1920s; third, his main character in these works spends a great deal of time in bars. What is strikingly consistent about these three facts is Fitzgerald's stress on the centrality of the bar in the texture of American life. Whether this is his sole intention or not, there is no doubt that his novels and stories that feature bars as settings represent bar visitation as the prevailing mode of life, fusing the typical with the universal and reflecting the mood of a whole society during the "greatest, gaudiest spree" (*CU*, 87) in American history.

The prominence of bars in Fitzgerald's fiction is in a large manner indebted to their role in this nationwide spree. It was Fitzgerald who named this period of "spree" the "Jazz Age," which ran its course excitingly for almost ten years, from the end of World War I to the "crash" of the stock market. In *The Crack-Up*, Fitzgerald wistfully proclaims that "it was an age of miracles, it was an age of art, it was an age of excess and it was an age of satire" (*CU*, 14). It created many stories of quick fortunes; it produced a configuration of quasi-mythic idols for the young generation, from sports heroes and movie stars to notorious gangsters; it nurtured a group of young writers who got both inspiration and recognition during the excitement of this decade. But World War I left some "shattering effects" on America and brought about a gap between the old and the young, who, as Mary Agnes Hamilton has noted, were so "apart in point of view, code, and standard, as if they belong to different races."[4] The old were disappointed because they believed that the war and, perhaps, the victory of that war had ruined the structure of their once stable society: morality, family values, religious belief, ideological direction, and the authority of social institution. The young were disillusioned because they felt embittered and betrayed by the sacrifice of their ideals, for which many of them had spilled their youthful blood and lost their friends on the battlefield. Young writers in the 1920s repeatedly blamed the war for whatever was reckless and libertine in the behavior of the young generation, and claimed that the young deserved the right to defy the past and search for a new future. Nevertheless, the new way of life that the young believed to be ideal was "an unchartered colony of freedom," and they were "refugees from reality."[5] For years, actually, many historians have metaphorized the 1920s as a "party," a "ten-year-long weekend party," and labeled the young people as the wildest "party-goers." By Fitzgerald's own definition, this young generation was one that "corrupted its elders" and pushed a "whole race going hedonistic, deciding on pleasure" (*CU*, 15). "In those days," as Fitzgerald fondly describes in *The Crack-Up*, "life was like the race in *Alice in Wonderland*, there was a prize for everyone." "Even when you were broke you didn't worry about money, because it was in such profusion around you" (*CU*, 21). But no one knew how long the "spree" would last. Almost everyone was perpetually haunted by their worries about the quick ending of their "party" and the imminence of death as well. Just as John F. Carter, Jr., a member of this young generation, proclaims in his article published in *The Atlantic Monthly*, the young "have been forced to live in an atmosphere of 'tomorrow we die,'" and quite naturally, they "drank and were merry."[6] Their disillusionment with the postwar society became an excuse for rejecting all the social and moral responsibilities, and their fear of sudden death drove them into the abyss of self-indulgence.

Apart from their voguish dress, fancy hair style, jargon, and candor toward sexuality, the most conspicuous outward sign of the young people's hedonistic life was drinking. Drinking was their magic joy because, as Fitzgerald explains in *The Beautiful and Damned*, "there was a kindliness about intoxication—there was that indescribable gloss and glamour it gave, like the memories of ephemeral and faded evenings" (*BD*, 417). Unfortunately, however, very few people realized at that time that drinking could also be destructive. The simple reason is that as Fitzgerald points out in *The Crack-Up*, "living wasn't the reckless, careless business these people thought" (*CU*, 87). Then, when the young men and women were awakened to the cruel realities of life, they had to face the hard fact of disillusionment. Drinking thus became the only evasive way they knew to deal with their emotional distress. Even though the Prohibition had taken effect nationally under the Eighteenth Amendment in 1919, there was more drinking than before. Society as a whole seemed to function on alcohol, and everything in American life hinged on the bottle. Day and night young people frequented the corner saloons in the neighborhood or the fancy bars in cities, and they stayed drunk all the time, or to be exact, all the time when they could afford it.

Without doubt, Fitzgerald was never far away from the general binge himself. It was not a secret that his life was marked by endless problems, from a ruined marriage, broken friendships, and fist fights to brushes with the law, all due to his excessive drinking. In fact, alcohol was not a rare commodity in his household when he was young. He recorded in his *Ledger*, "My father used to drink too much and then play baseball in the backyard."[7] According to an investigation on Fitzgerald's alcoholism conducted by Dr. Donald Goodwin in 1970, Fitzgerald drank heavily at Princeton; although alcohol in any form was strictly forbidden there, Fitzgerald drank beer to excess in the bars along Nassau Street. A few years after Fitzgerald made his debut as a writer, as Alfred Kazin once said, booze seemed to be a "natural accompaniment" of his literary life. During these years, which Fitzgerald spent alternately in America and Europe, his drinking problem became acute. Many of his friends were heavy drinkers, and he spent a lot of time touring various kinds of bars. Occasionally his drinking reached the point where he could no longer control himself in public, embarrassing both himself and his friends either in the bar or in someone's house. William L. Shirer wrote about one incident of Fitzgerald's drunken behavior. One midnight Fitzgerald showed up drunk at the *Paris Tribune*, where he sat on the copy desk, singing songs and ripping up copies. His friends, William L. Shirer, James Thurber, and Eugene Jolas, tried to take him home, but Fitzgerald insisted on touring bars. When he passed out, they took him to his apartment. But he refused to go in and fought with the three of them until they carried him into his room.[8] Frequently he would introduce himself to new acquaintances by announcing, "I'm an alcoholic." Busy hopping from one bar or a drinking party to another, Fitzgerald simply could not remain sufficiently sober to devote himself to his writing, although, as Hemingway recalled in *A Moveable Feast*, "he was always trying to work. Each day he would try and fail."[9] Consequently, his literary productivity waned considerably. It was quite a while before the heavy toll that his drinking took on his writing and life finally helped him understand the dangerous consequence of the wild binge in society, and forced him to confront his own bibulous indulgence. As a few of his notebook entries indicate, he knew that booze would ruin his work and eventually kill him. Starting from his early fiction, Fitzgerald's grappling with alcoholism is constantly reflected in his own writing. It is widely felt, though, that his treatment of drunks or drinking bouts bears an ambivalence toward alcoholism. By the time he wrote "Babylon Revisited," however, Fitzgerald accepted the painful fact that he was an obnoxious alcoholic, and drinking was ruining his writing career. Hence, drinking became a serious and recurrent subject in his work.

Rendering the "drunken outrages" in his fiction, the use of the bar as a recurrent setting seems to be the key to his phenomenal success. Given that the 1920s were the years when drinking virtually became a characteristic of American society, the bar seemed to be the most plausible symbol in representing the norm of life in Fitzgerald's time. As documented in various books and memoirs, it was common practice for writers and artists to hang out, or even to do their "creative work," at bars. For the public, the bar served as a gathering place, where one could sit for hours drinking and talking amid the smell of beer, wine, smoke, sweat, and odd perfume. Some bar-goers saw the bar as an extension of their house, or their apartment, where they could meet all kinds of people and share information in an exchange that they believed would make them feel connected with others and keep them close to the happenings in the world; some regarded the bar, not as an extension, but as a substitute for the residence they dreamed to have, a place where they could evade the unpleasant and harsh realities they were afraid to confront with; some, just like the characters in Theodore Dreiser's *Sister Carrie*, transformed the bar into an ideal shelter. There, sitting under the dim lights day and night, they would lose their sense of time and their memory of all miseries; there they could contemplate, dream, lament, and dupe themselves in endless intoxication. For them, that was the only way to maintain some minimal contact with society and to shield themselves from the pain of depression and, to borrow Albert Camus's words, "the terrors of solitude."[10]

BARS AND ILLUSIONS OF ROMANTIC EGOTISTS

A drinking writer himself, Fitzgerald enjoyed drinking in bars and knew them quite well. One interesting anecdote in Noel Riley Fitch's *Literary Cafés of*

Paris tells us that the Ritz Bar in Paris was virtually made famous by the regular visits of Fitzgerald and other wealthy Americans during the 1920s.[11] Back in America, Fitzgerald's name was also often associated with well-known bars from New York City to Hollywood. Although bars appeared in numerous fictional accounts, Fitzgerald seemed to be the first writer, if not the only writer, who thoroughly understood the indispensable role of the bar in the social formation of America in the 1920s and knew how to utilize the bar as a metaphorical milieu in probing and delineating the realities of life in fiction. From time to time, he either directly drew upon his own memory of the bars he used to frequent, providing them with real names and familiar features, or set his scenes and stories in bars without revealing anything specific about them, instead keeping their vague presence mainly as a backdrop. A perceptive reader of Fitzgerald's fiction is likely to be amazed by the diverse prowess Fitzgerald displayed in exploring the bar setting and by the tremendous effect the bar setting usually contributes to characterization and thematic development.

As can be readily seen, Fitzgerald's most deliberate and successful use of the bar setting is accomplished in his novels and stories that trace the downfall of seemingly ambitious and promising characters. What Fitzgerald does so consistently and so effectively in addressing their fall is to trace the close ties between their degeneration and the bar, or the bottle, in one way or another. One of the most convenient places to begin an examination of this issue is *This Side of Paradise*, in which Fitzgerald made his first attempt at exploring the bar setting. Although the novel is not primarily concerned with Amory's drinking problem and the bar is not always designated as the center stage of action in the novel, a recognition of the functional significance of the bar setting is crucial to an understanding of how each of Amory's bar visits symbolizes a different phase of his downward slip toward the ultimate failure. Amory is indeed a character who well fits the profile indicated by the first title that Fitzgerald had chosen for the novel: He is a "Romantic Egotist," full of youthful passion and ideals. Critics like James Gindin have called Amory a "Keatsian romantic hero strung between inevitably abstract polarities,"[12] a person always keenly aware of and helplessly torn by a paradoxical rivalry between the opposite sides of his own nature: idealism vs. materialism, nobility vs. snobbery, and sympathy vs. selfishness. Nevertheless, Amory does not take any constructive actions to suture the gap between the two extremes; instead, he remains disoriented and wastes most of his time either in savoring illusions or in wandering from parties to bars for drunken sprees whenever his illusions evaporate in the heat of harsh realities.

The image of Amory, bewildered and devastated, is most lucidly presented in a series of bar scenes immediately after his lover, Rosalind Connage, rejects his proposal for marriage. Prior to his encounter with Rosalind, Amory has already been hurt by several disastrous relationships. In his distress, Amory becomes "restless as the devil" and develops "a horror of getting fat or falling in love and growing domestic" (*TSP*, 163). Before long, however, Amory is again seized by his desire to enjoy life when he meets Rosalind, a light-hearted and irresponsible "debutante"; his sense of love is rekindled. In less than two weeks, he and Rosalind are "deeply and passionately in love" (*TSP*, 186), as if the memory of all his previous dismal encounters with other women has been swept away by a whirlwind. At this point, he is happily riding on "the great wave of emotion" (*TSP*, 186). For the first time in his life, Amory finds himself genuinely in love; he realizes that he simply cannot part himself from his godsend lover, as if he fears that the spell between them "would break and drop them out of this paradise of rose and flame" (*TSP*, 186). As Fitzgerald puts it, Amory has "closed the book of fading harmonies at last and stepped into the sensuous vibrant walks of life" (*TSP*, 186). For a brief moment, Amory's long and frantic search for an exciting and romantic life almost appears to have reached its triumphant end. Nevertheless, no matter how "genuine" this courtship may seem, it does not last very long, and it certainly does not lead him to a happy marriage; rather he ends up in a "genuine" emotional crisis. Contrary to what Amory has envisioned so far, Rosalind soon strips off her "golden girl" veil and reveals herself as a woman who pines for a life of extravagance and revelry, turning Amory into a victim of the sordid society by rejecting his proposal on the grounds of his financial deficiency. As a result, Amory is instantly hauled back into the world of despair, a world from which he has been trying so desperately to escape all along.

To see this more clearly, we need only look at the miserable appearance of Amory after that humiliating rejection. At the beginning of "Experiments in Convalescence," the second part of the novel, Fitzgerald presents a brief but striking description of Amory as he starts his three-week bender through the bars of midtown New York in an attempt to alleviate his grief. In fact, the word "grotesque" Fitzgerald uses in his scathing description of Amory says it all. The reader will have no problem in visualizing Amory's condition. Physically, he is in total exhaustion after "two days of worry and nervousness, of sleepless nights, of untouched meals"; mentally, he is flung into a void of numbness, the "emotional crisis" resulting from his lover's abrupt rejection having already deactivated "his mind into a merciful coma" (*TSP*, 198). To be sure, Rosalind is not the first girl in Amory's life; nor is this his first love affair. But Rosalind is the only girl who not only "had taken the first flush of his youth" but also "had drawn out [of him] what was more than passionate admiration" (*TSP*, 209). He has never been so serious in attempting a romantic relationship, nor so infatuated with anyone else. Because of such a deep and undying affection, the pain inflicted in Amory's heart by Rosalind's refusal becomes doubly unbearable.

In a scene inside the Knickerbocker Bar, the first of the bars that Amory will visit on that day, we see Amory fumbling at the table with his nervous hands and "knocking off the dish of olives to a crash on the floor" (*TSP*, 199) while talking mumbo jumbo to Wilson and Carling, his classmates at Princeton. What is especially revealing about Amory's despair is his own speech, "Seek pleasure where find it for tomorrow die. 'At's philos'phy for me now on" (*TSP*, 199).

One can easily picture Amory announcing to the bar at large that he is a "physcal anmal" and struggling to come up with an answer to this question from his audience:

"What are you celebrating, Amory?"
Amory leaned forward confidentially.
"Cel'brating blowmylife. Great moment blow my life. Can't tell you 'bout it'—." (*TSP*, 200)

In a sense, Amory's answer is very honest, although it is given with a tone of self-mockery. Deep inside his mind, Amory knows well that his breakup with Rosalind is by no means a cause for celebration. Ironically, the blow has come to him so suddenly that he simply cannot comprehend the whole thing himself. As if his mind is still in a perpetual spin, Amory is as much confused as those around him in the bar, who are listening to his raucous and incoherent speeches, apparently marked by the missing vowel in his words, and watching him smashing bottles.

From the Knickerbocker Bar to Shanley's, the Lethe Bar, the Biltmore, and then to the Coconut Grove, we see Amory garrulously arguing with his friends and other strange bar-hoppers, gulping one drink after another, and lamenting the great loss of his love with a streaming flood of tears. It is quite clear that what Fitzgerald tries to underscore in these bar scenes is not so much a melodramatic celebration as a long ordeal for Amory. Although different in physical signification, Amory's bar-to-bar drinking sprees can be perceived in only two ways: First, they are his desperate attempts to sort out the cause and effect of his love crisis; second, when he is unable to figure out what has gone wrong, they become the only means Amory can adopt to "shield himself from the stabs of memory" (*TSP*, 208), and thus put a stop to his grief.

What is notable about Fitzgerald's tactics in parading this series of bar scenes is the way in which he keeps Amory dangling between slumber and sobriety, unable to hide himself in that "merciful coma" induced by alcohol. The valiant message Fitzgerald intends to convey is that Amory's agony is far from over; his sorrow will not be easily washed away by drink, nor will "the bruised sports of his spirit" (*TSP*, 199) be soothed by his broken memories of happy days spent with his former lover. Ironically, this is something Amory soon finds out himself when his drunken bar-to-bar spree comes to a sudden halt with the advent of Prohibition. Once he is sober again, Amory realizes that alcohol is not a remedy for his problem, that drinking can relieve his sorrow by making his head spin so "gorgeously" that he can forget about his surroundings, but only temporarily. The stark truth, Amory discovers, is that after a lot of alcohol "tumbled into his stomach" in the three-week spree (*TSP*, 201), he is merely "over the first flush of pain" (*TSP*, 209); he is still trapped in the nightmare of his love crisis, "emotionally worn out" (*TSP*, 209).

Thanks to its graphic detail and dramatic contiguity, the episode of Amory's bar-to-bar spree is short, albeit quite entertaining and forceful; it is significant in the portrayal of Amory, for it establishes the distinguished quality of Amory's image as a "cynical idealist" amidst an emotional crisis, less by anything he says or does in these different bar scenes than by the way he responds to his friends and the people he meets in the bar and, particularly, by the way he communicates with himself, his memories, his past. It is also instrumental in that it demonstrates Fitzgerald's unique artistry in presenting each one of these bars as a setting perfect for Amory's whimsical moods and unpredictable actions during the drunken spree. What appears most extraordinary and therefore deserves more attention in the artistic features of this episode is Fitzgerald's hardly noticeable finesse in selecting and describing the physical features of these bars. The first thing that might appear a bit unusual to the reader is that Fitzgerald gives these bars real names; even their locations match their counterparts in real life. By introducing these well-known bars, which the author and his contemporaries used to roam during the 1920s, Fitzgerald injects into the story a strong sense of a particular time and a particular place—to which readers can easily relate based on their own experience in life—thereby enriching and empowering his story with a quality of immediacy and verisimilitude. Unlike many other writers, Fitzgerald made a conscious effort to give the depiction of these bars a poetic quality. His bar setting is well structured, not in the sense of an overall representation but, rather, in the sense of its characteristic features supported by carefully selected details. The language is terse, precise, and indicative of the occasion and the personality of the character; the imagery is vivid, familiar, and suggestive. Throughout this episode, one thing consistent in the description of bar settings is that almost nothing is told about the appearance or surroundings of the bars. Fitzgerald wastes no time by leading us into these bars right at the heels of his character, but not much is mentioned about the interior of the bars. The information Fitzgerald provides is, at most, quite sketchy, as if only one or two glimpses around the place are allowed. In Fitzgerald's view, what is essential to the function of a bar setting is not its physical integrity as a place, but its certain symbolic qualities, the kind of qualities that might correspond to and, more importantly, reflect the mentalities of the character. Precisely because of this belief Fitzgerald shows less care about the physical nature of each bar at the same time that he gives extra effort to make sure that each bar in this episode becomes not merely an object or a place for action but an integral part of the portrayal of the character.

Some analysis of the function of Fitzgerald's bar scenes might help us understand how the correlation between a bar setting and a character's personality becomes thematized. For instance, when Amory enters the Knickerbocker Bar, the bar is described as "well crowded" (*TSP*, 198), and nothing more. The image of the bar is an arresting one. However, while the reader is invited to envisage what is normally seen in a popular bar, Fitzgerald immediately brings Amory onto the scene. Similarly, nothing is said about

Amory's appearance; nothing in his physical condition indicates that he is still in shock over the abrupt end of his romance. What helps Fitzgerald to transpire the inner workings of Amory's mind is the brief description he gives to the bar. Highly symbolic, the word "crowded" contains multiple meanings in this particular context. Literally speaking, the word is suggestive of a typical scene we can easily imagine inside a bar around the corner of a busy street, a place packed with all kinds of bar-roamers, noisy with laughter and conversation. Figuratively speaking, however, the word "crowded" gives a genuine description of the comalike symptoms of Amory's mind. Within the two days after Rosalind removed his ring from her finger and returned it to him, Amory's mind has been congested with so much grief, worry, and regret that it has virtually fallen into shambles. In other words, it is no exaggeration to say that the "crowdedness" in the Knickerbocker Bar matches the chaos in Amory's mind and therefore underscores Amory's devastating emotional and psychological ordeal. The additional purpose of Fitzgerald's deceptively "sketchy" description is to accentuate that Rosalind's refusal is not so much a signification of Amory's sloppy stumble in love life as a truculent blow to his own unbridled ego, a blow that forces him to come to terms with himself honestly. Up to his break-up with Rosalind, Amory never had much doubt about his charisma and popularity. It is Rosalind's rebuff that delivered the first stunning revelation of his inferiority.

To further clarify the lingering aftermath of Amory's crisis, Fitzgerald resorts to the same strategy, exploiting Shanley's, the second bar stop in Amory's drunken spree, as another refraction of Amory's state of mind. Again, Fitzgerald's one-line description here, "Shanley's was very dim," is short but expressive. Fitzgerald puns upon the word "dim," as he has punned with the word "crowded." On the one hand, he uses the word "dim" to project another familiar sight in bars; most bars are poorly lit by design, with no windows and ceiling lights. On the other hand, he uses the word as a metaphor for the worsening condition of Amory's mind. Instead of focusing on Amory's "grotesque" appearance, as he did in the previous scene at the Knickerbocker Bar, Fitzgerald probes into the inner world of Amory's consciousness, which is jammed with all sorts of fantasies and delusions. Although he is talking in a loud voice, Amory is actually pondering his "desire to crush people under his heel" (*TSP*, 200). All of a sudden, Fitzgerald describes, Amory's mind wanders off: "Rosalind began popping into his mind again, and he found his lips forming her name over and over. Next he was sleepy, and he had a hazy, listless sense of people in dress suits, probably waiters, gathering around the table" (*TSP*, 200). Here, what is at work is Fitzgerald's subtle artistry in fusing the use of setting and characterization. The connection between the "dimness" in Shanley's and the "dimness" in Amory's mind is unannounced but can be felt by the reader with a discerning eye. To see the beauty of such a link, we need to look at this passage carefully. Worth noting is that Fitzgerald places this passage immediately after his description of the "dimness" in Shanley's. In so doing, he directs our attention to the image of the hero in the bar, rather than to the bar itself. Also, this passage is filled with a series of insentient snapshots broadly delineating Amory's mental tumult. His desire to crush people under his heel implies an uncontrollable rage on the verge of lashing out at anybody in his way; his ability to devour the three club sandwiches suggests his anxiety for revenge; the murmuring of Rosalind's name underlines his incessant lament for a painful and irretrievable loss; and the key words "sleepy," "hazy," and "listless" put the finishing touches on the vivid picture of a dimmed and disoriented Amory who is bound to lapse into delirium. When Amory wakes up again in a hotel room the next day, as we are told later, "his head was whirring and picture after picture was forming and blurring and melting before his eyes" (*TSP*, 201). Still, no light illuminates the tunnel of his mind.

Despite its sketchiness, Fitzgerald's description of the bar setting maintains its strong presence in the course of the story and makes its indispensable contribution to the characterization of the hero. Even though its effectiveness owes so much to the use of imagery, one can easily see a consistent pattern in Fitzgerald's use of bar settings; that is, all these bar scenes have great flexibility. Each is not a fixed stage for action: Sometimes a setting is more like a mirror, reflecting what is going on in the character's soul; sometimes it is designated as a particular episode, such as Amory's encounter with his former classmates in the crowd of the Knickerbocker Bar, his devouring of three sandwiches amid the dimness of Shanley's, the riot in the Biltmore, his sleep on the outside balcony of the Coconut Grove, and his exaggerated courtesy toward a famous cabaret star in Yonker's, but once you view them in sequence, they combine to project the whole story of the character as a montage. Between these episodes, Fitzgerald frequently shifts between the actual scene in a bar and the imaginary scene in Amory's memory or illusion. On several occasions, Fitzgerald jumps into the scene and interjects his own comments. All this, so to speak, helps to prove that Fitzgerald's bar setting in *This Side of Paradise* is simple and sketchy in physicality but sophisticated and profound in implication.

The significance of the bar setting could be further appreciated if we realize that as a representative figure of the entire young generation during the 1920s, Amory is not the only character in Fitzgerald's fictional world who feels lost and hurt, wavering between illusion and frustration, and that *This Side of Paradise* is not the only novel in which Fitzgerald relies heavily on bar settings in portraying his characters. In his later novels and stories, Fitzgerald created many characters who, like Amory, are so disillusioned and marginalized that they struggle to evade their predicament by getting themselves intoxicated. Roaming from one bar to another becomes the primary, if not the sole, routine in their daily life. Some of them assert that the bar is the only place they feel comfortable, and that their drinking buddies are the only companions they can find in society; some regard the bar as their only shelter on earth, a place where they can shield themselves from worry, sorrow, or pain, at least for a limited time. They drink endlessly. They are willing to give up meals, jobs, or marriages, anything but drinking. They drink in bars, and they drink at home as well. They drink by themselves and they drink with friends or strangers. They smoke, talk, and argue over their glasses. They even smash glasses on the floor and start brawls. A few of them turn their houses into bars, where one may see almost all the things and incidents you would usually see in public bars. However, as Scott Donaldson claims, drinking is not a "laughing matter in Fitzgerald's fiction."[13] Neither his portrayal of drunks nor his description of drinking bouts is intended purely for comic relief. Instead, both of them serve one single purpose: to convey the moods of a special historical period in American society in which alcoholism took a serious toll on so many people, including the author himself.

A deeper understanding can be achieved by examining a few more bar-hopping and alcohol-abusing characters in Fitzgerald's short stories. First of all, it is presumably not a mere coincidence that Fitzgerald's stories introduced a large cast of drunkards of various ages and backgrounds, who are hooked on booze for various reasons. All their alcohol-related miseries and tragedies combine to paint a sad picture of life during Fitzgerald's time, deploring human vulnerability in front of the temptation and destruction of addictive substance. By and large, the alcoholic addiction of Fitzgerald's "romantic egotists" seems to encompass two different forms: One is hedonism; the other escapism. They either believe that "stimulus" is what they need in pursuit of worry-free pleasure, and drinking is the way to get it, or they hope that the numbing power of alcohol could help them transcend a world of agony and shield them from lapsing into insanity.

What happens to the couple in "One Trip Abroad" (1930) is a telling example of this. As the story unfolds, Nelson and Nicole Kelly are presented as likable and decent people. At the time they leave for Europe in order to pursue a "richer and happier" life abroad, they cannot be called "drunkards" by any definition. On their way to Gibraltar, they deliberately stay away from the crowd that "leaned desperately on one another in the bar; instead, they seriously studied French, and Nelson worked on business."[14] But others just won't leave them alone. They send Nelson and Nicole an invitation for cocktails. The Kellys accept simply because they do not know how to refuse. Shortly afterward they regret their decision and feel guilty about it. As they travel around, they find that life in Europe makes them restless and that they "were at once too old and too young, and too American, to fall into immediate soft agreement with a strange land."[15] The "richer and happier" life they hoped to find abroad is nowhere to be found. To the contrary, they find themselves stuck in a place to which they do not belong. Before long, their yearning for attachment turns into a fear of alienation. In an attempt to seek the taste of life in this "strange land," they eventually turn to the stimulus of its wine. They start drinking a lot of *vin de Capri* and roam through famous bars and night clubs. For a moment they believe that this is the way to have fun, to gain recognition and acceptance, and to enjoy the best of their life abroad. However, what they have never expected is that the more bars they visit and the more wine they drink, the more bored they grow.

During a party in their hotel they are, "Trembling, they [cling] together." As they look around, they see only the clouds "merged into the dark mass of mountains," and "they [are] alone together in the tranquil moonlight."[16] By the end of the story, they have become real "strangers" in Gilbraltar, wanderers who have lost their "peace and love and health, one after the other."[17]

It seems ironic that while Nelson and Nicole count on wine bottles and bar visits for the fun and companionship they need to avoid feeling alienated in a strange land, Dick Ragland of "A New Leaf" (1931) ends up being socially ostracized because of his alcoholic behavior. In his portrayal of Ragland as a ruined, but not a despicable, man, Fitzgerald scored an extraordinary success in articulating misconceptions concerning the effects of alcoholism on characters like Ragland, whose life is disintegrated, but whose sensibility to the repressive contempt from his peers and his self-imposed sense of inferiority still remain strong. Fitzgerald writes meticulously to direct our attention to the way in which Ragland struggles to keep himself from further slipping into oblivion. His first move is to win some empathy from others by blarney; his second move is to satiate whatever "glory" he can score through deception. And it is his firm belief that drinking always helps him to do it. Occasionally, he feels a bit awkward about his own not-so-decent tactics, but he never feels sincerely shameful because of them. In answering why he drinks so much, Ragland explains: "I found that with a few drinks I got expansive and somehow had the ability to please people, and the idea turned my head. Then I began to take a whole lot of drinks to keep going and have everybody think I was wonderful."[18]

Ragland's words sound like a heart-felt confession and therefore make it a bit harder for us to question his honesty. The interesting and relevant point to present here is that, Ragland's desire to impress people parallels that of Fitzgerald. Those who know something about Fitzgerald's drinking history would probably agree that Ragland resembles his creator in many ways. They seem to be troubled by the same sense of insecurity and the urge for popularity. There are many stories about Fitzgerald's unpredictable alcoholic behavior. To please people, he would do anything, either getting attention through silly behavior or performing spontaneous acts of high-spirited charm. Fitzgerald knew that sometimes such a desire would be desperate, and that without "the stimulus of alcohol" it would not be sustained, let alone be fulfilled. He was also keenly aware that he was often torn between his growing dependence on alcohol and his fear for the physical and emotional toll his drinking was taking on him.

Fitzgerald's ambivalent feeling toward drinking is consistently prevalent and conspicuously enigmatic in his novels and stories. Apart from his rumination about the destructiveness of alcoholism, Fitzgerald also ponders the probability of freeing oneself from its spell-like dominance. One attempt at such speculation is Fitzgerald's portrayal of two kinds of alcoholic characters: those who cannot change and those who can. Characters like Ragland are always wavering between their almost incurable addiction and their capricious determination to change or to reform. Ragland, at the sincere request of Julia, promises to change, but change is something too painful for him to do. Drinking is what he can do to sustain the remnants of his self-worth and sanity. As Fitzgerald makes clear in the story, to ask Ragland to stop drinking is simply to ask him to stop breathing. Sadly, this is more or less the same case with the male alcoholic in "An Alcoholic Case" (1937), who is determined to drink himself to death despite the earnest persuasion of and repeated warnings from his nurse. The nurse laments at the end of the story, "It's just that you can't really help them and it's so discouraging—it is all for nothing."[19]

But "as a result of his attempt to adjust to the wreckage of his own career and his present condition,"[20] Fitzgerald created a few characters who somehow manage to emerge as new persons after going through an arduous recovery. The central character in "Family in the Wind" (1932), Dr. Forrest Janney, for example, used to be a brilliant doctor but, as we are told, ruined his own reputation and professional career "by taking to cynicism and drink."[21] After he is unexpectedly called to resume his professional role in a storm, when he must to treat injured people and perform brain surgery, his life is back on track and he becomes a decent and responsible man again, putting the bottle aside and adopting a young girl as his daughter. A similar miracle is dramatized in "The Lost Decade" (1939). Louis Trimple, an architect, has been "out of civilization" in the past ten years because of his alcoholism. As he comes back with a sober mind to the people and place that he left long ago, he surprises his host by walking away from the bar, leaving behind no sign that would make people associate him with drinking at all. Nevertheless, for Charlie Wales, the recovering alcoholic in "Babylon Revisited" (1931), it is never easy, since the road he is trekking is not merely the road to recovery; it is also a road to redemption. No matter how much he tries to redeem himself to wash away his guilt for all he committed during the drunken years, no one, especially his relatives, trusts him. No matter how long he is haunted by the painful memories of his drinking sprees, it seems that the end of his redemptive crusade is nowhere in sight.

It is not accidental that Fitzgerald's serious concern with alcoholism appears very early in his writing, and that many pivotal actions in his work are centered around the characters' drunkenness and their association with various bars. Although some of his stories have been criticized and even dismissed either as "hack writing" or as feeble attempts to address the issue of alcoholism through excessive sympathy for the characters, it is difficult to deny the courage and tenacity Fitzgerald has shown us in his persistent scrutiny of alcoholism or to overlook the finesse and effect his use of bar settings has accomplished for the thematics of characterization.

BARS AND MOODS OF SOCIETY

One thing that makes Fitzgerald's wide use of bar settings so unique and efficacious is what might be termed "theme-oriented flexibility." There is no regularly structured pattern in his creation of bar scenes. His treatment of bars varies in accordance with particular thematic and contextual needs. In *This Side of Paradise* and the stories discussed above, the bar setting is mainly, if not entirely, utilized as a foil, reflecting the mentality of the protagonist; it is one of Fitzgerald's principal descriptive strategies in characterization. But Fitzgerald's bar setting can also serve multiple purposes. Sometimes his bar settings, such as the night club "Marathon," Sammy's bar in *The Beautiful and Damned*, and the Ritz Bar in *Tender Is the Night*, "Babylon Revisited," and "The Bridal Party," far more adequately sets a mood than portrays a character, a mood that bears a profound implication of the social milieu and chimes in with his overall thematic development.

Fitzgerald's description of the midtown nightclub, Marathon, appears to be a forceful manifestation of this mood-setting strategy. During one of his dates with his girlfriend, Gloria, Anthony can hardly think of a place where they can go and have some fun. To please Gloria, who is obviously "in wretched humor," Anthony takes her to the Broadway area in an attempt to find a place that can cheer her up. As they pass "a dozen blocks down Broadway," their eyes are soon caught by a huge brightly lit sign "spelling 'Marathon' in glorious yellow script, adorned with electrical leaves and flowers that alternately vanished and beamed upon the wet and glistening street," and they hear "a colored doorman" saying, "Yes, this was a cabaret. Fine cabaret. Bes' showina city!" (*BD*, 68). Observant readers will instantly recall that no other Fitzgerald work has such a meticulous description of bar. As a matter of fact, this is one of the few relatively lengthy descriptions of the physical aspect of the bar setting Fitzgerald gives in his fiction. As suggested previously, Fitzgerald's style of presenting setting is mostly characterized by terseness and simplicity. The exception we see here is by no means unintentional, however. On the contrary, it is a deliberately calculated effort to draw upon *decor* in order to project a lifelike image of a typical cabaret in the city of New York. With the huge electric sign and colorful lights, shining and flashing, the Marathon is indeed pictured as a place that looks like a "Palace of Pleasure" (*BD*, 69) and thereby an epitome of the night life in the city. That Anthony readily believes the doorman's bragging about the place and instantly decides to "try it" together with Gloria seems to ratify its glamorous and joyous appearance. After all, the atmosphere of "festivity" is what Anthony and Gloria are looking for at this moment.

As soon as Anthony and Gloria enter the building, however, Fitzgerald's description of the Marathon takes on a sarcastic tone. He wastes no time in convincing us that this bar is not as spectacular as it looks. Even though his description of the interior scene works much the way his setting presentation operates throughout the novel, he avoids panoramic representation in lengthy passages and gives a sketchy account based on his sporadic observation of certain things inside the nightclub: From the "stuffy elevator" (*BD*, 69) to its dirty and infrequently changed "table-cloths" (*BD*, 71), its "Japanese lanterns and crape paper" (*BD*, 72), its squealing music of "careless violins and saxophones" (*BD*, 71), its casual performers and its boorish waiter, Fitzgerald singles out these key images one after another to divulge the Marathon's real identity as one of the "brummagem cabarets" (*BD*, 70). Moreover, the vulgar ambiance of the Marathon is thrown into relief by the "three qualifications" its patrons ascribe to the place: It is cheap; it imitates great cafes in the theater district; it is a place where one can "take a nice girl" (*BD*, 69). What we see in this scene contributes to a sharp contrast from what is projected in his initial description of the Marathon. The real nature of this place is thus pointedly dissected: Beneath its "imitated" glamour is only a "shoddy" place frequented by people "without money and imagination" (*BD*, 69). We learn without ever being told that these customers are lower-class people for whom the Marathon is a perfect hangout. The discrepancy between the cabaret's ostentatious appearance, which has just lured in Anthony and Gloria, and the interior scene Fitzgerald exposes to the reader shows the subtlety in Fitzgerald's presentation of setting.

The finesse with which Fitzgerald uses a physical condition of the bar setting to mirror the moral climate of a certain character, already analyzed in the early part of this chapter, can hardly be in question, but in this episode of the young couple's visit to the Marathon, one sees another remarkable technique of Fitzgerald's mood-setting artistry, namely, the organic fusion of setting and characterization. Fitzgerald elevates his use of bar setting to a new level by literally turning the patron characters into part of the cabaret setting. To a certain extent, these people are totally dehumanized, becoming objects that fulfill the same kind of functional role as the "table-cloths" and "lanterns." One discernible difference between his description of the nonhuman object and that of the human object is Fitzgerald's generous use of adjectives, each of which highlights one particular misery from which these patrons are suffering:

There on Sunday nights gather the credulous, sentimental, underpaid, overworked people with hyphenated occupations, book-keepers, ticket-sellers, office-managers, salesmen, and, most of all, clerks—clerks of the express, of the mail, of the grocery, of the brokerage, of the bank. With them are their giggling, overgestured, pathetically pretentious women, who grow fat with them, bear them too many babies, and float helpless and uncontent in a colorless sea of drudgery and broken hopes. (*BD*, 69-70)

Most remarkable about this human part of the setting is its double implication. Fitzgerald's sarcastic introduction of these patrons as the "abandoned people" (*BD*, 70) not only evinces the shoddiness of the Marathon in spite of its fake glamour but also delineates a social landscape by offering a glimpse of the life of the men and women who come from all social strata. Fitzgerald schemes to make the objects and faces in the scene reciprocate each other in both appearance and sentiment, so a careful reader can see that what begins as an account of Anthony's evening outing has now become a parable-like episode, emblemating the symbolic admixture of whole America.

To expand his point with a more poignant explication, Fitzgerald swiftly zooms in to his leading characters, as he often does in other works. In unmasking his characters, he applies the same strategy he uses to expose the nightclub's deceptive look. In many ways, the discrepancy between the Marathon's false glamour and its true shoddiness parallels the one between Gloria's gaudiness and the splendor attributed to her. Like the Marathon, Gloria has the beauty and charm that create illusions in the beholder's mind, but deep inside her is a kind of "cheapness," with which she was born. Her connection to this coarse world is ironically suggested by Gloria's own voluntary revelation. She tells Anthony bluntly that she can completely identify with these club customers, since she also has a streak of "cheapness" and "gaudy vulgarity" (*BD*, 73); she warns Anthony that he does not have the slightest idea about who she really is; she even implicitly compares him to those "clever men" who naively or arbitrarily label her personality. Strangely, Anthony shows no surprise nor offers any response, while Gloria keeps revealing how she truly feels about herself.

Nothing in Gloria's honest confession disturbs Anthony. To him, what she has just said is no more than a lovely and virtuous gesture of her openness. His perception of Gloria as the symbol of impeccable purity and beauty does not yield at all. On the contrary, he compares her to "a single flower amidst a collection of cheap bric-a-brac" and extols her as a "sun, radiating, growing, gathering light and storing it" (*BD*, 73). Here, Fitzgerald obviously tries to suggest not merely the discrepancy about the Marathon's or Gloria's character but, more importantly, the imminent disaster Anthony will run into because of his own blind obsession with this rosy but misty illusion. In a symbolic sense, Fitzgerald's ulterior intention is to point out the resemblance between Anthony's illusion about Gloria in the novel and his contemporaries's illusion about the American dream in real life, raising a serious question about America's identity—as a world of gaiety and prosperity or as "a colorless sea of drudgery and broken hopes"—and issuing the warning that anyone who fails to see the reality of life could end up in the same irreversible degeneration is awaiting Anthony. Thus, by the end of Chapter 2, Anthony has been well portrayed as a specimen for Fitzgerald's dreamers, and the scene in the Marathon episode has ultimately been transformed into a microcosmic picture of American society in Fitzgerald's time.

If the omen of Anthony's future disaster is first seen in this Marathon episode, then the last blow of his disaster is delivered in the episode of Sammy's bar toward the end of the novel, when Anthony is about to lose his sanity. Between, Fitzgerald offers considerable evidence to show the innate flaws of both Anthony and Gloria as well as the steady deterioration of their mentality, claiming that nothing in the world, not even the war, can halt their senseless pursuit of illusion. What makes Fitzgerald's claim so indisputable? It is his genuine illustration that Anthony and Gloria chart the course of their decline and never intend to look back along way. After returning from Europe, the only thing Anthony does is to await, idly and impatiently, his grandfather's death and his legacy, fantasizing the magic this money will create in his stale life. As the prospect of a large inheritance is fading away rather than drawing near, Anthony becomes increasingly restless and starts drinking heavily. For a short while, his courtship of and marriage with Gloria seem to halt his drinking and put his life back on track. But the excitement of his marriage evaporates as soon as the honeymoon is over. The spark between them soon dies out and gives way to lethargy. The same Anthony, Fitzgerald claims, is more and more "restless, inclined to quicken only under the stimulus of several high-balls" and taking on a "faintly, almost imperceptibly, apathetic" attitude toward his new bride, Gloria (*BD*, 192). His life is largely unchanged in spite of his new marriage, for he has reverted to the routine of his former life: waiting anxiously for the Patch family money. Heavy drinking becomes a daily ritual in the house, not only for Anthony but also for Gloria, who is drawn into this marriage primarily by the prospect of sharing a big fortune with Anthony. Ironically, it is during one of these drinking parties that Anthony's grandfather suddenly shows up and gets so angry that he almost disinherits Anthony on the spot. From that point on, Anthony's day begins and ends with drinking, as he waits for the court to make a decision about his challenge of his grandfather's will. Time is not on his side, though, and greedy obsession is the only card Anthony is holding in the matter. He has no control over the pace or the outcome of the draggy legal fight. Before he and Gloria realize it, for them to uphold their status as "beautiful" people is getting more and more difficult, for they have neither the necessary financial means nor the willingness to take action in changing their predicament. As Anthony fails in his half-hearted attempt to earn a living as a salesman and a writer of pot-boilers, their money problem becomes "increasingly annoying, increasingly ominous" (*BD*, 268). Anthony's only choice is to get himself drunk everyday, either "in Sammy's with these men" or "in the apartment over a book" (*BD*, 416). "As he grew drunker," Fitzgerald writes, "the dreams faded and he became a confused specter" (*BD*, 388). He has no core of self, no vision for his future, and no will to control his own destiny. In fact, he hates to be sober because sobriety would pin him down in gloomy realities and make it impossible for him to ignore the people around him," the "struggle," the "greedy ambition," and the "despair" (*BD*, 417).

Anthony's uncontrollable dependence on liquor is brought into focus by Fitzgerald's description of the scene at Sammy's, where Anthony is visiting, as it turns out later, for the last time. This is one of the few bar scenes whose setting and characters Fitzgerald describes in detail. The most salient detail here is that Fitzgerald's keeping track of the time of Anthony's arrival and departure. The whole episode at Sammy's is accordingly centered around "pretension." Large sections of Fitzgerald's description represent interior viewpoints that places Fitzgerald's characterization of Anthony beyond the image of an ordinary bar-hopper, emphasizing Anthony's keen awareness of his own plight and his uncontrollable impulse to regain his lost status. By using contrast, imagery, and selected diction, Fitzgerald persuasively exhibits Anthony's pretension in a process of integrating his basic inner conflicts at this moment—shame and dream, inferiority and vanity.

"It was just after six o'clock," Fitzgerald writes; the "accumulation of cigarette butts and broken glass" (*BD*, 430) that Sammy, the owner of the bar, is sweeping into the corner suggests that business has peaked for the day. The timing of Anthony's visit is tactfully chosen, coming at an hour when the bar is almost empty, Anthony does not have to face his old acquaintances and struggle with their questions. Unlike other customers, Anthony is here not to seek company, but to quench his irresistible thirst for a drink. "Nervous" and "shivering" (*BD*, 429) only a moment before, Anthony is greeted by two men and then invited to their table. The Anthony we see in Sammy's is not the same Anthony who at the Marathon had every right to feel he belonged to the class superior to that of the crowd he and Gloria were watching. Here at Sammy's, Anthony is only a cheap customer, who after a long contemplation of his purchasing power walks into the bar with less than four dollars in his pocket. The irony is that he must put on a "higher, rarer air" (*BD*, 70), pretending by gestures and words that he still belongs to the same class as the customers with whom he is drinking at the bar. While speaking to his friends "jovially" (*BD*, 430), Anthony reveals no clue that he has been counting his money and calculating how many drinks he can afford to buy. Here we see a sharp contrast between the double images of Anthony, a man totally desolated by the terrible pain of his disintegration. At this moment, nevertheless, Anthony is still totally subjugated by the indescribable gloss and solace only intoxication can offer him. "At half past seven," Fitzgerald writes, Anthony had already finished six rounds with his buddies; and was feeling "happy and cheerful now—thoroughly enjoying himself," but he felt that his bibulous "desire" was still not satisfied. If he could "take just one more drink he would attain a gorgeous rose colored exhilaration" (*BD*, 430-31).

Apparently, Anthony does not have the slightest idea that this very "desire" for one more drink has been, and still is, dictating his consciousness, dragging him toward his ultimate demise. Like Amory during his three-week-long bender, Anthony has become a man who has allowed his vanity and illusion to be self-destructive. At this moment, what he yearns for most is a drink that will help him transcend all the unpleasant things in his life; what worries him most is the danger of disgracing himself in front of his friends if he is not careful enough to conceal his financial predicament. Here, Fitzgerald's unique métier as a "bar explorer" is on full display, catching Anthony's every discernible physical move and emotional shift. Since so much of his personal prestige is at stake, from the minute he enters the bar, Anthony has been extremely cautious in every gesture he makes and every word he says. Ironically, this is the first and perhaps the only time throughout the entire novel that Anthony appears so articulate and so determined in doing something for himself. The pity is that what he is doing in this scene is just a pathetic and fruitless game of "pretension." Nothing is more suggestive of Anthony's art of pretension than the wry performance he gives before leaving Sammy's:

Artfully, he fished in his vest pockets, brought up his two quarters and stared at them as though in surprise.

"Well, I'll be darned," he protested in an aggrieved tone, "here I've come out without my pocketbook."

"Need some cash?" asked Lytell easily.

"I left my money on the dresser at home. And I wanted to buy you another drink."

"Oh—knock it." Lytell waved the suggestion away disparagingly. (*BD*, 431)

Judging from the seriousness of his gesture and the sincerity of his voice, the image of a perfect gentleman-like Anthony emerges again in Sammy's, as if the same Anthony we saw in the Marathon long ago has just been resurrected. The irony is all the more bitter when Fitzgerald wastes no time to ridicule his hero as a drunkard who "staggered to his feet and, bidding them a thick good night, walked unsteadily to the door, handing Sammy one of his two quarters as he passed out" (*BD*, 431). We cannot fully understand the irony, however, unless we notice one small but critical detail in Fitzgerald's description: Having been drinking for more than three hours at Sammy's, Anthony only reluctantly paid Sammy one quarter while he kept the other in his pocket. Once we realize how much a quarter means to Anthony in this Sammy's episode, we need no more details to measure the degree of Anthony's plight.

Of more importance is what happens to Anthony after he leaves Sammy's, even though Fitzgerald shifts his focus from the inside of the bar to the scene in the streets. Suddenly remembering that he has left home with the task of getting cash for Gloria, Anthony goes to several loan offices and pawnshops only to find them all "shut and barred" (*BD*, 431). He decides to come back to the bar to ask Park Allison for a loan, but the door is already locked. The closing of all these places, especially Sammy's, symbolically represents the indifference and alienation prevailing in society. Up to this point, Sammy's has been the only place Anthony could go to get consolation by savoring the days of his past. Now he has no place to turn. "With growing discouragement, with growing befuddlement" (*BD*, 432), Anthony is utterly at a loss, wandering like a ghost in the dark and deserted streets. His eyes light up when he runs into Manny Noble, his friend at Princeton, but his sense of shame nullifies his courage to ask for a $10 loan from his friend, who is actually in no mood to talk to him. For a second, it seems as if Fitzgerald deliberately freezes the scene with the image of Anthony standing by himself under the dim street, out of words, but full of rage. "He [is] furious," Fitzgerald describes, because he has been "snubbed" by all people, including his friends of the old days.

The scenes inside and outside the bar combine to provide a double message that seems epitomized by the key word "snubbed" in this passage: First of all, Anthony is "snubbed" by himself in the sense that he is not aware of his own continuous degeneration and the unacquitable part he has played in it; second,

Anthony is "snubbed" by the apathy of his friends and hence the alienation in society. Inside Sammy's, which is in many aspects depicted as a microcosm of the world outside the bar, Anthony tries to hold onto his crumbling social status, to avoid being "snubbed" by his peers. In the end, however, he is doomed to fail both inside and outside Sammy's, as he gets beaten up in a brawl and soon loses his sanity altogether.

Fitzgerald's treatment of Anthony's last visit to Sammy's is unique in structure and description. It is sparse and comic, almost ludicrous except that he underscores the tremendous ordeal in which Anthony wrestles with his inner conflicts. Apart from enriching the texture of the novel, the symbolic significance of the Sammy's environment adds dimension to Fitzgerald's artistry in using bar settings. The beauty of such an artistry is even more enjoyable when one realizes that Fitzgerald's depiction of these two bars, the Marathon in the early part of the novel and Sammy's near the end, is organically crafted. The settings not only help to create the linear structure of the plot development and project the mood but also enrich Fitzgerald's characterization through the corresponding effect between these two bar scenes, which, in turn, formulate an implicit but detectable contrast of Anthony's persona before and after his degeneration.

CHEERS AND TEARS IN THE RITZ BAR

Fitzgerald's selection and treatment of settings backs up his insightful probe into various thematic issues. He places the actions in a series of scenes, instead of one. As the story moves on, the focus of his narrative shifts from one scene to another in a chain of events. Most, if not all, of the bar scenes are carefully arranged and distinctive in their visual appearance and functional significance. Unlike the scenes of the Marathon and Sammy's in *The Beautiful and Damned,* which are basically designed to create a half-satirical and half-farcical moment in the protagonist's downfall, some bar scenes in Fitzgerald's novels and stories are rendered with more significance in their structural function. The Ritz Bar, one of the famous bars that appears again and again in Fitzgerald's fiction, is arguably the best example of all. It is the setting for "The Bridal Party," in which major actions are staged. It is also the setting for key events in the first section of *Tender Is the Night,* in which the brutal demise of Abe North, one of the main supporting characters, is meant to foreshadow Dick Diver's gradual deterioration. It has a much greater functional significance in the structure of "Babylon Revisited," a story many critics regard as Fitzgerald's most famous and spectacular exploitation of bar settings. But another difference between the Ritz Bar and the Marathon, or the Sammy's, deserves special recognition. The Ritz Bar is not fictionalized; it was made famous by Fitzgerald and other wealthy Americans during the 1920s, and later by Hemingway. Before the Depression, it used to be the gathering place for the Americans to throw lavish and wild parties. As his friends recalled, Fitzgerald drank to excess many nights in the Ritz Bar and was taken home dead drunk on more than one occasion. It is inevitable, therefore, that Fitzgerald's fictional account of the Ritz Bar presents some deep insights about his personal life and the life of the American expatriates in Europe as well.

Although "The Bridal Party" is among the least commented on stories written by Fitzgerald, it is certainly better than average. For a short and simply plotted story, "The Bridal Party" is much more meaningful and sophisticated than it seems. It displays a notable improvement of Fitzgerald's skill in thematic development and style, especially his use of the bar setting in short stories. Before writing "The Bridal Party," Fitzgerald had produced quite a few love stories between poor boys and rich girls in his novels and short stories, reiterating his belief that only money could make a man special and attractive. But this time Fitzgerald wrote "The Bridal Party" as a variation on the theme. After the double reversal of fortunes between the two leading characters, Fitzgerald gives the story an unexpected ending that is totally different from that of *The Great Gatsby*. The rich boy who won the rich girl suddenly goes broke because of his sudden loss in the stock market crash, but he is determined to regain his position and succeed on his new job; the poor boy who had lost the rich girl suddenly becomes a quarter-of-million-dollars richer because of an inheritance from his grandfather, but he has learned a valuable lesson about life through his failed love affair and frees himself from grief and delusion; the rich girl values the character more than the wealth of her suitor and decides to marry her newly bankrupted fiancé.

One might wonder how Fitzgerald is interested in and capable of writing nifty stories like this. The answer is simple. He was familiar with this type of entangled relationships because he had his share of the same frustration in his early years. He wrote these stories not just to recount the drama about the riches and rags; he aimed to link the issue to the moral values of his time. Put briefly, Fitzgerald's heightened preoccupation with morality sets "The Bridal Party" apart from other conventional "poor boy and rich girl" romances. It shows Fitzgerald's contemplations of the true value of money and love in one's life at the time when the sensational 1920s were about over. Does this mean that the story is filled with more autobiographical revelations than those of Fitzgerald's contemporaries? The answer is no. This is evidenced by his indifference toward the organizational details of this "bridal party." Nothing in his depiction suggests that this is a happy and romantic occasion, signifying a new beginning in someone's life. There is little doubt that Fitzgerald is more interested in uncovering the predicament of those at the party. Fitzgerald's montage of the "party," as he constantly swivels around and zooms in on his characters, outlines the anxiety common among his peers and their futile attempt to cope with it through excessive drinking. Fitzgerald does not hesitate to announce that these people are hopeless, for they are "too weary to be exhilarated by any ordinary stimulant."[22] Week after week, Fitzgerald continues, they keep searching for a magical "stimulant" to suit their needs; "they had drunk cocktails before meals like Americans, wines and brandies like Frenchmen, beer like Germans, whisky-and-soda like the English," but what they have found "served only to make them temporarily less conscious of the mistakes of the night before."[23] Fitzgerald wants us to see their sad "tears," rather than their gleeful "cheers."

The presence of the Ritz Bar plays a preponderant part in "The Bridal Party." Even before the scene of the bachelor party for Rutherford unfolds, the Ritz Bar has already been mentioned twice in the conversation between the two characters. While being introduced to each other, Rutherford and Curly realize that they have met one year before in the Ritz Bar. Though simple and casual it may seem, such a detail carries an overtone that layers its significance beyond a passing reference: the Ritz Bar is a popular and magnificent gathering place for the wealthy and important Americans, a place they must frequent for the sake of good business opportunities and personal prestige. Therefore, when Rutherford says to his rival, Curly, "I'm taking the Ritz Bar from nine o'clock on,"[24] it is not so hard to detect the pride he takes in associating himself with the Ritz Bar. By the time we reach the scene of the bachelor party, Fitzgerald's observational depiction of the guests has given way to a meticulous account of the rowdy festivity in the Ritz Bar: "The Ritz Bar had been prepared for the occasion by French and American banners and by a great canvas covering one wall, against which the guests were invited to concentrated their proclivities in breaking glasses."[25] Here, as we have seen in his description of the Marathon in *The Beautiful and Damned*, Fitzgerald balances his representation of the setting with his portrayal of the characters in it, another perfect example of his organic fusion of setting and character. Even though Fitzgerald does not bother to enumerate the physical details about the bar or the personal features of the guests, the "banners" and "great canvas" are suggestive enough to help us visualize the grandeur of the scene, and the "trembling hands," "tide of laughter," and "bursts of song" enable us to envision what kind of crowd is attending Rutherford's bachelor party. Moreover, Curly's asseveration upon his arrival at the Ritz Bar that "for the first time since he had left college he felt rich and assured himself; he felt that he was part of all this" surely adds another explication to the atmosphere of this occasion.[26]

What gives "The Bridal Party" more profound social implication, though, is the well-construed connection between the scene of the story and the world beyond. For instance, the bachelor party at the Ritz Bar bears striking parallels to Gatsby's grand party at his mansion. Apart from the ostensible glamour and gaiety, a lot of events are taking place both before the scene and behind the scene. Rutherford, the man of honor at the bachelor party, is nowhere to be seen mingling with the guests because he is keeping a watchful eye on the prices on the stock market. Similarly, Gatsby does not care to know any of his uninvited guests and, despite his obligation as the host of the party, repeatedly retreats from the scene to attend his bootlegging business. Whereas Rutherford is caught off guard by an unexpected female visitor with an intent to blackmail, Gatsby is agitated by the phone calls from the mysterious man, Wolfshiem. Such a strategy exhibits Fitzgerald's skill in emphasizing the social implication of his work by dropping a hint at the close, though invisible, link between the current and actual scene of action—namely, the Ritz Bar—and the scene of action in the remote and imaginary business world. Through this strategy, without much actual depiction, Fitzgerald transmits images of the chaos on the stock market and the mystery of the hideous underworld. As we witness what is going on in each story, we are also keenly reminded of what America was going through during those eventful years.

"The Bridal Party" is short, but its brevity belies its rich implications. Its value goes beyond that of a pot-boiling story of an entangled love affair, for subtly and distinctly presents a last but serious look at the life of American expatriates in Europe as well as the life of the author's generation in the America of the 1920s. It also shows the widespreading disillusionment with the false promise of the Jazz Age. In many ways, the story is a parable for the times when "flappers and egoists" learned their hard lessons and searched for a new hope for the future. As a paradigm of the unsolvable discrepancies between ideals and realities, the story might as well be seen as a tale about the "last party" of that ten-year-long spree. In this context, the story is Fitzgerald's portrayal of those who were running from the past but did not know where they could run to.

Of course, Fitzgerald does not use the same strategy all the time. He knows how to alter the presentation of bar setting when necessary. By contrast, the same Ritz bar takes on a different look in the first section of *Tender Is the Night*, where one of the main supporting characters, Abe North, sits at the bar alone, pondering deeply what he should do next with his life. In sharp contrast to what we see in the scene of Rutherford's bachelor party, the Ritz Bar here has no "banners," no "great canvas," nor anything else that suggests grandeur or festivity. On the contrary, here is a much shabbier and, therefore, much gloomier bar: "Abe North was still in the Ritz Bar, where he had been since nine in the morning. When he arrived seeking sanctuary the windows were open and great beams were busy pulling up the dust from smoky carpets and cushions" (*TIN*, 101). Here is at work the same skill with which Fitzgerald has described the sordid ambiance in the Marathon. The "dust" and the "smoky carpets and cushions" constitute a familiar picture of the inside of a bar. Everything about the Ritz Bar is virtually shown in a dismal mist of apathy and may be construed as a reminder of the mood in the bar as well as the state of Abe's mind. But Fitzgerald's narrative does not linger long on the physical aspect of the setting. As in his previous novels and stories, he turns his attention from the bar to its patrons, featuring them as part of the whole bar setting. Even though we are not given much information about what North has been thinking before his arrival, the fact that he has been in the Ritz Bar for so long in order to seek "sanctuary" signals that he is in deep trouble. Although it is common for patrons to spend hours in a bar, this scene is not as ordinary as it seems. Fitzgerald layers meaning to reflect the dismal mentality of his character. Evidently, Abe is a troubled soul in a "cheerless" bar, and he has no one else to "cheer" with. Were we to visualize what he looks like in the bar, we would immediately recall the gloomy scene at Sammy's in *The Beautiful and Damned*, where Anthony is visiting for the last time before being beaten and losing his sanity. As Fitzgerald tells us in the second section of *Tender Is the Night*, this also turns out to be Abe's last visit to the Ritz Bar, for he soon takes a ship to New York, is brutally beaten in a speakeasy, and crawls home to the Racquet Club to die.

Although created only as a supporting character for Dick Diver, Abe dominates the scene at the Ritz Bar. Such an arrangement is appropriate and indicative of the designated function of the bar setting in Fitzgerald's fiction. Abe, associated as he is with men like Diver, is certainly a specimen of Fitzgerald's disillusioned dreamer, a representative figure of what Gertrude Stein called "the Lost Generation." In the novel, he is a composer whose creative energy has been irrevocably destroyed in war. He has given up on every hope he used to have. In fact, he has not done anything for the last seven years, except drink. Deep inside him is this strong urge to abandon everything, to cut off his every link to the present world, and to hide himself in the oblivion of alcohol. Nothing interests him anymore, not even his food. Seeing other people order luncheon, "Abe did likewise but scarcely touched it. Afterwards, he just sat, happy to live in the past. The drink made past happy things contemporary with the present, as if they were still going on, contemporary even with the future as if they were about to happen again" (*TIN*, 103). Evidently, there is no place for the present or the future in Abe's mind. He never has the chance, or the will, to recover from his loss of zeal and aspirations during the war. At this moment, his illusion about an instant return to the past reigns in his memory and his soul. But Abe soon comes to realize that such a return can happen only in dream. Not surprisingly, once his illusion is shattered, as Bruce L. Grenberg argues, "his departure from Paris clearly signals the end of life, not a new start," and his journey ends quite fittingly in the death that he has been longing for all along.[27]

Even though it may seems so, Fitzgerald is not making fun of the laughable stupor of his characters. He renders their preoccupation with the past and its heartrending consequences with great care and sincerity. He urges us to question why Abe can peacefully remain in the world of his past only by ending his life at present. In a way, Fitzgerald provides us with an answer to this question in "Babylon Revisited," a story that Fitzgerald wrote a few years after the Jazz Age. What happens to Charlie Wales, the protagonist, shows us how difficult it could be to transcend an undesirable past to face a harsh and exclusive present. Whereas for Abe the past seems to be a consoling haven for which he pines, to Charlie the past means a haunting nightmare from which he must try to, but still cannot, run away. This magnificent story, as Fitzgerald called it in one of his letters,[28] is a profound study on the relationship among the past, present, and future based on the author's retrospective reflection upon what had happened during the nearly ten-year-long "spree" in his time. What makes the story magnificent is not merely its plot or characterization; rather, it is Fitzgerald's bar setting, which moves the theme of the story with poignancy and forcefulness.

Unlike the Ritz Bar we see in "The Bridal Party" or *Tender Is the Night*, the Ritz Bar in "Babylon Revisited" is a framing device. The story begins and ends in the Ritz Bar, but the background is set in Paris, considered by Fitzgerald, as the title implies, as a modern Babylon, a place of luxury and wickedness, during the days before the crash. Although no specific description of the bar is given, the name of the bar itself is enough for us to visualize the scene in the bar. We learn from the outset of the story, when Charlie is asking about his former drinking buddies, that the Ritz Bar must have been a popular haunt for rich American expatriates. Moreover, judging from what has happened to Charlie's friends, Campbell and Fessenden, it is easy to imagine what they used to do every day in the Ritz Bar. Besides, Fitzgerald illuminates a subtle contrast between the Ritz Bar before and after the stock market crash by describing Charlie's reaction to what he sees. He is a bit stunned to find Paris so "empty," but he does not feel extremely "disappointed" about it. "But the stillness in the Ritz Bar was strange and portentous. It was not an American bar anymore. He felt the stillness from the moment he got out of the taxi and saw the doorman, usually in a frenzy of activity at this hour, gossiping with a *chasseur* by the servant's entrance."[29]

Through Charlie's recollection, Fitzgerald attempts to re-create the Ritz Bar of the wild decade of reckless drinking and gambling. Yet he does not dissect the bar scene of the past, for he safely depends on the reader to complete the scene based on Charlie's surprise at the absence of "frenzy" in the Ritz Bar, a place Charlie and his American friends had always treated as if they owned. The changes in milieu are epitomized by the word "stillness." Charlie does not see anything that would resemble the kind of grandeur and festivity in the Ritz Bar of "The Bridal Party" or the noise and crowd in the Ritz Bar of *Tender Is the Night*. But neither his reactions nor his questions about his former drinking buddies reveal any overt sign of shock or regret. His inquiries about his cronies of old days come from his mechanical curiosity. To this end, the primary function of the opening scene is to thrust Charlie back into the same but drastically changed Ritz Bar to show that he has separated himself from the blurred life before the crash, that he has come back as a new and sober man. In this profile, Charlie is utterly different from Abe North in *Tender Is the Night*, who values the past more than the present and attempts to defy the transition of time at any cost, even if it means to end his existence. From our first sight of Charlie, we get the impression that he is optimistic about his prospect of regaining custody of his daughter and idealistic about their future life together. But Charlie knows well about the daunting task ahead of him. He allows himself only one drink every afternoon; he stays out of trouble; he tries hard to impress the Peters about his "change" and his ability to raise his daughter.

Nonetheless, it would be too naive to say that Charlie has thus been set completely free from the curse of his past. For him, it is impossible to forget all the pains his bibulous indulgence has inflicted on his family, especially the death of his wife and the loss of his daughter's custody. As he tells Paul, the head barman of the Ritz Bar, "I lost everything I wanted in the boom."[30] Charlie is deeply aware of his own responsibility for all this. As he returns to Paris, he is on his way to his resurrection and redemption, ready to do penance for what he did during that boom. He wants to forget the horrors of the past and embrace a bright future. Seymour L. Gross pointed out, "Charlie Wales' return to Paris is an attempted return to fatherhood, and an attempt to lay the ghost of his past childishness through the recovery of his lost child, Honoria."[31] After Charlie walks out of the bar and into the street, Fitzgerald explicitly stresses the splendid achievement of Charlie's reform with a series of scenes. We see Charlie promising Marion that he will remain sober permanently, and we watch him have lunch with his daughter in "the only restaurant he could think of not reminiscent of champagne dinners and long luncheons that began at two and ended in a blurred and vague twilight."[32]

No matter how determined Charlie is to go on with his reform and start a new life, it is by no means an easy task. The curse of his past follows him around closely. At times Charlie's efforts seem useless because he feels so powerless, as if he is being simultaneously pulled or pushed back to the old days by several forces. First of all, "the memory of those days swept over him like a nightmare."[33] Then, his former cronies, Duncan and Lorraine, chase him around like "ghosts out of the past,"[34] interfering with his plan for a new life and haunting him to defeat. They seem to remain as "wild" as they were in the "spree" years. In a sense, their reckless intrusion into the Peters' apartment directly jeopardizes Charlie's likely chance of winning the battle for the custody of his daughter. More disheartening, however, is the insurmountable obstacle to Charlie's wishes: the mistrust of his sister-in-law, Marion, whose extreme self-righteousness and unrelenting obsession with Charlie's responsibility for the death of her sister have erected an unbreakable high wall separating Charlie from his daughter. Symbolically, Marion's reluctance to relinquish her guardianship of Honoria is, as Charlie himself realizes, a sharp reminder of the dark shadow his own irresponsible behavior during the boom. It is ironic, but fitting, that Charlie is snubbed in Marion's house and has no place to go, but returns to the Ritz Bar, where he had started his crusade in the first place. His return to the bar ends the story, as well as Fitzgerald's structural maneuver of his bar setting in it. Such an ending creates "the double effect." On the one hand, the circular pattern of the narrative does more than offering the story a close-knit structure; it suggests a sense of hope, convincing us that the story does not render Charlie's return to Paris a total failure because, as we see in the end, Charlie is not weeping over his glass in the Ritz Bar but is tenaciously determined to come back for another try in the near future. On the other hand, Charlie's final conversation with Paul, which touches upon his big loss in the stock market crash, like Rutherford's in "The Bridal Party," reiterates Fitzgerald's persistent demand that his readers see and ruminate on the connection between what happens in the Ritz Bar scene and what was happening in real-world America.

NOTES

1. I am indebted to Ray Oldenburg in formulating this observation. He claims that human experience is divided mainly into three realms: the first is "domestic," or home; the second is "gainful and productive," which take place in the office or workplace; the third is "social and communal," which is conducted in public places like hotels, malls, and mostly bars (14). A more comprehensive analysis can be found in Ray Oldenburg, *The Great Good Places* (New York: Paragon House, 1989).

2. For more information, see Joseph Wechsberg's "The Viennese Coffee House: A Romantic Institution," *Gourmet* 26 (December 1966): 16, 90-99.

3. Carl Bode, *The Young Mencken* (New York: Dial Press, 1973), 197.

4. Mary Agnes Hamilton, "Where Are You Going My Pretty Maid?" *Atlantic Monthly* 138 (September 1926): 298.

5. See Frederick J. Hoffman, *The 20's* (New York: Free Press, 1965), 418. This book is perhaps the most resourceful study of American life during this decade. Here, I cite and address only some of the issues associated with the topic of my discussion.

6. John F. Carter, Jr., "These Wild Young People," *Atlantic Monthly* 126 (September 1920): 302.

7. Matthew J. Bruccoli, introduction to *F. Scott Fitzgerald's Ledger: A Facsimile* (Washington, D.C.: NCR/Microcard Editions, 1972), 160.

8. For more detail about this incident, see William L. Shirer, *20th Century Journey* (New York: Simon & Schuster, 1976), 231-33.

9. Ernest Hemingway, *A Moveable Feast* (New York: Bantam Books, 1970), 180.

10. Albert Camus, *A Happy Death*, trans. Richard Howard (New York: Knopf, 1972), 51.

11. Noel Riley Fitch, *Literary Cafés of Paris* (Washington D.C.: Starrhill Press, 1989), 67.

12. James Gindin, "Gods and Fathers in F. Scott Fitzgerald's Novels," in *F. Scott Fitzgerald*, ed. Harold Bloom (New York: Chelsea House Publishers, 1985), 110.

13. Scott Donaldson, *Fool for Love: F. Scott Fitzgerald* (New York: Congdon & Weed, 1983), 173.

14. Matthew J. Bruccoli, ed. *The Short Stories of F. Scott Fitzgerald: A New Collection* (New York: Charles Scribner's Sons, 1989), 578.

15. Ibid., 582.

16. Ibid., 597.

17. Ibid., 596.

18. Ibid., 637.

19. Malcolm Cowley, ed., *The Bodley Head Scott Fitzgerald*, vol. 6, "Short Stories" (London: Bodley Head, 1963), 322.

20. Arthur Mizener, *The Far Side of Paradise: A Biography of F. Scott Fitzgerald* (Boston, Houghton Mifflin, 1951), 284.

21. Cowley, *The Bodley Head Scott Fitzgerald*, vol. 6, 276.

22. Bruccoli, *The Short Stories of F. Scott Fitzgerald*, 565.

23. Ibid.

24. Ibid., 562.

25. Ibid., 569.

26. Ibid.

27. Bruce L. Grenberg, "Fitzgerald's 'Figured Curtain': Personality and History in *Tender Is the Night*," in *Critical Essays on F. Scott Fitzgerald's Tender Is the Night*, ed. Milton R. Stern (Boston: G. K. Hall, 1986), 223.

28. F. Scott Fitzgerald, in *The Letters of F. Scott Fitzgerald*, ed. Andrew Turnbull (New York: Charles Scribner's Sons, 1963), 64.

29. Bruccoli, *The Short Stories of F. Scott Fitzgerald*, 616.

30. Ibid., 633.

31. Seymour L. Gross, "Fitzgerald's 'Babylon Revisited'," *College English* 25 (November 1963): 129.

32. Bruccoli, *The Short Stories of F. Scott Fitzgerald*, 620-21.

33. Ibid., 633.

34. Ibid., 622.

4

SCHOOLS: CRADLES
OF THE ELITE

In Fitzgerald's time, school, especially a private school, was a very remote but exalted place in people's eyes. It was, and perhaps still is today, regarded as a cradle of the elite in society. Rich, lucky, and smart young men used school as a gateway to future success, wealth, and prestige. As a literary setting, however, school did not attract much attention from American writers before Fitzgerald. Even in Fitzgerald's novels and stories, school does not feature as prominently as it does in British novels or as frequently as home and bar do. Apart from his Basil stories, *This Side of Paradise* seems to be the only work in which Fitzgerald explores prep school and, particularly, college as settings, seriously addressing the issue of adolescent education by examining various aspects of life on campus.

BILDUNGSROMAN AND THE AMERICAN COLLEGE NOVEL

Although it is difficult to find any evidence that Fitzgerald was consciously borrowing from the instructive and edifying novels written in the well-known European literary form of the *Bildungsroman*—the novel of youth's formative education—*This Side of Paradise* not only uses the same kind of theme and artistry one would see in the masterpieces of this genre but also reflects Fitzgerald's concerns and assumptions about a series of issues ranging from education to self-realization. The novel's most unique quality is that it goes beyond *Bildungsroman*'s conventional prototype for adventure seeking and wisdom learning, assimilating elements from *Erziehungsroman* (novel of upbringing), *Entwicklungsroman* (novel of character development), and the novel of school education. For years, however, critics have downplayed the importance of *This Side of Paradise,* claiming that in spite of its huge commercial success at the time of its publication and its limited literary influence since then, it is not an especially well written novel and that it is important only as the novel that established Fitzgerald's reputation as a serious writer. Indeed, there is no doubt that *This Side of Paradise* is not as subtle and profound as Fitzgerald's later novels. Certainly it does not strictly meet all the criteria for a college novel, or academic fiction, but this is the first American novel in which an American school and one of its best universities are featured so prominently. Fitzgerald deserves our praise for taking the lead in pioneering this genre with a compelling and artistic vision, and *This Side of Paradise* deserves a unique place in the history of American literature, first, for inventing a very needed American variation of these German novelistic genres that deal with youthful development and, second, for projecting an insider's perspective of campus life and a bipolar view of the elite educational institutions in America, both of which have become principal characteristics of the American college novel ever since.

The so-called insider's perspective Fitzgerald offers in his presentation of college life originates from what I would term "an organic fusion" of his personal experience and fictional account, a fusion so craftily done that it not merely gives his work a sureness of tone, a precision of discourse, and a value of verisimilitude that prevent the flow of narrative from becoming loose and discursive but it also helps Fitzgerald to set off various incidents and fancies, and to interject his own illuminating and, at times, amusing insights. The so-called bipolar view is the ambivalent feeling Fitzgerald expressed toward the disparity between what these famous schools mean to the career of a young man and what they actually deliver. A strong tone of irony and even cynicism underlies Fitzgerald's descriptions of college and college students. He recognizes what colleges like Princeton stand for in America; he knows what advantages they offer to young people ambitious and determined enough to climb high within the social order; he romanticizes Princeton and other Ivy League schools by delineating parameters for a successful performance on campus. Yet he also seems to believe, particularly as his later stories indicate, that ultimately going to Princeton or other elite schools may not be a proper path to one's success and happiness in life. Sometimes he does not even bother to hide his dissatisfaction with or mistrust of the attitudes so prevalent on college campuses, the insincerity and snobbery, yet he stops short of trying to convince the reader that American college life is either wonderful or altogether worthless. This is not to suggest that Fitzgerald does not clearly understand school life in America. Such an assertion would miss the vital part of his vision, namely, that what schools should offer their students is not just prestige but the ability to triumph in the real world. To understand Fitzgerald's vision completely, we need to investigate the "organic fusion" strategy through which he effectively represents campus life, and we must consider his ambivalence toward the educational institutions of his time.

Before delving into Fitzgerald's work, it seems imperative to look briefly at the tradition of *Bildungsroman*. We know that *Bildungsroman* is a German term for novels of coming-of-age adventures, and J. W. von Goethe's *Wilhelm Meister* was the first classic work to establish such a genre in German literature. To call *Bildungsroman* a European tradition in novel writing is appropriate because such a form has been extant in European literature both before and after Goethe. Jean-Jacques Rousseau's *Confessions* is a case in point. It became a popular and intellectually important literary form in Europe after the turn of the nineteenth century and won further popularity with works like Wordsworth's autobiographical account of his early life, *The Prelude*. Soon it became a dominant form of novel writing in Europe, especially in England thanks to the widely read *David Copperfield* of Dickens and *Pendennis* of Thackeray. Between the beginning of the twentieth century and the end of World War I, almost every British novelist tried the form, from Compton Mackenzie in *Youth's Encounter* and its sequel, *Sinister Street,* to Somerset Maugham in *Of Human Bondage,* D. H. Lawrence in *Sons and Lovers,* and James Joyce in *A Portrait of the Artist as a Young Man.*

What seems a bit peculiar is that such a well-established genre did not find its first American counterpart until *This Side of Paradise.* Even though many American writers before Fitzgerald, the Romantic writers in particular, had made attempts to address issues regarding the education and training of youth, they were more interested in creating a story of lost childhood, as we see in Mark Twain's *The Adventures of Huckleberry Finn,* but less concerned with the misery and agony of late adolescence, which might be considered an extension of one's growing up. Before the publication of *This Side of Paradise,* the only eminent American book that is close to the combined form of *Bildungsroman* and *Entwicklungsroman* is *The Education of Henry Adams.* Although a truly great work of imaginative art, the book is, after all, an autobiographical account of the author's own career, as Rousseau's *Confessions* had been. Proportionally, his schooling experience is nothing more than an insignificant fraction narrated tongue-in-cheek. It can hardly be classified under this literary genre, along with the novels like Mackenzie's *Youth's Encounter* or Joyce's *A Portrait of the Artist as a Young Man.* In addition, Adams's book was first printed privately in 1907 and for more than ten years was circulated basically among a hundred or so friends and famous figures mentioned in the text. The book's first edition for public sale was not available until 1918. Only after Adam's death did the book reached a much wider reading public. Judging from its form and its critical and public reception, it seems safe to say that *This Side of Paradise* is the first American novel to explore an individual's "formative education" through real school education; at least it is the first American novel to probe the mysteries of campus life in America.

Nonetheless, for all the differences in form and tone, *This Side of Paradise* and *The Education of Henry Adams* are quite similar in several respects. Fitzgerald might have learned something from Adams. Even though the two authors had limited direct contact, there was a special connection between them. The years during which Adams's book was gradually gaining its popularity coincided with Fitzgerald's coming to the East Coast and his subsequent secondary and college education. Adams was no stranger to Fitzgerald at all. In his letter to Maxwell Perkins in 1919, Fitzgerald wrote, "I knew him when I was a boy," through Sigourney Fay.[1] Having carefully read and studied *The Education of Henry Adams* before starting his writing career, Fitzgerald eventually reiterated some of Adams's assumptions in his own novel. The most conspicuous one has to be the "miseducation" by family and school, which both Adams and Fitzgerald believed to be the root cause for their "failure."

To a certain extent, it is no surprise that Fitzgerald found in Adams's book a model for the thematic development in his novel. What does seem remarkable is that Fitzgerald's models for the form of his novel are Mackenzie's *Youth's Encounter* and its sequel, *Sinister Street,* rather than the masterpieces of Lawrence or Joyce. According to several of his biographers, Fitzgerald had not read or even known much about the best novels of this literary genre at the time he was writing *This Side of Paradise,* but he did know Mackenzie's novels. As we learn from one of Sigourney Fay's letters to him, Fitzgerald admired Mackenzie's two novels so tremendously that he wrote a story himself imitating what he liked in Mackenzie's novels and sent it to Sigourney Fay for comment.[2] Even though Mackenzie does not now hold an eminent place in literary history, his two novels did receive strong and favorable response from many critics during his time. One of these critics, M. R. Proctor, claims in his book, *The English University Novel* that *Sinister Street* is the best among the novels dealing with aspects of college life.[3] In spite of his narrowness of view and his lack of artistic subtlety, Mackenzie presents a prudent look at the school system by chronicling his protagonist's life from nursery school through college education, and he urges the reader to question the role that schooling plays in one's coming of age. Mackenzie's strong influence on Fitzgerald is an undeniable fact, well documented by the common theme and parallels in the plot development of Mackenzie's two novels and Fitzgerald's *This Side of Paradise.* Mackenzie starts his story in *Youth's Encounter* from the childhood and early education of the hero, Michael Fane, and then moves on in its sequel, *Sinister Street,* to Michael's days at Oxford, his involvement with several women, and his job survival in London. Fitzgerald unfolds his story in *This Side of Paradise* with a brief account of Amory's life up to his enrollment at a secondary school on the East Coast, and he then traces his days at Princeton, his repeated failure in his relationship with women, and his job and struggle in New York.

Much of the success of *This Side of Paradise* derived from what Fitzgerald learned about the school setting from Mackenzie.[4] His depiction of Princeton helped to generate some of the novel's immense popularity in the 1920s and win its fame as the first realistic American college novel. It was, and perhaps still is, widely hailed as a real and intimate study of college life, revelatory and subtle. It portrays, better than any other American novel dealing with college life, the atmosphere of one of the most prestigious universities in this country. David W. Bailey, a Harvard undergraduate at the time, wrote a review of the novel for his school newspaper, the *Harvard Crimson,* calling *This Side of Paradise* "a slice carved out of real life."[5] Bailey's comment represents the general feeling about the novel among 1920s youth, since they could easily identify Amory's experience as the average experience. To them, the novel was a comment on the times. It abounds in juvenile and adolescent problems, many of which had never been addressed in American novels. And there is in it much of the attempts of youth and collegians of the time to rebel against the old taboos and reticence, to struggle for fame and status, and to find new meaning for their lives in the postwar era. Many of the incidents depicted in the novel might have taken place at Harvard or Yale or at any other university in America. With the portrait of Amory as essentially an American "college man," the novel definitely presents a picture of the daily existence of other American collegians in Fitzgerald's time. Following Amory through his years at Princeton, we look into the heart of American youth; Amory is thinking about and doing what hundreds of thousands of other young people were thinking about and doing in colleges all over the country. Thus, the publication of the novel was perfectly timed, which in turn magnified its appeal among young readers looking for inside information about the study and life in a glamorous university like Princeton so that they would know how to succeed both intellectually and socially when they themselves got there. In addition, the novel has a fresh intellectual flavor that enticed the readers to indulge themselves in literary learning. While depicting how Amory and his friends attempt to search for a satisfactory philosophy, Fitzgerald promoted the enlightening and instructional value of literature by alluding to or citing from a long list of well-known books and writers (sixty-four titles and ninety-eight writers are mentioned in the novel).[6] Consequently, Fitzgerald launched a new trend among young readers to seek inspirations and models in literature.

Yet this "intellectual flavor" is by no means the only characteristic Fitzgerald initiated for the American college novel, or is his triumphant exploration of the school setting limited to *This Side of Paradise*. Fitzgerald frequently featured Princeton and Yale in his other works. During his first trip to Hollywood, Fitzgerald presented to United Artists a script entitled "Lipstick," in which Princeton appears as the setting of a seminatural story about a girl who has been put in jail unjustly and now has a magic lipstick that lures men to kiss her. Soon after this short screenplay was rejected, Fitzgerald used Yale as the major setting for his Basil stories. Although he never used college again as a central setting for his later works, Fitzgerald did make frequent references to colleges of the Ivy League, from Princeton to Harvard, Yale, and MIT. Also, many of his characters, both in his major novels and in his stories, are Ivy Leaguers: Tom Buchanan in *The Great Gatsby,* Dick Diver in *Tender Is the Night,* Anson Hunter in "The Rich Boy," Philip Dean and Gordon Sterrett in "May Day," and Benjamin Button in "The Curious Case of Benjamin Button" all go to Yale; Anthony Patch in *The Beautiful and Damned* goes to Harvard; George O'Kelly in "The Sensible Thing" goes to MIT. Such a long list of Ivy Leaguers, a list that cannot possibly be compiled in the works of any other American novelist, is an indisputable evidence that Fitzgerald's repeated exploration of school setting, especially during the first ten years of his writing career, was not entirely haphazard. Whenever he is setting his story in school and college, Fitzgerald appears in total command of his subject. The school setting affords him an opportunity, not merely to tell stories about flappers but, rather, to dramatize the American college experience, which was still an uncultivated territory in American literature at that time. That he did brilliantly through an organic fusion of his personal experience with fictional imagination.

Like most of Fitzgerald's novels and stories, *This Side of Paradise* is highly autobiographical. Autobiographical representation in fiction is not completely an invention of Fitzgerald. "Subjective intrusion," as critics often call it, has been a long tradition or even a well-established strategy in fiction. John Gardner once remarked, "Keeping personal ego out of one's art is one of the hardest things about writing fiction."[7] To some writers, "subjective intrusion" is not so much a problem as a challenge to their creativity. In effect, most, if not all, of Fitzgerald's favorite works—he deemed some of them his models—are filled with their creator's personal experience and emotions. Writers like Charles Dickens, James Joyce, William Golding, Samuel Beckett, Doris Lessing, Thomas Wolfe, and Saul Bellow frequently drew, sometimes heavily, on private experience, even though they differ greatly from each other in style and content. Speaking of his own role in *The Tropic of Cancer,* Henry Miller felt no compunctions in declaring, "I have painstakingly indicated throughout the book that the hero is myself. I don't use 'heroes,' incidentally, nor do I write novels. I am the hero, and the book is myself."[8] To these writers, the fusion of personal experience and fictional account is definitely helpful not only in presenting an emotional development or sensibility the sympathetic reader might share but also in enriching their representation and circumscribing the range of invention in the novel.

To Fitzgerald, such a fusion is more than a novel-writing technique; it is an advantage, if not entirely an expedient. When he first started writing *This Side of Paradise*, Fitzgerald was young and still at Princeton University. His social experience was therefore limited. What he knew best at the time was naturally what he had just experienced at St. Paul Academy, Newman School, and Princeton, that is, the life of adolescents and undergraduates in schools and colleges. As he was able to extrapolate almost anything from these areas of American life, his ability to use school settings became a great advantage for him. Helped by the general ignorance of and curiosity about prep school and college life among his readers, this fusion of personal experience and fictional imagination made Fitzgerald extremely effective in asserting the authority of his descriptions in *This Side of Paradise* and the Basil Duke Lee stories, and he instantly turned him into a pioneering writer of college novel in America. Some people at the time of its publication viewed *This Side of Paradise* as "immature," but most critics were unanimous in praising the accuracy of Fitzgerald's representation of school life. Although, as Malcolm Cowley argues, Fitzgerald often "changed or disguised the events, as stories always do, but the best of them served as a faithful record of his emotions."[9] Since *This Side of*

Paradise was written not long after Fitzgerald left Princeton, what is depicted in the novel inevitably reveals his own deeply felt and mixed sentiments about the romantic and competitive life in college, a life to which, he knew, he would never be able to return. His fusion strategy creates immediacy, enabling the reader to perceive an invisible, but palpable, link between the protagonist and the author himself. Thus, the story seems realistic and touching.

Unlike *This Side of Paradise*, the Basil stories were written more than ten years after Fitzgerald's college life was over, and he had already obtained the fame he wanted. It is highly possible in these stories that his reflection upon his college life would have been affected by the drastic change in time and in his status; and for that reason, the stories are more contrived, lacking the direct personal feeling evident in *This Side of Paradise*. A comparison between what Fitzgerald had actually experienced and the major events in which Fitzgerald places Amory and Basil in the stories will demonstrate how he projects his own failings and wishes onto his characters, and how he fictionalizes the zany and sneering events to scathe the schools for failing their youngsters. Such a demonstration will, in turn, clarify misconceptions about the self-reflective trait in Fitzgerald's narrative, shed some light on how Fitzgerald's fusion strategy works through facts, changes, and disguises, and introduce a new dimension to his work for a better appreciation.

THE FUSION OF THE ACTUAL, THE FICTIONAL, AND THE WISHFUL

Given the autobiographical nature of Fitzgerald's fiction, it seems helpful to make some consideration of his own schooling history and to examine his stated view of campus life in particular. From the day in March 1900 when, as he records in his *Ledger*, "his parents sent him to school but he wept and wailed so they took him out again after one morning"[10] to the time in 1911 when he was about to leave St. Paul Academy, Fitzgerald's early education was generally a less than happy experience. As a young boy, he had the same aspirations for glory and prestige as others, but he was seldom successful in garnering either. While still young, he became an avid reader, spending much more time than his friends on voluminous and varied books. One thing he learned well from his reading was how popular a boy with extracurricular talents could be in school or college. He became anxious to shine among his peers. Although he was not physically built for sports and he had little appetite for rough games, he forced himself to play football and basketball. When he realized that sports could not help him gain the kind of popularity he needed, he diverted his efforts to stage performances, where he believed he could enhance his visibility among his peers by showing off his dramatic talent. Contrary to what he had hoped, his glory on stage failed to turn around his reputation in school. Hence, he could take refuge only in writing. In his brief autobiographical essay "Who's Who—and Why," Fitzgerald recalls: "When I lived in St. Paul and was about twelve I wrote all through every class in school in the back of my geography book and first year

Latin and on the margins of themes and declensions and mathematics problems" (*AA,* 83). However childish it may sound, this recollection underscores an obsessive fascination with writing at such a young age. He did have a predilection and an imagination for writing. After his debut piece, "The Mystery of the Raymond Mortgage," in 1909, Fitzgerald published in school magazines, first in *St. Paul Academy Now and Then* and later in *Newman News.* His fledging writing, which includes verses, plays, articles, and short stories, is unusually phenomenal in variety and in quantity. To his distress and that of his family's as well, Fitzgerald's success in writing did not bring the glory and fame that he craved. Conversely, it became a cause of others' envy of him and thus furthered his unpopularity. Also, because of his obsession with writing, he was never able to concentrate on his schoolwork and get good grades.

Many years later, through the penchant he had displayed in his school papers, the matured Fitzgerald plunged back into his past experience, reliving the innocent laughters and cries, the childhood games and mischiefs, the adolescent anxieties and conflicts. In *This Side of Paradise,* Fitzgerald is virtually telling his own story as he takes Amory from his childhood through prep school, Princeton, and a short way into the business world. Like Fitzgerald, Amory is a "rather tall and slender" (*TSP,* 7) boy who always likes to keep to himself. "His chief struggle," as Fitzgerald tells us, "had been the concealing from 'the other guys at school' how particularly superior he felt himself to be, yet his conviction was built upon shifting sands" (*TSP,* 8). Like Fitzgerald, Amory knows the importance of popularity in school. What bothers him is not his poor grades but his weakness and disadvantage in sports. He is keenly aware that athletic ability is "the touchstone of power and popularity at school" (*TSP,* 9), which cannot be replaced by any other means. Unlike Fitzgerald, however, Amory makes "furious and persistent efforts to excel in the winter sports" (*TSP,* 9), willing to risk injuries. Even though his goal is to be a good hockey player, Amory cannot help wondering whether he would ever be able to hold a hockey stick properly. Despite his acute awareness of the importance in being popular, Amory simply does not know how to impress others. He becomes more and more doubtful about his hope to be a young man, who is physically handsome, socially charming, and mentally superior (*TSP,* 18). By the time he is about to go away to a new school in the East, Amory is still "drifting" on his way to adolescence without obtaining the popularity he has pined for.

By comparison, Fitzgerald dips much deeper into his own early experience in writing the Basil stories. Each of the eight published stories recounts what Fitzgerald personally experienced during his childhood and adolescence. Taken together, these stories could assemble a very good autobiography. Critics differ in their assessments of the Basil stories. According to Kenneth Eble, these Basil stories "are as excellent in craftsmanship as any Fitzgerald ever wrote."[11] But critics like James Nagel believe that these stories do not "constitute his [Fitzgerald's] finest efforts in fiction."[12] Unlike his other novels or stories, the Basil stories considerably minimize the fictional part of Fitzgerald's fusion strategy. The hero, Basil, is clearly portrayed as Fitzgerald's alter ego, whereas other characters can be easily identified with his friends in real life. The incidents in the stories are conceived and developed in accordance with Fitzgerald's recollection of real events, and no change or disguise has been made. Like Fitzgerald, Basil's early education is marked by mishaps, unfulfilled wishes, and failed attempts at popularity. What Henry Adams said in *The Education of Henry Adams* about his school experience sounds so fitting to Fitzgerald and Basil: "Most school experience was bad. Boy associations at fifteen were worse than none."[13] Recalling his own notoriety among his classmates, Fitzgerald quoted a line from his school paper in his *Ledger*: "Will someone poison Scotty or find some means to shut his mouth."[14] Later, the same incident turns up in his Basil story, "The Freshest Boy" (*TAR*, 29). Like Fitzgerald, Basil is concerned with his status among his peers, and makes great effort in extracurricular activities and other things, such as discovering a sense of self-confidence and self-esteem in his relations with the opposite sex. It must be understood, though, that what Fitzgerald meant to suggest is nothing like sexual awakening. To Basil, perhaps to Amory and Fitzgerald as well, "A girl's heart and lips," as Andre Le Vot has pointed out, "were symbols for him: more than awards, they were the tangible signs of a victory over his rivals, even, sometimes, over himself. Will, not the senses, was the motor."[15] We recall Amory's strong sense of shock and abhorrence after kissing Myra for the first time: "Sudden revulsion seized Amory, disgust, loathing for the whole incident" (*TSP*, 14). He became so nervous that he "wanted to creep out of his body and hide somewhere safe out of sight, up in the corner of his mind" (*TSP*, 14). To the young and naive Amory, being with a girl who is fond of him is a rare opportunity to assert and relish his own self-worth. But the excitement is short lived as his usual sense of insecurity returns. Similarly, in the Basil story "A Night at the Fair," we see Fitzgerald's reiteration of this point in his description of Basil's encounter with the girls at the fun fair. The pity is that the fun Basil enjoyed with the girls does not last very long; other than a brief sensation, it offers no help to elevate his miserable status in school.

For Fitzgerald, a chance to end his misery at St. Paul Academy came when his family decided to move him to the Newman School, a Catholic prep school located less than an hour from New York, a move his family hoped would give him a bit more discipline and the stimulus to study harder; but Fitzgerald saw the move as an opportunity to go to a new and famous place, where he could be happier and have a fresh start of his crusade for glory. Interestingly, the same wishful thinking is captured, not once, but twice in his fiction. In *This Side of Paradise* and the Basil stories, Fitzgerald gives his two alter egos, Amory and Basil, the same chance to go to the fabulous East for schooling. Through them, Fitzgerald reopens his bittersweet recollections of his adolescent past, recounting not only his romantic anticipation about his adventures at Newman and in the East but also his unexpected setbacks and failures during those years. Amory wants to go away to school in the East not merely because "everybody in

Minneapolis is going" but because the East is "the Land of Schools" (*TSP*, 22-23), full of the kind of excitement he has found in books and dreams. Basil is "terribly happy" when he learns that he is "starting away to school" in the East (*TAR*, 8); as he says in the story, being at school in the East will give one a feeling of "certain superiority" (*TAR*, 56), which is exactly what he, and Amory as well, has been desperately yearning for over the years. Basil's remark about feeling "superior" in going to school in the East echoes what Henry Adams said when he was complaining about being sent to Harvard College. To Adams, it was not a choice but a matter of following suit; "All went there because their friends went there, and the College was their ideal of social self-respect."[16]

To be superior, not merely among the boys in school but over all the people around him in society, is what Fitzgerald's youthful ambition was about. His arrival at Newman School marked his renewed endeavor toward this goal. The adaptations and transferences of his ups and downs in the prep school constitute the most impressive, if not the best, episode in *This Side of Paradise* and the Basil stories. For one thing, Newman School is now fictionalized as "St. Regis" in *This Side of Paradise* and the Basil stories. In the former, Fitzgerald takes time for a brief explanation of how he perceived the school. It is primarily one in a network of eastern "prep schools"—Andover, Exeter, Groton, Powfret, St. George's, Taft, Kent, "and a hundred others." It is a school dedicated to turning out proper and distinguished social types for the top universities in the Ivy League, the new blood of the social elite in American society. Toward the end of this short introduction, however, Fitzgerald cannot help interjecting his own comments about the schools: "Their vague purpose set forth in a hundred circulars as 'To impart a Thorough Mental, Moral, and Physical Training as a Christian Gentleman, to fit the boy *for meeting the problems of his day and generation,* and to give a solid foundation in the Arts and Sciences'" (*TSP*, 23).

Here, two things need our extra consideration. One is the retrospective nature of this comment; the other is the word "vague," which is the key to understanding Fitzgerald's perception of St. Regis and, in a broader sense, his judgment on the whole prep school system in America. Of course, as a boy who was lucky enough to enter one of these schools, Fitzgerald must have been overwhelmed by satisfaction and expectation at the time. Whatever the tone of doubt or resentment that the word "vague" in this passage may divulge, it is only something that Fitzgerald, the author, came to realize eight years after he first enrolled there as a fifteen-year-old boy. Like Fitzgerald, Amory and Basil will find out whether the education they are about to receive is as impeccable as promised only as they encounter life's problems. Their discovery turns out to be both perplexing and frustrating because they find themselves totally consumed and ruined by their endless struggle for visibility and self-knowledge. It is no surprise that neither of them is fully prepared for the grueling challenges each is about to face.

To depict that struggle with clarity and forcefulness, Fitzgerald puts his fusion strategy into a remarkable play by exploring his own experience at

Newman, including trivial events as well as crucial incidents. One trivial detail is that Basil's job at the Great Northern car shop is based on Fitzgerald's actual experience; the other is that Basil's letter to his mother, requesting more pocket money because "all the boys have a larger allowance" (*TAR*, 30), is based on the letter Fitzgerald wrote to his mother from a summer camp in Canada.[17] Though minor in their significance to the overall plot development, details like these do more than afford a sneak view of a young man's anxiety to remain competitive among his peers; they enliven the pages with realistic and amusing feelings and contribute to the richness and persuasiveness of the stories.

Of more importance is Fitzgerald's exploitation of his meeting and hence his close relationship with a priest, Father Sigourney Fay, a mentor and friend he found while he was at Newman School, on whom Fitzgerald based his characterization of Monsignor Darcy in his first novel, *This Side of Paradise*. This relationship proves to be a crucial turning point in the growth of Fitzgerald as well as his fictional soulmate, Amory. Fitzgerald met Sigourney Fay, who was then thirty-seven, at the start of his second school year. Apart from the difference in the time of their meeting and Fay's age, what Fitzgerald tells about Amory's relationship with Monsignor Darcy applies with equal force to his own relationship with Fay. When the forty-four-year-old Darcy meets Amory during the young man's tutelary visit, they "[take] to each other at first sight" (*TSP*, 24). Darcy is depicted as "the jovial, impressive prelate" who has the intelligence and charm to "dazzle an embassy ball," whereas Amory is given the typical image of a "green-eyed, intent youth," looking for companionship and guidance (*TSP*, 24). Like Fitzgerald, Amory felt a mutual and instantaneous attraction between Darcy and himself. Obviously, Darcy feels the same way. The two "accepted in their own minds a relation of father and son within a half hour's conversation" (*TSP*, 24). Amory has never imagined that such a visit would bring him a friend, a mentor, a spiritual guide, whose impact on him would last for the rest of his life. He is delighted to know a priest who presents religion not as an arduous road to salvation but, instead, as a way of "appreciating life to the fullest, if not entirely enjoying it" (*TSP*, 24). Darcy even offers a cigarette to Amory. What makes Amory feel more deeply touched is that Darcy is the first adult, a male adult, who is willing to listen to, understand, and inspire a young man with so many tumultuous feelings. In this scene, one may find the most unquestionable instance of Fitzgerald's verisimilitude in all his fiction because there is no tangible distinction between Amory and his creator here. For many years in his young life, as in Fitzgerald's early years when his father was always away on business, Amory's emotionally unstable and unbearably doting mother is often the only adult in the house to whom he can go for consolation and instruction. The lack of male presence in his young life has left a visible dent on his personality, a dent he has never been able to eradicate.

That Fitzgerald depicts the meeting between Darcy and Amory so meticulously demonstrates his own strong anxiety to relive that unforgettable moment in his life. Some critics insist that the Father Darcy/Amory relationship is Fitzgerald's conscious imitation of the Father Viner/Michael connection in Mackenzie's novel *Sinister Street*. This conclusion is, at best, inaccurate. It is true that Fitzgerald's indebtedness to Mackenzie is a widely acknowledged fact, Fitzgerald's primary source of this touching relationship is undoubtedly his own personal experience. Furthermore, the Viner-Michael connection in Mackenzie's novel is never developed beyond the boundary of an ordinary acquaintance between a minister and his parishioner. By comparison, the Darcy-Amory match is a very intimate relationship, which is made all the more remarkable by a dual quality in its chemistry: the father-son-like attachment and the candid friendship. This is particularly encouraging to a sensitive young man like Amory because he can see in Darcy not only a nurturing father figure but also an understanding partner with whom he can feel comfortable sharing all his joy and pain. In his comment on Fitzgerald's indebtedness to Mackenzie, Jack Hendriksen argues that "Fitzgerald has transformed Mackenzie's material" while appropriating it.[18] In my view, Fitzgerald certainly deserves more credit than just "transforming"; he seems to have perfectly interwoven with his own personal experience what he might have adapted from Mackenzie's novel. He always stresses the inner communication, rather than the nominal contact, between Darcy and Amory. He also intentionally designates this relationship as an instrumental part of Amory's psychological profile.

Throughout this episode, Fitzgerald appears extraordinarily in control of his material and his maneuvering of the narrative. Everything that Darcy and Amory do and talk about together is presented with great care: They have lunch together; they talk about school, religion, and even Amory's feelings of inferiority concerning his Irish ancestry. Considering how drastically Amory changes after this meeting, it is fair to say that the appearance of Darcy opens up a world of new ideas Amory has never encountered before. The immediate impact on Amory's, or rather Fitzgerald's, life from such a meeting is aptly summarized by Fitzgerald's figurative but sincere description: "Amory's mind turned inside out" within this "wonderful week" (*TSP*, 26). For a moment, Amory felt as if he had been transformed into a new being, whose hundreds of doubts and worries had not only been clarified, but also "crystallized into a thousand ambitions" (*TSP*, 26). Now everything about him seemed to suggest his readiness to deal with any bumps on his road to maturity.

Unfortunately, Amory's optimistic attitude does not last for long. Everything soon goes back to its original state of disarray. Despite Darcy's help and guidance, Amory is still unable to adapt himself swiftly enough to the status quo at St. Regis. All his preconceived notions run into a course of blunt confrontation against various odds at the school: snobbery, mistrust, jealousy, rivalry, alienation, and lack of discipline. It is clear that Amory has brought his personality problems with him to St. Regis. The strong and almost rigid sense of conceit and the austere attitude he has acquired while growing up in the Midwest just cannot fit in with his new learning environment. It is therefore predictable to see Amory's experience at St. Regis taking a dismal course right after his arrival. From the very beginning, we are told, things do not start off properly for him. He always has this odd feeling that he is "universally detested" (*TSP*, 27). Perhaps he is more perturbed by everybody's attempt to impose a kind of "authority" over him, however, and this is becoming something more than he can endure. Soon frustration leads to disillusionment and, ultimately, isolation. He has no mood for study or for interaction with others; he takes "to sulking in corners and reading after lights" and is "unbearably lonely, desperately unhappy" (*TSP*, 27-28). One thing he still will not give up, though, is to be a part of the elite in his school. He, like Fitzgerald, remembers what he has learned from his days back in St. Paul Academy: Popularity in school does not always come from one's intellectual success. Instead, it typically begins through athletics and other activities. He decides to play football, write poems for the school magazine, and take active part in theatrical activities. Owing to distractions like these, "it was temperamentally impossible for Amory to get the best marks in school" (*TSP*, 28). Consequently, Amory fails badly on both fronts: His efforts to win popularity through extracurricular activities never really paid off; his poor performance in study cost him what was left of his reputation among his teachers and fellow students.

Clearly, this is not a plausible way to achieve success in school. Fitzgerald learned this lesson the hard way. It did not work for Fitzgerald at Newman; it caused a lot of pain to Amory at St. Regis; and it will also fail Basil at St. Regis later. What Fitzgerald went through during his two years at Newman was chiseled so deeply into his mind that it would not easily vanish from his memory. Eight years after he adapted this episode of his life into Amory's story, Fitzgerald used it once again in his Basil stories. Among the eight published stories in the Basil series, more than half are set at St. Regis, the fictional substitute for Fitzgerald's Newman School. Like Amory, Basil's greatest and never-diminishing problem at St. Regis is his unpopularity. For Amory, things all went wrong at the outset; but Basil is not any luckier than Amory either. Within a week or two, Basil is involved in two fights. He is not only bullied by the captain of the football team but also ostracized by everyone. Before the first month is over, he is already fully aware of "the extent of his unpopularity" (*TAR*, 34). The initial shock at this unexpected discovery gradually turns into a vexing bewilderment. He tries different means to alleviate his misery, from crying to hiding. Nothing works. "Puzzled and wretched, he looked at his face in the glass, trying to discover there the secret of their dislike—in the expression of his eyes, his smile" (*TAR*, 34). To rescue himself from his dilemma, Basil resorts to the strategy he had tried in his hometown school before coming to the East: becoming popular through extracurricular activities. First he decides to play football, but he is soon accused of being "yellow" during a football game. Then he writes stories and takes an active part in drama, but the honor he earns never lasts. To his dismay, he is criticized for being a showoff. At first Basil is determined not to give up his ambition so easily. As Fitzgerald's title for one of the Basil stories suggests, "He Thinks He's Wonderful" because "he believed that everything was a matter of effort—the current principle of American education" (*TAR*, 53). For "a long hard time," ever since his first year at St. Regis, Basil "made numberless new starts and failed and tried again" (*TAR*, 51) in his effort of self-discovering and self-improving, displaying an admirable spirit of resilience much stronger and more tenacious than Amory's. Ultimately, however, "the supreme self-confidence with which he had come to St. Regis in September was thoroughly broken" (*TAR*, 34). The fabulous dream he has carried from boyhood into adolescence has culminated in a nightmare.

If compared carefully, one can see that Fitzgerald's treatment of the St. Regis episode in Amory's and Basil's stories is distinctly different in theme and characterization. In Amory's story, Fitzgerald pictures Amory as a hypersensitive and insecure egoist. Thus, details and incidents are carefully selected and analyzed in the most expressive way to expose the dimensional aspects of Amory's egotistic spirit. The focus of Fitzgerald's depiction is placed on Amory's inner strife. Yet in the Basil stories, Fitzgerald does a better job in capturing the doubt, pain, and triumph of a young man who is trying to fulfill the goal he has cherished since childhood. In his portrayal of Basil, Fitzgerald does not want to impose any specific label; he simply aims to present him as one of the young boys in prep school who were searching for the knowledge, guidance, and ideal in their life. Unlike Amory, who appears far more introverted and melancholic, Basil has a common boyish quality in his character. He is more open minded and more sophisticated to see through the problems he is facing, and he never hesitates to adjust himself to new challenges accordingly because he knows what it takes to be a tough competitor in school. Besides, the portrayal of Basil is better contrived with more and fresh details and incidents, most of which are represented as ongoing actions, in the form of dialogues between Basil and other characters, rather than in the frequently listless and sporadic narration as used in *This Side of Paradise*. The effect of such an approach is that Basil appears more real and believable than Amory, for we have seen him constantly struggling against the same odds an ordinary schoolboy has to face.

One issue to which Fitzgerald has given more importance in Amory's story is the American "success ethic." By devoting a special section, "the philosophy of the slickers," to the discussion of this issue, Fitzgerald offers his definition of the "slicker": clean-looking, well dressed, endowed with "social brains," skillful in the use of "all means on the broad path of honesty to go ahead, be popular, admired and never in trouble," "always a little wiser and shrewder than his contemporaries, managing some team or other, and keeping his cleverness carefully concealed" (*TSP*, 35). What is implied in Fitzgerald's definition is his ironic criticism of American prep schools for being a training ground, not for those who can meet their responsibility to society, but for those who are interested only in paving their own path without disclosing any larger aim. Here Fitzgerald presents some cogent reasons for questioning the function of American prep schools as the "cradle of social elite" in America. He believes that what grows out of this "cradle" is not an "elite" of future leaders, devoted to the well-being of their society, but an "elite" of self-centered "slickers" driven by their greed and ambition.

Knowing that Fitzgerald established his interpretation of the American prep school by adapting his own experience, one can see poignancy in his message. The function of such adaptation goes beyond contributing to Fitzgerald's characterization of Amory and Basil and reflecting Fitzgerald's evaluation of his past experience, however. It gives us a touching and amusing view of life in private school, demonstrating the significance "the American 'prep' school has to American life in general" (*TSP*, 27), as well as "the intricacies of a university social system and American society" (*TSP*, 26). The more profound implication about Fitzgerald's adaptation is what is not said, but subtly hinted. As Arthur Mizener says in his introductory note to one of the Basil stories, Fitzgerald's adaptation "has transmuted actually and made the personal experiences into the representative occasions of the young manhood of the American middle class."[19] As compared to boys like Mark Twain's Huck or Sherwood Anderson's George, who came from a poor family and had to start their own life at an early age without any chance of going to school, boys like Amory and Basil were much luckier. By going to school, they had the privilege of an extended growing process, and they did not have to face the harsh realities of life totally by themselves at a vulnerable young age. Ironically, however, this extended "growing process" might not be a "blessing"; it could be a disaster in disguise. By depicting what happened to Amory and Basil in the prep schools, Fitzgerald is able to compress this irony into a simple question: Does the American prep school have any significance in American life?

Amory's answer to this question is "very little," given at the beginning of the section of "The Egotist Down." Fitzgerald gives a similar answer in his autobiographical essay "What I Think and Feel at 25." Fitzgerald claimed that the two years he spent at prep school "were wasted, were years of utter and profitless unhappiness."[20] But he had not realized that at the time he was leaving Newman School. He still had not grasped "the philosophy of the slicker," which would probably help him to avoid making the same mistakes at college. He had no idea whatsoever that the burden of unpopularity, by which he had been baffled throughout his stay at Newman, was following him again to college. Only eight years later was he able to discover the truth about education and life in American prep schools, and to articulate that truth in fiction based on his own experience. The young Fitzgerald who was leaving Newman, just like the young Amory who is leaving St. Regis, "had not in himself changed" (*TSP*, 32); his youthful hope to become a Big Man on the college campus remained as strong as ever. The campus of his choice was Princeton.

Why Fitzgerald tapped Princeton as his favorite college has been a frequent subject of conjecture, including a number of published comments from Fitzgerald himself. In fact, the real reason was twofold: First, he was able to make a choice; second, Princeton was his top choice. With a large estate that his family had just inherited from his grandfather, Fitzgerald did not have any financial worries while considering his college choice. Since he would be the first member of his family to go to college, the choice was essentially left to him. He was able to confine his final choices among the colleges in the East, within the Ivy League of course. It was totally up to him to drop local schools like the University of Minnesota off his list and to turn down his Aunt Annabel's offer to pay for his expenses if he would study at the Catholic Georgetown University. In contrast, Fitzgerald was much luckier than the Basil boy in "Forging Ahead," who is having a tough time begging his mother not to send him to the cheaper but infamous state university, even though he is willing to "take care of furnaces," "shovel snow off sidewalk and tutor people" (*AA*, 35), in working his way through college. Fitzgerald gave various explanations for his choice of Princeton, such as his fond memory of Princeton's stunning victory in the 1911 Princeton-Harvard football game, his good impression of Princeton men as "slender and keen and romantic,"[21] and his interest in its Glee Club's concert and Triangle Club's play. In his essay "Who's Who—and Why," he explains that the decisive factor of his final choice is his discovery of a new musical-comedy score;

It was a show called *His Honor the Sultan,* and the title furnished the information that it had been presented by the Triangle Club of Princeton University.

That was enough for me. From then on the university question was settled. I was bound for Princeton. (*AA*, 84)

Clearly, all these explanations add up to the fact that Fitzgerald regarded Princeton as the best place for him.

What Fitzgerald wrote of Amory's decision to go to Princeton is apparently autobiographical. "Amory had decided definitely on Princeton" (*TSP*, 36), Fitzgerald tells us in the novel. Amory discusses his decision on this matter in his conversation with Darcy. "I want to go to Princeton" (*TSP*, 25), he tells Darcy, without any trace of hesitance in his voice. He does not give his mentor a specific reason, only a vague explanation: "I think of all Harvard men as sissies, like I used to be, and all Yale men as wearing big blue sweaters and smoking pipes. . . . I think of Princeton as being lazy and good-looking and aristocratic— You know, like a spring day. Harvard seems sort of indoors—" (*TSP*, 25).

Two things in the quote are worthy of note. One is that Amory's seemingly innocent impression of these schools contains a salient observation of America's leading institutions in higher education. The other is that no word about any complications and hesitations, especially Fitzgerald's problems with the entrance exams, is uttered. What we see is a different approach at work in Fitzgerald's fusion strategy, that is, to use his personal experience selectively. Fitzgerald's description of Amory's transition from his St. Regis days to his new life at Princeton is notably brief and smooth, without any reference to his potential catastrophe of having to settle for a state university, a catastrophe that might as well have occurred had he not inherited a fortune after his grandfather's sudden death. By telling the reader that Amory is the only one entering Princeton from St. Regis that year, Fitzgerald is applying a note of honor to Amory's admission to Princeton. Ironically, however, Fitzgerald's own admission to Princeton did not come so easily. His scores for the entrance exams were not good enough to win admission. Thanks to a personal interview that gave him a chance to persuade the admission committee at Princeton, Fitzgerald was accepted conditionally.

The omission of these details is by no means an inadvertent neglect on the part of Fitzgerald. Similarly, the variation of actual event is a well-designed move of his fusion strategy. Given the widely known autobiographical nature of the novel, a move like this might be risky, but Fitzgerald never doubted that it would work to his advantage. From one point of view, such a move is legitimate because no writer working so hard on a first and conspicuously autobiographical novel would be willing to expose too much personal information. From another angle, however, this move exemplifies Fitzgerald's dexterous tactics to ensure that what is, or what is not, drawn from his personal life will put feathers in his character's cap. In pragmatic terms, Fitzgerald is actually doing what has been done by all his literary predecessors, paving his way to the first sensational success in his writing career. Knowing this fact immediately enables us to understand what the romantic image of Amory symbolizes in the social context of the 1920s and to better appreciate the unique way in which such an image is presented so compellingly in the novel.

The various aspects of Amory's image coincide with the different pictures of Basil in the Basil stories. Both Amory and Basil have the strong desire to be Ivy Leaguers, although for Basil the choice is Yale. In fact, as Fitzgerald tells us, Basil has made the decision years before he actually reaches college age. Even before leaving for St. Regis, his anticipation of becoming a Yale man, as Fitzgerald's description in "The Scandal Detectives" about what is going through his mind during a summer night reveals, makes him "terribly happy" all the time: "This summer he and his mother and sister were going to the lakes and next fall he was starting away to school. Then he would go to Yale and be a great athlete. Everything was fine. He had so many alluring things to think about that it was hard to fall asleep at night" (*TAR*, 8). The reference to "many alluring things" and "Basil's difficulty in sleeping is vital in judging how much Yale weighs in Basil's youthful mind, in other words, how much an ingenuous and romantic ideal like Basil's means to a young man coming of age. In a symbolic sense, the night scene transforms Basil into a universal figure representing all the boys and girls whose heart beats fast with expectations as well as uncertainties about their dream of the future. In all great coming-of-age novels, such a mixture of emotions is projected as the initial impact of youthful dreams and is frequently depicted as an expression of the dreamer's anxiety. Whether Fitzgerald is consciously appropriating this tradition into his story is difficult to say, but what he does here has the exquisite resemblance to it. A brief comparison between Fitzgerald and his predecessors might help us to affirm

Fitzgerald's descriptive power, which gives color and substance to a scene as simple as this one.

Basil's sleepless night is very much like the night George Willard, the country boy in Sherwood Anderson's story "Departure," endures before he leaves for his new adventures in the city. Like Basil, George is a young man from the provinces who is leaving his hometown to meet the adventures of life "despite the uncertainty of his future life in the city."[22] Now that the day he has been expecting for so long has finally arrived, he cannot wait one more minute to part from his old life: "Young George Willard got out of bed at four in the morning. . . . Since two o'clock he had been awake thinking of the journey he was about to take and wondering what he would find at the end of his journey."[23] Although there is a big difference in personality and background between Basil and George, and even though their destinations are not the same, both of them are going through the same kinds of growing pains; both have been "carried away by their growing passion for dreams."[24] In comparing Basil and George, we see the reflections of Fitzgerald and Anderson over the common conflicts and transitions that American youth was experiencing during a crucial time in history. If Anderson captured every youngster's tantalizing dream of going to the city at the end of the nineteenth century, Fitzgerald certainly helped to transform it into the dream of going to an eastern prep school and then a prestigious Ivy League college. In essence, the dream of going to the city is tantamount to the dream of going to college, for both are cherished as the best and fastest way to a bright future.

Earlier in England, one may recall, Thomas Hardy had presented a combined version of these two dreams in his brilliant novel *Jude the Obscure*, whose protagonist, Jude, a country boy, dreams of going to university in the city. To a greater degree, however, Basil's sleepless night resembles the numerous sleepless nights in the young life of Jude. As the well-named title indicates, Jude is "obscure" not only in that he is unknown and has no social status but also in that he is enigmatic. Unlike Basil, Jude is an orphan who knows next to nothing about his ancestors, even his own parents. The bleak condition of his everyday environment is so devastating that it is almost beyond his ability to get by day by day, let alone to have a chance to go to prep school like Basil. Mentally, nevertheless, as Hardy suggests in the novel, Jude is no ordinary boy; he is a child full of impulses and ideals. He is "crazy for books" and deeply consumed with desires and aspirations those around him cannot understand. In spite of all the misfortunes in his young life, Jude is still hoping to rise in the world; he yearns for a life that is intellectually and morally better than the one he is expected to lead in the future. In Jude's faith, all this can be realized through acquiring scholarly distinction. The seed of this scholarly ambition is planted in Jude's heart by the schoolmaster in his village, who is saying goodbye to Jude before leaving for a university in order to pursue an advance degree:

Well—don't speak of this everywhere. You know what a university is, and a university degree? It is the necessary hallmark of a man who wants to do anything in teaching. My scheme, or dream, is to be a university graduate, and then to be ordained. By going to live at Christminster, or near it, I shall be at headquarters, so to speak, and if my scheme is practicable at all, I consider that being on the spot will afford me a better chance of earning it out than I should have elsewhere.[25]

Every word of the schoolmaster's parting speech leaves a mark in Jude's mind. Now that he fully understands the reason behind the schoolmaster's departure, he believes that he should to go "there" too if he wants a better chance for his future. Soon the anxiety of embarking on his own adventure makes him restless every night, just as Basil's thought of "the glamorous miracle of Yale" (*TAR*, 51) and so "many alluring things" (*TAR*, 8) at that campus makes him sleepless all the time. Since the departure of the schoolmaster, just as Basil is enraptured by the tops of spires and towers in New Haven, Jude becomes infatuated with the lights of Christminster, the University City. Nothing can take his mind off the university, or the city. Whenever possible, Jude steals off to the Brown House on the hill to catch a glimpse of the far-away city. Through this imagery of lights in dark night, as Bruce Johnson's comment on Hardy's novel suggests, "we are accustomed to seeing in the luminous symbol of Christminster (looking in the distance like 'the heavenly Jerusalem') a mixture of Jude's desire for learning with a youthful, romantic enthusiasm to escape from home and enter a larger social world."[26] What Johnson says here can also be applied to Basil, for in the eyes of Basil and Jude, both New Haven and Christminster are the Mecca of learning, or in a symbolic sense beacons of their hope, "a sort of gate-way to that deeper, richer life" (*AA*, 34).

If it is safe to say that Jude is obsessed with the lights over the sky of Christminster, it should not be an exaggeration to say that Basil cherishes Yale with equally utter ebullience, for as Fitzgerald tell us in "Forging Ahead," "Yale was the faraway East, that he had loved with a vast nostalgia since he had first read books about great cities" (*AA*, 34). As we have seen in Jude's story, what makes Basil's young heart tick is the university and the city where the university is located. On more than one occasion, Fitzgerald asserts, "the Mirage of Yale," coupled with the thought of going there, snaps Basil out of the abyss of frustration with the magic of excitement and expectation. No one, nor anything, can make Basil change his mind. Perhaps the most egregious evidence is a conversation between Basil and John Granby in "The Perfect Life." After making a high point in a football game for his school by running sixty yards for an unallowed touchdown, Basil suddenly becomes a hero on campus. He even receives flattering praise from Granby, a former St. Regis alumnus and now a "Big Man" at Princeton. Granby invites Basil for a chat late that afternoon. During their conversation, Granby brags about Princeton, but as soon as he finds out that "Yale was an abstract ideal deep in Basil's heart" (*TAR*, 106), Grandy immediately gives up his attempt to "recruit" Basil. As a sixteen-year-old prep school student who still has a year to go before college, Basil has already perceived Yale as the best place for him, a place where he would be able to improve himself and prepare for social success.

Despite almost ten years between the dates of their publication, *This Side of Paradise* and the Basil stories betray little essential difference in Fitzgerald's descriptions of Amory's romantic fantasy about Princeton and of Basil's about Yale. One striking point must be admitted, though, namely, that Fitzgerald was being straitlaced and even a bit obdurate when he wrote of Basil's bumpy journey to Yale. As mentioned previously, Fitzgerald presents a short but plain-sailing transition between Amory's departure from St. Regis and his new life at Princeton, without touching on any of his dismal memories about his own failure in make-up exams or the potential financial difficulty that might have led his family to send him to a state university instead. To avoid any conceivable damage to his own public image, Fitzgerald took great care in selecting real events from his personal experience and changing them to fit the positive image of Amory as a typical romantic hero of Jazz Age America. By sharp contrast, however, Fitzgerald devoted lengthy episodes to Basil's transition from St. Regis to Yale, relying heavily and candidly on of events and affairs that occurred during his vacations in Minnesota, particularly his poor scores in exams and the financial threat to his plan for college. Throughout these episodes, which spread over the second part in "Forging Ahead" and the first in "Basil and Cleopatra," Fitzgerald did not shy away from any disparaging personal information that could potentially damage his own reputation.

In "Forging Ahead," Fitzgerald is, as usual, brilliant in details. In this story, Basil is almost seventeen, wandering at the crossroads between his prep school, St. Regis, and his undecided college. His mother comes home one day with the terrible news that they have lost $22,000 in a business investment. Given the huge cost Basil's education at Yale may incur, his mother urges him to give up Yale and go to the state university instead. Due to this unexpected turn of fortune, it seems that Basil is about to lose his hope for the "halo" he believes only an Ivy League school can offer him. After hearing what his mother said, Basil's heart "tumbled into his stomach; the future, always glowing like a comfortable beacon ahead of him, flared up in glory and went out" (*AA*, 33). Fitzgerald's description of Basil's reaction to this bad news is immediately followed by the image of Basil left alone to ponder the nightmarish infringement of his plan for college:

Basil sat thinking in the dark parlor. For the present the loss meant only one thing—he wasn't going to Yale after all. The sentence itself, discovered from its meaning, overwhelmed him, so many times had he announced casually, "I'm going to Yale," but gradually he realized how many friendly and familiar dreams had been swept away. (*AA*, 34)

Here, Fitzgerald shows his best in using room setting to reflect the character's state of mind. The time is way after seven in the evening; the room is dim and probably has no lights at all; Basil is the only person there. The dimness sets up Basil's mood. He still has not recovered from the terrible shock he has sustained from the bad news, and the emptiness of the room symbolizes the blankness of his delirious mind. With all the dreams and fantasies about his prospect of going to Yale completely blown away, Basil is literally at a loss what to do next with his life. In *This Side of Paradise,* Amory's mother, Beatrice, provides Amory with the kind of romantic background Fitzgerald never had the luck to enjoy; here in the Basil stories, Fitzgerald shared his own dreams of school and college with Basil and deliberately mixed these dreams with the actualities of his own experience. Although Fitzgerald did not face the same situation as Basil, he was very close to it. He must have known what it is like to be in such a dilemma because had his family not gotten an inheritance from his grandfather in time, Basil's heart-breaking frustration could have certainly been Fitzgerald's. The point of comparison is that by taking a realistic approach to self-revelations, Fitzgerald did not lose any dignity or popularity among his readers simply because of a few setbacks in his personal life or a few difficulties in his family. On the contrary, Fitzgerald's profound fusion of actual events and fictional works presented an unrebukable social implication: Money has irreplaceable importance in any young American's pursuit of any wishes, from personal growth to social success.

In "Basil and Cleopatra," the last and the best story in the Basil series, in which Basil is enrolled at Yale, Fitzgerald's depiction of Basil's failure in his make-up exams is revealing. Its significance lies in Fitzgerald's apparent reluctance to willfully glorify his characters all the time. Some might argue that Fitzgerald's fusion strategy clearly tilted toward the actual side simply because this particular story was conceived and published after his sensational success with *The Great Gatsby,* when his reputation as "the representative voice of the Jazz Age" was already solid enough to withstand any negative self-exposure. That might be a factor in Fitzgerald's boldness, but without doubt the details of Basil's frustration over his poor scores and his ineligibility to play freshman football because of them help to turn him into a more lifelike representative figure among the Ivy Leaguers of Fitzgerald's generation. Fitzgerald's depiction of Amory's fantasy about being a hero at Princeton and of Basil's determination to be a "Big Man" at Yale is another example of how his fusion strategy operates in various capacities. The way in which he conducts the vigorous probe into the life on American campuses laid the groundwork for what was to be labeled the "college novel." First of all, it should be noted that Fitzgerald resembles Amory and Basil in numerous ways. Fitzgerald's Princeton is as much as Amory's Princeton and Basil's Yale, but the differences between them may well be as many as the traits they share. The tough challenge to the reader is to define correctly what is similar and what is different between Fitzgerald and his two fictional characters.

THE POWER OF FITZGERALD'S "PARADOXES"

Since Fitzgerald's fiction constantly and considerably depends on a mixture of the events he actually experienced, the events he fictionalized, and the charming qualities he wished he had possessed (like the heroes in his fiction), it is not easy to draw a clear-cut distinction between the actual, the fictional, and the wishful. Furthermore, it becomes a more formidable challenge when his treatment of school setting is swayed by his fluctuating and often contradictory mentality toward those elite schools in America. In discussing Bernard Malamud's view of the university expressed in *A New Life*, James M. Mellard points out that "the academic or, more strictly, the college novel displays an author's reactions to the college institution itself, its faculty, and the cycle of events linked to an academic calendar."[27] In my view, Fitzgerald's "reaction" to colleges in the 1920s is conspicuously characterized by a strong sense of ambivalence and energized by the power of his "paradoxes." As we discover in his fiction and essays about Princeton, Fitzgerald perceived schools like Princeton at once with feelings of excitement, admiration, contempt, and resentment. Whenever romantic speculation awoke in his mind, he would be overwhelmed with pride and expectation at the thought of Princeton; but whenever he stumbled over something, not even disastrous, but merely unpleasant, he would be instantly bereft of hope and fumed with complaints and grudges toward his school. The expression of his ambivalent feelings appeared as early as in his *Ledger* and later found its way into his novels and stories. It is therefore not surprising at all to see Fitzgerald continuously wrestling with his notion of what these elite schools, Princeton in particular, mean to him. Since his perspective shifts so often in his fiction, sometimes it is extremely difficult to tell whose feeling or notion it is, Fitzgerald's or his character's. Like Fitzgerald, Amory and Basil swing between love and hate all the time. The only time they have no doubts or animosities toward their beloved colleges is when they are romanticizing the Ivy League in their prep school days. Once they enter college, what they encounter there is not exactly what they imagined or expected. Inevitably, disappointment drives away the initial euphoria; frustration takes over from excitement. Before long, they start to grapple with intriguing new questions: What does the college really stand for? Why does one have to be popular in college? What type of elite men will the college turn out into society? Sometimes the ambivalent feeling is overtly configurated by a kind of anti-Princeton sentiment or a mistrust of college study in general.

Since Princeton is the principal model of the college setting in his fiction, Fitzgerald's ambivalent feeling toward college is directed mainly at his alma mater, with a scattering of brief comments on other Ivy League schools. Critics have never agreed with the argument that Fitzgerald is a writer whose career is most closely associated with his university. In a sense, this dispute may easily be solved by what his daughter, Scottie Fitzgerald Smith, said of her father's relationship with his alma mater: "My father belonged all his life to Princeton."[28] It is absolutely true. From the night in 1905 when the nine-year-old Fitzgerald came to know about and love Princeton after attending its Glee Club concerts to the moment before his death, when he was reading a football game report in the Princeton alumni bulletin, his life had been inseparably tied to the school. It does not seem farfetched to say that without Princeton there would not have been a great writer like Fitzgerald, and that perhaps America would have had to wait some more years before it could see its first college novel.

Fitzgerald came to Princeton full of ambition. Of course, his long-term goal was to prepare himself for a successful career in society; but for a start, as William Goldhurst writes, "the most important part of Fitzgerald's program, it seems, was to become a popular figure, a football hero, and a member of the most prestigious eating club on Prospect Street."[29] One thing Goldhurst failed to mention is that Fitzgerald also wanted to be a hero in theatricals, for Fitzgerald believed that he would have a better chance to stand out among his classmates in sports and theatricals, not in intellectual achievements. That does not mean that he had no confidence in his own intelligence. The real reason is that these nonintellectual activities, which were well sponsored at Princeton, would not require much extra effort from him. In a sense, this is the most memorable lesson he learned from his years at St. Paul Academy and Newman School, and it was one of his major considerations in choosing Princeton. Throughout his years at Princeton, Fitzgerald never took his academic program seriously. In the classroom, he was a poor student; outside the classroom, he was an arduous worker on almost everything else but his studies. His obsessive interests in sports, theatricals, writing for school magazines, and other campus activities diverted him from all academic responsibilities and resulted in his weak showing in school records. In his junior year, he left Princeton partly because of malaria, but mostly because of his fear of flunking. Years later he regretted having left. When he learned that his daughter was devoting much of her time to writing a musical comedy, Fitzgerald sent her a serious warning right away, telling her that he did not want to see such a mistake repeated twice in two generations.[30]

For decades the question of whether Fitzgerald was intellectually equipped to be a Princetonian or the writer of influential novels about Jazz Age America has been examined by critics, especially Fitzgerald's contemporaries, from nearly every conceivable perspective. Yet few thus far have seriously probed how Fitzgerald felt and what he said about this issue himself. People tend to base their negative conclusions solely on Fitzgerald's bad grades. One of Fitzgerald's Princeton professors, Gordon H. Gerould, doubted that a student with such a dismal performance in English classes could have written *The Great Gatsby*.[31] It is only in recent Fitzgeraldian scholarship that distortions about his intellectual ability have been rectified. Deborah D. Schlack has observed that "Fitzgerald's relatively weak showing in his Princeton English classes may reflect only that Fitzgerald was intrigued more with the social than with the academic side of college life."[32] Some critics have acknowledged that it is quite an accomplishment to have twenty-one selections published in Princeton's *Nassau Literary Magazine* during Fitzgerald's three-year stay, and that it is remarkable enough to show that "the undergraduate [Fitzgerald] always on the verge of expulsion was beginning to exhibit a high level of literary craftsmanship."[33] Fitzgerald's "warning" to his daughter further convinces us that he never doubted his own talent and that he deeply regretted not using it more sensibly, even though he deemed it an innocent misjudgment at a time when socializing in college was considered more important than learning and one's prestige could come only from one's popularity among peers rather than one's academic excellence. Had he a chance to do it again, he would probably not repeat the mistake.

This, in fact, is one aspect of Fitzgerald's Princeton experience that he never hesitated to share in his writings. Through Amory and Basil, Fitzgerald kept poring over this issue. Even though Fitzgerald did not go so far to recount all the details of his academic failure in *This Side of Paradise,* Amory's accomplishments in studies were about those of his creator. Amory's entire crusade for his romantic ideal, including his ups and downs in extracurricular activities, his relationship to the young men he meets, his romance with Isabelle, his friendship with Monsiñor Darcy, his involvement with Clara and a number of other romantic effusions, is immediately drawn from Fitzgerald's own adventures at Princeton. Amory's belief that one can shine in college only through sports and theatricals accompanies him to Princeton very little changed from his childhood. It is not accidental, therefore, that during his exploratory tour of the campus Amory could not help "stopping to investigate a display of athletic photographs in a store window" (*TSP*, 37). Amory's keen interest in this window is further conveyed by another scene in the same chapter. When he sees Princeton's football team marching across the campus, his eyes are fixed on Allenby, the football captain, who is leading "the white platoon" (*TSP*, 42): "He sighed eagerly. . . . Fascinated, Amory watched each rank of linked arms as it came abreast, the faces indistinct above the polo shirts, the voices blent in a paean of triumph—and then the procession passed through shadowy Campbell Arch, and the voices grew fainter, as it wound eastward over the campus" (*TSP*, 42).

It is apparent that what Fitzgerald tries to emphasize in these two scenes is definitely more than a newly arrived freshman's curiosity in college football. The sight of these athletic heroes on campus strikes a responsive chord in Amory, giving him a strong sense of euphoria and solemnity. The two words "platoon" and "marched," which present a vivid military imagery in the above scene, have apparently conveyed Amory's conception of and high admiration for a hero on campus. But the word "sighed" betrays his concealed frustration over his slim chance in being a sports hero, the best way to gain the popularity and prestige everyone dreams of on campus. Here, Fitzgerald lets us peek into his ambivalent sentimentality toward the football glory on campus during his time. What we see is a mixed bag of awe, bewilderment, and disappointment, which has been a key element in his exploration of school setting, recurrent in many of his stories, from "Reade, Substitute Right Half," his 1910 selection in *Saint Paul Academy Now and Then* to *This Side of Paradise* and the Basil series.

Although Amory, like his creator, does not fully comprehend why football has such a magic power on campus, he does try his luck in football before turning to other means of becoming a hero on campus. Amory wrenches his knee and is cut from the freshman football team almost immediately.[34] He soon switches his time and energy to creative efforts, working and writing for school magazines. As he tells his classmate Kerry, Amory is determined to become "Princetonian chairman or Triangle president." He "wants to be admired" (*TSP*, 47). Brilliant, witty and strong-willed, Amory has accomplished his plans one after another on the social front of his college life, earning membership of the Triangle Club and a seat on the editorial board of the *Princetonian*, and attracting "the intent eyes" of his classmates with the eloquence and knowledge he has demonstrated in literary discussions. Thus, it may be said, Amory has become exactly the kind of campus hero Fitzgerald had always wanted to be. Yet no matter how much prestige Amory enjoys among his less successful undergraduates, he is still an egotist, a self-centered and emotionally unstable man who fears "crowds unless the crowd was around *him*" (*TSP*, 77), someone who dislikes the dark forest when he is "particularly imaginative" (*TSP*, 129). He is simply too romantic and immature to brave the world off the campus. Evidently, what Fitzgerald intends to show is that the popularity of a campus hero does not necessarily guarantee his maturity.

In the portrayal of Basil, the conception of hero on campus remains Fitzgerald's major theme, although he has covered only Basil's freshman year and replaced Princeton with Yale as setting. As Arthur Mizener's note in *Afternoon of an Author* suggests, "The real source of Basil Duke Lee's inner experience at Yale was Scott Fitzgerald's experience at Princeton."[35] As we discover, Basil possesses most of the traits that Fitzgerald had given to Amory. Like Fitzgerald and Amory, Basil comes to college with a lot of romantic dreams. What he wants to accomplish in college has been a goal formulated well before his arrival on campus. He is smart, but not talented; he is conscientious, but not committed; he is full of sensitivity and vanity, but lacks self-confidence and vision. Unlike Amory, who regards being a sports figure only as one of the fast ways to be popular on campus, Basil always equates his desire to be a great athlete on campus with his romantic perception of a college leader. Fitzgerald writes in "The Scandal Detectives," the first story of the Basil series, that Basil wants to "go to Yale and be a great athlete" (*TAR*, 8); he tells us again in "He Thinks He's Wonderful" that Basil "wanted to be a great athlete, popular, brilliant and always happy" (*TAR*, 53).

Even though this difference between Amory and Basil is something above the surface, it does imply the kind of guileless, or even provincial, quality in Basil's vision of college life, the same quality that writers like Joyce, Anderson, Dreiser, and Mackenzie have stressed while depicting their young character's quest to the city. Although drastically different in circumstances, Basil reminds us of the boys in James Joyce's *Dubliners*, of George Willard in Sherwood Anderson's *Winesburg, Ohio*, and of Sister Carrie in Theodore Dreiser's namesake novel. Being fundamentally a midwestern boy, Basil sees college life in the East as little different from the way these characters see the life in the city.

All of them tend to fantasize about the new and strange world they are about to enter; they are naive and vulnerable, anxious and ambitious; but they are not aware of their own weaknesses as these writers see them—vanity, self-suspicion, and lack of experience, courage, and perseverance. Coming to the East for schooling, Basil believes that this is "the golden time" (*TAR*, 62) to begin his conquest of "the successive worlds of school, college and New York" (*TAR*, 50). He deems being an athletic star on campus the first and most effective step to accomplish his conquest. In "The Freshest Boy," Basil gives his friend Lewis patronizing advice: "You'd probably be a lot more popular in school if you played football" (*TAR*, 28). In "Basil and Cleopatra," Basil admits to William that to play football is "the greatest ambition in his life" (*TAR*, 53). Later in the same story, after having been promoted onto the freshman team because of the starting quarterback's unexpected injury, "Basil felt the old lust for glory sweep over him" (*AA*, 62). When his poor marks in trigonometry prevent him from playing football during the first half of the freshman football season, Basil feels so sad that he begins to "look around him gloomily to see if there was anything left in life" (*AA*, 60). Once he drives his team to a close victory over Princeton, the first thing that comes to his mind is the joy over his sudden emergence as a hero in the eyes of his estranged girlfriend, Minnie, and his classmates. But the biggest irony in Fitzgerald's portrayal of Basil is that no matter how much and how hard he tried, Fitzgerald never had a chance to enjoy the kind of pride and prestige awarded to a football star in college. All his life Fitzgerald wished that he could have been a great football hero like Basil. Regretfully, it is only through his portrayal of Basil that Fitzgerald had an opportunity to taste the "awe" of football glory.

Dissecting the stories of Amory and Basil side by side, one would easily figure out Fitzgerald's artful use of paradox in order to stress the futility in overcoming what may be termed "the popularity syndrome" rampant on American campuses. In his belief, however, neither being a sports hero nor being a social club leader will suffice. In the Basil stories, the point Fitzgerald wants to strike is to win popularity by using the football field as a public platform; whereas in Amory's story the advice Fitzgerald tries to offer is to win fame by seeking a role as champion of the class clubs, editorial boards, and theatrical groups. Basil did enjoy being an athletic hero after winning a game, but it did not last long; Amory did achieve some successes in his extracurricular activities, but they are still not good enough to get him to the top rank of popularity among his classmates. During his own years at Princeton, Fitzgerald tried both strategies, but the pity is that only one of them worked for him. He had Amory's imagination and theatrical skills, but he did not have Basil's athletic talent. That is why he portrays Amory as someone who is romantic and self-determined, constantly changing and developing himself internally, but he turns Basil into someone who is intellectually less mature and less sophisticated, eager to be a football hero on campus but lacking an inner drive to be a real leader in society. Personally, Fitzgerald really wished that he had an ideal combination of Amory's imaginative power and Basil's basic instincts. To his regret, such a perfect mix is seldom, if ever, found in real life. To his consolation, though, he was able to reassess this dream from two opposite points of view by writing *This Side of Paradise* and the Basil series.

The Princeton Fitzgerald attended was essentially an undergraduate college, "set in what is for America an ancient village; the aura of history surrounding Nassau Hall; the neo-Gothic splendor of dormitories and chapel."[36] Andre Le Vot once claimed that Fitzgerald always saw Princeton through a lover's eyes.[37] Le Vot's remark seems too ambiguous to reflect what Fitzgerald really felt about Princeton over the years. In the eyes of the young Fitzgerald, Princeton was a beautiful and romantic place, worthy of his dreams and expectations. His initial fantasylike perception of Princeton is typically characterized by his own comparison of Princeton to "a green Phoenix" (*AA*, 71) in "Princeton," an essay he wrote almost ten years after he left the school. Toward the end of this essay, however, his perception of Princeton has lost its romantic touch, and his narrative has turned into a voice of deep regret, lamenting:

Looking back over a decade one sees the ideal of a university become a myth, a vision, a meadow lark among the smoke stacks. Yet perhaps it is there at Princeton, only more elusive than under the skies of the Prussian Rhineland or Oxfordshire; or perhaps some men come upon it suddenly and possess it, while others wander forever outside. (*AA*, 79)

The tone of his voice suggests a murky, but thought-provoking, message for a new generation of Fitzgeralds and Amorys, young men about to start their adventure on this campus. The same ambivalent feeling toward his alma mater is also unleashed paradoxically in his fiction. Amory's changing, and sometimes even confusing, concept of his mission at Princeton reflects Fitzgerald's initial speculation of what Princeton really symbolizes to him. It is quite certain that the young Fitzgerald saw Princeton as Amory saw it in *This Side of Paradise*. Amory comes to Princeton because Princeton has the "atmosphere of bright colors" and the "alluring reputation as the pleasantest country club in America" (*TSP*, 36).

In view of Amory's divergent sentiments before and after his arrival at Princeton, it is clear that Fitzgerald's delineation of how Amory perceives Princeton is tinged with a paradoxical combination of ebullience and perplexity. On the one hand, by romanticizing Princeton as a country club, Fitzgerald tries to attach an idyllic and elite quality to the school and thus accentuate Amory's anxiety for his association with it; on the other hand, he deliberately makes a trenchant point about Amory's agonizing sense of nervousness about his own appearance during his first walk on campus, as if Amory is struggling with his guilty conscience about being here. Perhaps, he wonders, a midwestern boy like him simply does not belong here after all. For a moment, Amory, the protagonist of the novel, seems to have been reduced to a human foil whose humbleness is exposed to reflect the grandeur of the campus surroundings. Swiftly, Fitzgerald shifts the focus of his imagination back to the surroundings again. To transform

Princeton into a paradise worthy of Amory's romantic dreams, Fitzgerald bestows a group of contemporary buildings with deceptive historical splendor by using personification and animal imagery. Amory, who now seems to have recovered from his self-consciousness, is enjoying his exploratory tour of the campus: "He wanted to ramble through the shadowy scented lanes, where Witherspoon brooded like a dark mother over Whig and Clio, her attic children, where the black Gothic snake of Little curled down to Cuyler and Patton, these in turn flinging in the mystery out over the placid slope rolling to the lake" (*TSP*, 42)" Again, Fitzgerald's superb descriptive ability is on full display. With this articulate imagery of these oddly named buildings based on their architectural formation, Fitzgerald completely covers Princeton with a traditional and romantic patina. In fact, many buildings on the campus were very young; even the Gothic towers that inspired "great dreams" were no more than a quarter-of-a-century old.

It is true, though, that the beauty of the campus is not the only thing that triggers Amory's romantic illusion about Princeton; he likes the "handsome, prosperous big-game crowds" (*TSP*, 43); most of all, he likes its promised cachet for social prominence. For the same reason Anthony Patch of *The Beautiful and Damned* goes to Harvard: Schools like Harvard "open doors," and "it would be a tremendous tonic, it will give him innumerable self-sacrificing and devoted friends" (*BD*, 7). Again, for the same reason Basil never hesitates to make his quick decision to go to Yale, and whenever the word "Yale" pops up in conversation, "a new pleasurable thought occurred to him" (*TAR*, 74).

As soon as a setback strikes, however, their romantic illusions about their schools vanish immediately and their fantasized world of glory and success falls apart completely. When Fitzgerald failed to make the football team he felt that he had lost a great opportunity to shine as a campus hero; when his poor marks prevented him from taking the presidency of the Triangle Club, he was devastated by missing his last chance to stand out among his classmates. In his letter to Edmund Wilson, Fitzgerald complained that "Princeton is stupid" and that he was "rather bored" in school (*CU*, 248). He even blamed the courses, the professors, and the departments for his own poor intellectual performance. In his 1927 sketch of Princeton, Fitzgerald singled out its English department for ridicule, calling it "a surprisingly pallid" one, "top-heavy, undistinguished and with an uncanny knack for making literature distasteful to young men" (*AA*, 75). He also claimed that his instructors were inept and his preceptors even worse.

The resentment is deeply seated. Fitzgerald's frustration with Princeton followed his characters into *This Side of Paradise*. His characters help to express his own admiration and resentment toward Princeton, a familiar cynical paradox in his treatment of school setting. Like Fitzgerald, despite all his pride of and romantic conceptions about Princeton, Amory "was far from contented" because "he missed the place he had won at St. Regis', the being known and admired" (*TSP*, 44). His farewell to football, a result of his leg injury takes a big toll not only on his vanity but also on his self-confidence. Similarly, even Basil, whose utter devotion to Yale is repeatedly stressed in the stories, has ambivalent feelings toward his school. Perhaps the most evident example can be found in a scene in which Basil comes back to school and finds out that he has failed an exam and therefore will not be eligible to play football. He "threw himself on his bed," laughing wildly, not sure if there is anything meaningful left in his life, "only now did he begin for the first time to be aware of Yale" (*AA*, 60).

Shortly after the novel was published, Fitzgerald was astonished by the bitter reaction against his novel, particularly by the reaction of the president of Princeton, John Grier Hibben, who wrote a reproachful letter criticizing the book for giving such a wrong impression about the school as "a country club," a place of calculation and snobbery. Even from the standpoint of Amory, this accusation was not entirely a fabrication. One can tell from reading *This Side of Paradise* that the "impression" was deliberately intended. But it was not wrong. The Princeton section is largely designed to impart an avocation of the campus life at the time, vivifying the "country club" quality of Princeton, exhibiting its alluring charm to youthful ideals and fantasies scoffing at its stodgy and even deceptive guidance for its romantic egotists, and satirizing the philistine ambition for popularity and prestige. That Fitzgerald seldom, if ever, touches upon the academic rectitude and intellectual learning on campus reiterates his (and his contemporaries') lack of keen interest in the integrity of educational programs at Princeton. In addition, he expressed his bitterness toward Princeton in letters to his daughter, and he made the same flippant remarks about Princeton's approach to education in his essays and interviews. It was only in his later years that Fitzgerald became more and more supportive of Princeton, even though he continued to express some bitterness toward Princeton in letters to his daughter.

One phenomenon worthy of mention is that in his later novels and stories Fitzgerald portrayed many of his characters as Yale men, without any flagrantly demeaning or sarcastic intention. It seems reasonable to speculate that Fitzgerald did so because of his ambivalence toward Princeton. Looking back at his own not-so-fantastic experience at Princeton, perhaps he believed that Yale would have been a far better choice had he made the same decision as Basil or Dick Diver did. Nonetheless, no matter how much bitterness and animosity Fitzgerald revealed in his fiction and essays, it was not his intention to dismiss everything he had learned from his college experience. Conversely, he had admitted on many occasions that Princeton helped to sharpen his social sensibility and supplied him with so many inspirations. His attitude toward Princeton is, at worst, a paradox. Whenever Fitzgerald recalled his days at Princeton, as James L. W. West, III has observed, "one part of him wished profoundly that he fit in there and he had been successful during his undergraduate career. Another part, however, knew that his motivation and drive as an artist depended in important ways on his having failed at Princeton—that he wrote well about Princeton and, in a larger sense, about the level of society that Princeton represented precisely because he had been an outsider and a failure at that university."[38] Some critics went so far to label Fitzgerald's criticism of some colleges' weakness as "anti-intellectualism." It is presumptuous to make such a judgment based on Fitzgerald's intriguing, sometimes even paradoxical, contemplations of the campus. As a matter of fact, Fitzgerald's mistrust of education is not totally unfounded. What he tried to suggest is that education has its limitations because a man's learning goes far beyond his graduation from prep school and college, and also because what he has learned has to be tested in a much more complex life off the campus. It is a tough issue and difficult to find a perfect answer. The depiction of the adventures of Amory and Basil in prep school and college is Fitzgerald's attempt to explore this issue. To a certain extent, the ambivalence he revealed in his depiction symbolizes the complexity of this issue. At least Fitzgerald created Amory and Basil, who are not merely the mirror images of himself, but more importantly two representative figures of 1920s youth, suffering growing pains and developing from "egotist" to "personage." Moreover, the fusion strategy Fitzgerald used to portray his characters has established a new approach to the European tradition of the *Entwicklungsroman*. The use of paradox that enriched Fitzgerald's sentiments toward school has set up a new pattern to be found in the American college novel after Fitzgerald, especially in the novels of Joseph Heller, Joyce Carol Oates, Bernard Malamud, Philip Roth, and Saul Bellow.[39]

NOTES

1. F. Scott Fitzgerald, *The Letters of F. Scott Fitzgerald*, ed. Andrew Turnbull (New York: Charles Scribner's Sons, 1963), 138.

2. Matthew J. Bruccoli and Margaret M. Duggan, eds., *Correspondence of F. Scott Fitzgerald* (New York: Random House, 1980), 21-22. It is imperative, I think, to read the correspondence between Fay and Fitzgerald. It will help to illuminate the connection of *This Side of Paradise* to the tradition of the American *Bildungsroman*.

3. M. P. Proctor, *The English University Novel* (Berkeley: University of California Press, 1957), 154.

4. For a more detailed comparison between Mackenzie and Fitzgerald, see Jack Hendriksen, *This Side of Paradise as a Bildungsroman* (New York: Peter Long, 1993).

5. David W. Bailey, "A Novel about Flappers for Philosophers," *Harvard Crimson* (May 1, 1920): 3.

6. For more information, see Dorothy B. Good, "'Romance and a Reading List': The Literary References in *This Side of Paradise*," in *Fitzgerald / Hemingway Annual*, 1976, 35-64. The author offers a complete summary and analysis of Fitzgerald's use of literary sources in the novel.

7. See the afterword in *John Gardner: Critical Perspectives*, eds. Robert A. Morace and Kathrya Vanspankeren (Carbondale, Ill.: Southern Illinois University Press, 1982), 149.

8. Quoted from *New Republic* (May 18, 1938), by Steven G. Kellman in *The Self-begetting Novel* (London: Macmillan, 1980), 122.

9. See Malcolm Cowley's editor's note in *The Bodley Head Scott Fitzgerald* vol. 6 (London: Bodley Head, 1963), 9.

10. F. Scott Fitzgerald, in *F. Scott Fitzgerald's Ledger: A Facsimile*, ed. Matthew J. Bruccoli (Washington, D.C.: Bruccoli Clark, 1972), 154.

11. Kenneth Eble, *F. Scott Fitzgerald* (Boston: Twayne, 1977), 23.

12. James Nagel, "Initiation and Intertextuality in *The Basil and Josephine Stories*," in *New Essays on F. Scott Fitzgerald's Neglected Stories*, ed. Jackson Bryer (Columbia, Mo.: University of Missouri Press, 1996), 265.

13. Henry Adams, *The Education of Henry Adams* (Boston: Houghton Mifflin, 1973), 38.

14. F. Scott Fitzgerald, *Ledger*, ed. Matthew J. Bruccoli, 163.

15. Andre Le Vot, *F. Scott Fitzgerald: A Biography*, trans. William Byron (Garden City, N.Y.: Doubleday, 1983), 18.

16. Henry Adams, *The Education of Henry Adams*, 54.

17. See the letter Fitzgerald wrote to his mother from Orillia, Ontario, at the age of ten, collected in *The Letters of F. Scott Fitzgerald*, ed. Andrew Turnbull (New York: Charles Scribner's Sons, 1963), 449.

18. Jack Hendriksen, *This Side of Paradise as a Bildungsroman*, 76.

19. F. Scott Fitzgerald, *Afternoon of an Author*, ed. Arthur Mizener (Princeton, N.J.: Princeton University Library, 1957), 15.

20. Matthew J. Bruccoli and Jackson R. Bryer, eds., *F. Scott Fitzgerald in His Own Time: A Miscellany* (Kent, Ohio: Kent State University Press, 1971), 217.

21. Scottie Fitzgerald Smith, Matthew J. Bruccoli, and Joan P. Kerr, eds., *The Romantic Egotists: A Pictorial Autobiography from the Scrapbooks and Albums of F. Scott Fitzgerald and Zelda Fitzgerald* (New York: Charles Scribner's Sons, 1974), 13.

22. Sherwood Anderson, *Winesburg, Ohio* (New York: Modern Library, 1974), 302-303.

23. Ibid., 299.

24. Ibid., 303.

25. Thomas Hardy, *Jude the Obscure* (New York: Dell Publishing, Laurel Edition, 1959), 14-15.

26. Bruce Johnson, *The Correspondence: A Phenomenology of Thomas Hardy's Novels* (Tallahassee, Fla.: University Press of Florida, 1983), 132.

27. James M. Mellard, "Academia and the Wasteland: Bernard Malamud's *A New Life* and His View of the University" in *The American Writer and the University*, ed. Ben Siegel (Newark: University of Delaware Press, 1989), 54.

28. Quoted from Scott Donaldson's *Fool for Love: F. Scott Fitzgerald* (New York: Congdon & Weed, 1983), 18.

29. William Goldhurst, *F. Scott Fitzgerald and His Contemporaries* (Cleveland: World Publishing, 1963), 44.

30. F. Scott Fitzgerald, *The Letters*, ed. Andrew Turnbull, 70.

31. Scott Donaldson, *Fool for Love*, 151.

32. Deborah D. Schlack, *American Dream Visions: Chaucer's Surprising Influence on F. Scott Fitzgerald* (New York: Peter Long, 1994), 5.

33. Robert Roulston and Helen H. Roulston, *The Winding Road to West Egg: The Artistic Development of F. Scott Fitzgerald* (Lewisburg, Pa.: Bucknell University Press, 1995), 11.

34. In fact, Fitzgerald himself lasted only one day on the freshman squad. He made a reference in *The Crack-Up* (p. 84) to the "shoulder worn for one day on the Princeton freshman football field."

35. Quoted from Fitzgerald's *Afternoon of an Author*, 72.

36. William Thorp, ed. *The Lives of Eighteen from Princeton* (Princeton, N.J.: Princeton University Press, 1946), vii.

37. Andre Le Vot, *F. Scott Fitzgerald: A Biography*, 33.

38. James L. W. West III, "Did F. Scott Fitzgerald Have the Right Publisher?" *Sewanee Review* 100, no. 4 (fall 1992): 652.

39. One book that offers a close look at the American college novel after Fitzgerald is *The American Writer and the University* edited by Ben Siegel (Newark: University of Delaware Press, 1989). The portrayal of universities by these writers is carefully reviewed in respective chapters.

5

CITY: A LAND OF GLAMOUR AND DESPAIR

If settings like home, bar, and school in Fitzgerald's fiction accentuate the unbridgeable gap between youthful romantic ideals and harsh realities, his city setting presents an even fresher, wider, and bleaker view of the increasingly urbanized American society of the 1920s. For one thing, the city setting claims more space in Fitzgerald's world than any other setting he exploited, featuring New York and other American cities preeminently in most of his novels and short stories. More important, however, Fitzgerald's novelistic representation of city life brilliantly caters to the public's emerging curiosity about the excitement and opportunity in urban areas. Its irresistible charm for and its unmeasureable impact on the reading public might better be understood if we know the astounding changes America was undergoing through urbanization. By the time Fitzgerald started his writing career, the city had become the center of modern life. Blanche H. Gelfant said in her book *The American City Novel*, "As a shaping influence upon the modern American literary mind, the city has made its impression not only as a physical place but more important as a characteristic and unique way of life."[1] Its impact reached everyone and every corner in society. Ben Hecht describes it well in *A Thousand and One Afternoons in Chicago*: "No matter who they are or where they live, or what their jobs are they can't escape the mark of the city that is on them."[2] Fitzgerald was no exception; the fast-growing dominance of the city in modern American life dazzled him and instigated his literary impulse—an impulse that grew stronger and more clearly articulated as his writing career went on—to discover the essential meaning of city life.

THE DOUBLE FUNCTION OF THE CITY SETTING

Probably no one would argue that the city setting features more frequently and prominently than any other setting in Fitzgerald's fiction, however, it operates in still more diverse ways. Fitzgerald renovated and expanded this scheme of setting exploration consistently adopted in his portrayal of home, bar, and school. Throughout his writing career, Fitzgerald derived his social vision and the intrinsic material of his art from his own quest in the American city; yet as any great writer would do, he drew upon the rich tradition of the city novel in European and English literature. As Ann Ronald argues, "No work stems solely from the mind of its author."[3] An avid reader since childhood, Fitzgerald read numerous novels that explore cities in Europe and America as literary tropes. In many ways, it was these novels that impelled him to set out on a quest in the city. Again, when he started to write about his own quest in the city, the novels offered him the inspiration and model he needed to orchestrate his interpretation of city life in America. It seems unnecessary to trace the origin of the city novel in early literature, although it would be helpful to redefine the imperatives of the city novel that have left a mark on Fitzgerald's perception of city life and his dramatization of it.

There have been many explanations of the origin of the city novel, some ambiguous, some specific. Critics like Burton Pike contend that the city "has been a powerful image in literature since literature began" because "it is an artifact deeply rooted in our civilization and the Western mind."[4] But most critics believe that, to borrow Hana Wirth-Nesher's words, "the development of the novel, and the rise of modern cities have taken place concurrently."[5] Despite the equivocal relationship between the novel and the city, city novel as a genre has flourished since the nineteenth century, becoming a big topic of novel criticism after Ian Watts offered his first standard discussion of urbanization in the English novel. Given the obvious historical reason, the city novel in America did not catch up until the latter part of the nineteenth century. The main reason is that, as John Raleigh has observed, "America had no dominant City, as was the case with London and England, and no Dickens or Thackeray to portray it if in fact it had existed. De Tocqueville had noticed this in the 1830s, and James Russell Lowell lamented continuously the lack of a literary capital, such as London provided for England and Paris for France."[6] It was only after the beginning of the Jazz Age that America founded for itself a "literary capital" in New York and Fitzgerald became the novelist to portray it, at least during the roaring twenties.

How did Fitzgerald represent the city in America? To answer this question, one has to find out what he had learned from his European and American predecessors. Through his reading of city novels and his experience of city life, Fitzgerald was keenly aware of the city's magnetic power over its citizens, especially those young romantic dreamers. He was quite familiar with the recurrent theme in the city novel: the adventures of a naive and ambitious young man or woman in the big and strange city, from Fielding's Tom Jones to Balzac's Eugène de Rastignac, Hardy's Jude, Anderson's George, Dreiser's Sister Carrie, and Joyce's Stephen. One thing that fascinated and baffled him most was the paradoxical nature of the city. On the one hand, the city embodies the glorious accomplishment of civilization, mesmerizing people with its promise of marvelous joys and endless opportunities. On the other hand, the city is a hideous and amorphous place, constantly threatening people with its depersonalizing and corrupting evils. It is, as Diana Festa-McCormick has observed, "in the grips of decadence, abandoning old ideals and values."[7] Writers before Fitzgerald found this intriguing and dramatized their dreams and fears about the city in their writings, which include almost all genres. Susan M. Squier claims, "From the town-country debates in Virgil's *Eclognes* to T. S. Eliot's urban wasteland, the city has provided a moving metaphor for the human condition. And ambivalence has always been a vital part of this literary response."[8]

Fitzgerald's writing about the city shows his profound knowledge of various archetypes and approaches widely adopted in early city novels. Essential to the influence on Fitzgerald is the notion about the double function of the city setting: One might be termed a "physical locale," the other a "psychological emblem."[9] By drawing the reader's attention to the physicality of the city, namely, the actual compound of streets, structures, clothes, smells, sounds, temptations, and strangeness, the novelist creates a realistic scene of the city and exacts a distinctive impression upon the mind and senses of his reader. Because Fitzgerald sees city life as an organic whole, his depiction of each physical object is only part of his total scheme to express a coherent and organized vision of the city, or to offer an interpretation and a judgment of certain aspect of city life. Almost invariably, therefore, such an approach contains social implications, even though these implications are conveyed through creative and artistic expressions, rather than blunt propaganda.

A salient example is Dickens's description of London in his novels. Dickens begins his presentation of London with certain conventions for describing cities and modifies them based on his experiences in London and his response to them. In the novels in which London is used as the setting, the city is conceived as a "physical locale"; each aspect of city life is treated as a historical reality. Taken as a whole, the city becomes a socially and morally charged metaphor of human conditions, which offers a context for the ideas and values he intended to express. Dickens relied on different scenes to address different issues in society, from noise, dirt, crime, and disease to injustice and corruption. To dramatize loneliness as the common miserable condition of urban men and women, he turned his focus to street scenes in London. In "Thoughts about People," for example, he laments: "It is strange with how little notice, good, bad, or indifferent, a man may live and die in London. He awakes no sympathy in the breast of any single person; his existence is a matter of interest to no one save himself; he can not be said to be forgotten when he dies, for no one remembered him when he was alive."[10] This is, of course, not a description of a particular scene, but it does offer a pictorial image of humanity's bleak existence in the city. Nothing Dickens said in this passage alludes to any of the city's "wonders." Confined in layers of walls and streets, social laws and religious creeds, the individual in Dickens's London does not have much private space, either physically or spiritually. Images like these are everywhere in his novels; each of them carries a clear and sharp social implication and stands out as a part of the panoramic view of London. Although there is a touch of sadness and cynicism in his tone, Dickens seems more inclined to expose the ostracizing nature of the city by stressing the "indifference" among people rather than to offer genuine insight of what devastating impact such "indifference" would impose on the state of these people's minds. George Eliot once highly praised Dickens's "power for rendering the external traits of our town population," but she did not hide her regret about Dickens's lack of skills to depict the city setting as a "psychological emblem" to dramatize a character's inner experience in depth.[11]

When the city setting is treated as a "psychological emblem," however, the novelist's approach is totally different from the one Dickens took in his novels. The novelist shifts his or her primary interest away from the object, or the scene. He or she is not likely to offer much detail about the physicality of what he or she is describing. One conspicuous difference is that the setting is no longer described; it is, instead, dramatized as an inner experience. The novelist's emphasis is not upon what one sees in the scene but, rather, upon the way one sees the scene. The real meaning of the scene is not explicitly shown by the novelist's description; it may be implied through the selective process that appropriates the details of an object, or a scene, for description. Thus, the function of city setting is changed and expanded from what it used to be. It has become more than mere setting and more than a "locale" of action. Reflecting an awareness of the city as psychological emblem, the physical scene is presented as subjective experience.

One of the most effective patterns to present the city setting as a psychological emblem can be found in James Joyce's *A Portrait of the Artist as a Young Man*. Although Joyce exploited so many modernist devices, such as episodic structure, shifting narrative mode, and inner monologue, setting still plays a major role in the whole novel. All the action takes place in or about the city of Dublin. The unity of the city as setting is as scrupulously organic as that of time. Even though Joyce does not describe scenes or use street names that adequately resemble the actual cityscape of Dublin, or place his characters in events modeled upon well-documented incidents in real life, he does make many topical allusions to characteristic sights of streets in Dublin, to anecdotes and personalities of Dublin's culture and history. Unlike Dickens, who always gives his primary attention to the physicality of the city setting, Joyce seldom begins the action with a description of the surroundings or pauses somewhere to offer readers some glimpses of the background against which the action is staged. He puts most scenes in motion, forcing readers to follow the characters from one part of the city to the other. In doing so, readers may have a sound grip of the setting by piecing together all the physical details he has gathered from different scenes. But it is the character, not the narrator or author, who leads the reader through these sequential scenes. In other words, the focus of the narrative never veers away from the character; the reader sees the changing scenes through the character's eyes. The following passage from Joyce's *A Portrait of the Artist as a Young Man* is a good example, which is long but worth quoting at length:

Dublin was a new and complex sensation. . . . The disorder is settling in the new house left Stephen freer than he had been in Blackrock. In the beginning he contented himself with circling timidly round the neighbouring square. . . . He passed unchallenged among the docks and along the quays. . . . The vastness and strangeness of the life suggested to him by the bales of merchandise . . . wakened again in him the unrest which had sent him wandering in the evening garden in search of Mercedes.[12]

In this passage, everything is meticulously depicted, as if Joyce resists any urge to hurry through these scenes. From the new house where Stephen is staying to the square, to one of the side streets, to the custom house, to the riverside, the scene is shifting incessantly. The unifying parallel is the visible "wandering up and down" of Stephen's body and the invisible "wandering up and down" in his mind. Passages like this apparently have a dual effect. First, they draw a neat sketch of Stephen, the young artist. What Stuart Gilbert said about Bloom in *Ulysses* can also apply to Stephen, who is "a Dubliner undistinguished by any particular virtue or vice," yielding himself to the ambiance, "like the Homeric wanderers."[13] Second, although what we see in these passages are fragmentary scenes in the city, they represent various institutions and sectors in society—from residential houses and neighborhood to customhouse, docks, and steamers—thus presenting a panoramic picture of Dublin. One must understand, though, that Joyce's purpose is not just to set up Dublin as a "physical locale" for action; rather, he makes Dublin a "psychological emblem" that generates and molds the secret desires, fears, memories, and fancies in the mind of Stephen-like city wanderers.

What Dickens and Joyce did in their exploitation of London and Dublin as the setting of their novels was to establish two archetypes in the city novel. There are many American writers whose city novels bear great resemblance to those of Dickens and Joyce, such as Adams's description of Boston in *The Education of Henry Adams* and Dreiser's description of Chicago in *Sister Carrie*. However, the distinction between these two archetypes in their treatment of city setting might not be as clear as the one we have seen between Dickens and Joyce. Frequently, writers may want to adopt both archetypes at the same time, appropriating different details about the city setting for different purposes: to reflect a character's personality, to enhance the mood of the story, or to symbolize the underlying mentality of a whole society. Fitzgerald was one of these writers. His treatment of city setting is often a blend of Dickensian and Joycian tactics. The reason I chose Dickens and Joyce for a long comparison is that each has accomplished considerable success in his approach, and their respective achievements represent the major polarities between these two approaches. A comparison between Dickens and Joyce offers a feasible premise for the analysis of Fitzgerald's treatment of city setting and provides a solid understanding of that treatment.

Looking at Fitzgerald's use of city setting in general, however, one sees a clear distinction between the traditional city novels and Fitzgerald's novels that feature cities. There is an unmistakable difference in the thrust of the story and the function of the city setting as well. The traditional city novels tend to investigate the myth of the city as an emblem of the modern life, dissecting its complex structure into bits and pieces and defining its impact upon behavior of its citizens. To put it in a simpler way, these novels are about cities, in which the city is not just a setting; it is *the* story. In Fitzgerald's fiction, the city is basically presented as an occasional locale. More accurately, most of his stories do not use the city as the dominant or unifying setting at all. The focus is his characters, not the city in which the story takes place. To a certain extent, Fitzgerald's practice seems akin to the use of city setting in novels like Dreiser's *Sister Carrie*, James's *The Bostonians*, and Joyce's *A Portrait of the Artist as a Young Man*. Even though they set respectively in Chicago, Boston, and Dublin, none of them is a story about the city. What all these writers intended to show the reader primarily, is the nature and the transformation of that nature in their character, not the city. Fitzgerald adopted the same approach, but he executed it in an innovative way. The city in his fiction is more frequently designed as backdrop for the interactions among his characters, functioning symbolically as an agent of the social milieu or the villainous antagonist in the story. Sometimes the role of city setting goes beyond being a fixed "backdrop" for real actions; it engages the protagonist in psychological "maneuvers"; it takes on changing impetus, either nurturing or corrupting, and exacts it upon the protagonist, whose response varies from time to time, either acceptance or defiance. It is a constantly altering and interactive process, through which Fitzgerald presages and captures the protagonist's adventure for self-perfection, or his journey of self-destruction.

A question immediately arises of determining what Fitzgerald discovered about the American city of the 1920s, or how he dramatized his discoveries and presented his interpretations about city life in his fiction. To give a perfect answer to this question, we must consider background information about the American city and Fitzgerald's fascination with it. By the end of the nineteenth century, the city had apparently produced a distinctive way of life in America. When Fitzgerald first used the city as setting for his novel, *This Side of Paradise*, the population of America had reached 105 million. The figure had almost doubled in less than four decades. The whole country was becoming intensively urban. According to the report of some sociological studies at that time, nearly 40 per cent of Americans were living in urban areas. The city started to serve as the political, economic, and cultural center of the country and became the embodiment of hope, joy, success, and prestige in life. William Cowper once wrote in his poem, "God made the country, and man made the town."[14] What people saw in the city was not merely a new mode of life; they also saw a place full of excitement and opportunity. In their eyes, the city was a man-made paradise where they would fulfill their American dream. Cities, especially those along the coasts, not only attracted waves after waves of foreign immigrants but also lured thousands of young Americans from different parts of the country who came in the hope of discovering new value and meaning in their life. Writers and artists followed on the heels of other city adventurers, believing that the distinctive qualities of the city could offer them fresh material and new inspiration with which to write about the new modernity and Americanness of urban life and reveal how cities create and definitely mark the people living in them, especially people like Nick Carraway, the narrator in *The Great Gatsby*, and Robert Walmsley, the hero in O. Henry's short story "The Defeat of the City." Coming back from the war, Nick becomes too "restless" to stay in the Midwest, where his family has lived for three generations; "Instead of being the warm center of the world, the Middle West now seemed like the ragged edge of the universe" (*GG*, 6). Like Nick, when Robert is tired of living on his upstate farm, he comes to New York, searching for new excitement in his life. Before long, he is transformed by the city: New York City "remodeled, cut, trimmed and stamped him to the pattern it approves."[15]

Fitzgerald's personal experience offers another example of the shaping influence of the city on one's life and writing career as well. It would be a mistake to ignore the presence and influence of the city in Fitzgerald's writing career because city life provided opportunities for his personal and professional growth. What he knew about and learned from city life was a vital source of his inspirations and visions, and hence an indigenous part of his fiction writing. That cities are so central to his life and work should not be something shocking at all. He spent most of his years living in, traveling to, and writing about cities. Although he was not a city boy by nature, Fitzgerald had always associated his ambition with all the romantic assumptions about the city, New York in particular, since his early childhood in the Midwest. There was no doubt in his young mind that his bright future was in the city because the city epitomized all the wonders and values in life. Apparently for this reason he was anxious to go to Newman School and Princeton, both of which are in the vicinity of New York; it was also for this reason that he returned to New York to start his writing career right after he left the army training camp. His quest for the city, which he initially began by coming East for prep school, and later continued by making frequent excursions to New York, never stopped; instead, it picked up momentum after he entangled himself in the real hustle and bustle of the city. What he discovered about city life in his quest was constantly transmuted into his fiction. The way he used the city as setting in *This Side of Paradise* proves that he had a sound grip on the heartbeat of city life: He understood its cultural and economic structures; he knew its system of tenuous and yet complex social relationships; he felt its tensions and tempos; he liked its breathless, though sometimes absurd, atmosphere; he recognized its tremendous impact upon a person's imagination and spirit. As Fitzgerald's quest in the city went on, his concept of the city as a somewhat peculiar and unprecedented way of life fluctuated and matured.

Because he was a writer living in and writing about the city, his writing became an integral part of his quest, constantly elevating to a new level his perception of what the city stands for, good or bad. After a careful review of his writing, one finds that most of Fitzgerald's novels and short stories have something to do with city life. While depicting all sorts of city-life scene, they either truly represent or indirectly reflect every change and progress in Fitzgerald's understanding of various city problems as well as his vision of the city's future. Taken together, these novels and short stories not only compile a detailed chronicle of Fitzgerald's own quest in the city but also produce a panoramic and inside view of the American city in his time.

Judging from the number of his works in which New York City features as the central setting and from the variety of themes he developed about New York, Fitzgerald is absolutely a writer of New York, the "literary capital" of America. In *This Side of Paradise*, much of the action takes place in or around New York; the action in *The Beautiful and Damned* takes place mainly in New York, except during the young couple's honeymoon trip to San Francisco, Colorado, and Washington, D.C.; his masterpiece, *The Great Gatsby*, is entirely set in Manhattan and the suburbs of New York; only *Tender Is the Night* takes us to cities in Switzerland and France, but as the death of Abe North indicates, the novel maintains its connection to New York. New York also serves as the setting for Fitzgerald's major short stories, such as "The Rich Boy" and "May Day."

The domineering presence of New York in Fitzgerald's writings is not incidental by any means, for New York played as big a part in both his personal and professional life as it did in the national life before and after the turn of the century. Eugene Arden suggests, "The basis for the New York of romance and achievement is easily understood. Throughout the nineteenth century, New York was a dynamic center of growth and activity unparalleled in the New World."[16] At the time of Fitzgerald's arrival in the East, New York probably more than any other city in America embodied the boundless optimism and prospect of a new era after World War I. For many, New York was the most exciting city in the country, the most diverse in social and cultural customs. Skyscrapers were erected one after another in the wake of business expansions; they rapidly changed the geometrical pattern of the city's skyline, giving New York the image of a modern city. As Leon Trosky once remarked, "More than any other city in the world, it is the fullest expression of our modern age."[17] During the Jazz Age, a period characterized by high living, big spending, and pleasure seeking, New York became a timeless place and the center of a glamorous existence unavailable anywhere else in America. Saul Bellow puts it well, "What is barely hinted in other American cities is condensed and enlarged in New York."[18]

Although New York made its appearance in literature soon after the 1524 visit to New York Bay of Italian explorer Giovanni da Verrazano, it is only after the turn of the century that New York started to play a unique role in American literature. The biggest change about its role in literature was that it no longer served as a mere setting for a story; instead, it was more and more frequently portrayed as a symbol of glamour, ideal, and despair in modern society. The importance and charm of New York in literature are underscored by the large number of writers it attracted from different parts of the country and by the large number of stories they wrote about young people coming to New York in search of a new life. Fitzgerald was one of these writers who came to New York to establish a writing career in the city. On his return from the army training camp, as the record in *Literary New York* shows, he lived in a cheap room on Claremont Avenue, worked for an advertising agency and tried to launch his career as a writer.[19] Being a midwestern boy, he was dazzled by what he saw in New York. It was as if he was wandering in a dream world of surging crowds, theaters, glowing bars and restaurants, and long stretches of streets lined with awesome and high stone buildings. Once he finally married Zelda Sayre in 1920, after the publication of *This Side of Paradise*, Fitzgerald "plunged" into the glamorous life of New York. For three years, he and his wife were popular in the New York literary circle, well known for throwing lavish and wild parties at their Westport, Connecticut, and Great Neck, New York, houses. All those years in New York provided Fitzgerald with the social background for his novels and short stories and even clues for certain characters. One typical example, as critics have speculated, is that Fitzgerald's own West Side neighborhood may well have served as the setting for the apartment in which *The Great Gatsby*'s Tom Buchanan keeps his assignations with his mistress, Myrtle Wilson.

As his life experience in New York furnished the physical details for the city setting, what he felt about New York laid down the foundation of his perspective on urbanization. For the first few years, New York had a special meaning for him: It "had all the iridescence of the beginning of the world" (*CU*, 25); it was a symbol of all these things that seemed important to him; it was a "dreamland" to him; and, to borrow Alfred Kazin's words, "the name of the American dream was New York."[20] Later, as New York changed and his own mind "unwillingly" matured, the symbolic image of New York, which had been so real, turned into a mirage. Before long he discovered and abhorred the city's disheartening and degrading erosion of individual hopes and choices. John Dos Passos, another famous writer of New York, once said that he was both fascinated and saddened by the contrasts he found in Manhattan. He found New York both marvelous and hideous. His big wish in writing *Manhattan Transfer* was to present the changes "always as seen by some individual's eyes, heard by some individual's ears, felt through some individual's nerves and tissues."[21] Fitzgerald was equally distressed in his groping for the paradoxical nature of New York. He questioned and rejected some of the assertions he held so firmly. His mature concept of the "real" New York, which derived from his disillusioning experiences and observations, modified his interpretation and judgment of New York and of city life. Fundamental to his new concept of city life is a clear recognition of the disappointing, almost appalling, dichotomy between its dreamy attractions and its treacherous evils. In other words, Fitzgerald showed in his writings a strong intention to explore New York, to show what it is, what values it lives by, what problems it faces and creates, and what impact it exerts upon one's character and destiny.

To convert these values and problems of New York into dramatic and symbolic realities in fiction, writers need to do more than absorb the city into their consciousness. They must have the kind of artistic talent with which to exploit, portray, and ultimately judge the city they are describing; they must also know how to incorporate the legacy of their predecessors into their own imaginative processes to create settings peculiarly their own. Fitzgerald proved that he had done that. He gives his New York setting multiple functions and puts it in different pictorial images. When he explores New York as a physical locale, his sense of place is pervasive and vibrant, and his mode of description is deliberately realistic and discursive, with his focus constantly shifting from the urban scenes to domestic ones, from New York's physical outlook to its individual residents, or vice versa; when he explores New York as a psychological emblem, his sense of scene is stronger, and his mode of description is subtle and fanciful. He shows consistent excellence in using symbols and metaphors to conjure a dramatic situation that corresponds or reflects the inner workings of the character's mind. His portrait of New York is a blend of insight crystallized through what he actually discovered and what his artistic imagination saw in this mysterious city. He tried the different techniques in setting exploitation used by earlier writers and presented in earlier novels, from Dickens and Joyce to Dreiser, Dos Passos, and Wolfe. By transforming traditional settings and expanding traditional techniques, Fitzgerald created a completely original presentation. His greatest achievement is his ability to make his city setting so vital to the whole structure of his fiction that it not only functions at once literally and symbolically in its roles but also contributes to the roles of each of the other elements found in fiction, namely, theme, characterization, plot, and description. It is this ability precisely that enabled Fitzgerald to artistically render New York City as a composite of experience and sentiments in his fiction, artistically re-creating its bright and dark images as a city of glamour, opportunity, degeneration, and despair.

NEW YORK: A CITY OF GLAMOUR AND OPPORTUNITY

One thing that always frets writers who feature New York in their writings is to define for what the city stands. So far, no single definition seems to have fully decoded its seemingly simple but profoundly paradoxical nature. That New York's paradoxical nature has caused so many opposing views indicates, to some extent, the complexity underlying the ambivalent reflections exercised by writers and critics. Donald Barthelme called New York "the most exquisite mysterious muck."[22] This image of "muck" implies metaphorical interpretation of the city's nature as a quagmire composed of sticky and messy mud and filth.

Barthelme's remark is quite similar to Irving Howe's notion of the city in twentieth-century American fiction. To Howe, the city is "a maze beyond escape."[23] Anyone who has been lured and trapped there has no chance to totally break away from it.

No doubt this is a lesson Fitzgerald learned through his experience in the city, and he was determined to pass it on to his readers. Fitzgerald had a feeling for the texture of the metropolitan glamour of New York, a discerning eye for all kinds of spectacles and sorrows in the city, and the ability to articulate what he saw and felt. In his exploitation of New York, Fitzgerald's use of city setting reaches a kind of fullness and perfection in terms of its contribution to plot development, characterization, and location. He is in no way like Victor Hugo, who took the idea of description to its most inclusive conclusion, spending hundreds of pages describing Paris in *Les Misérables*, from street scenes to gamins, customs, and even the history of its sewers. Nevertheless, Fitzgerald has the ability to evoke the spirit of New York by depicting some well-selected and yet highly suggestive details of the city scene, such as the spectacular view from the Queensboro Bridge, the narrow lanes lined with skyscrapers, the "enchanted metropolitan lights," the people who are like "the forms leaning together in taxis," and the endless flow of cars and limousines. There is no doubt that in his glamorization of the city's image, Fitzgerald re-creates, as Henry James has said, a "remarkable, unspeakable New York."[24]

This image, which had only just begun to emerge as the symbol of the most sophisticated and glamorous qualities of urban life, is first presented in *This Side of Paradise*; but more descriptions about its emergence and symbolic significance are given in Fitzgerald's short story "May Day." Although it appears to be a simple story about Gordon Sterrett, it is actually a somber attempt to capture the ambiance of postwar New York City and the beginning of the Jazz Age. The story starts with a description of the victorious and joyful mood in the city, which "was crossed with triumphal arches and vivid with thrown flowers": "The returning soldiers marched up the chief highway behind the strump of drums and the joyous, resonant wind of the brasses, while merchants and clerks left their bickerings and figurings and, crowding to the windows, turned their white-bunched faces gravely upon the passing battalions."[25] In a sense, Fitzgerald is not writing about an individual character or about the city. His real subject is a piece of social history. To be more specific, as Fitzgerald commented when the story was collected in *Tales of the Jazz Age* (1922), it is about "the general hysteria of that spring." Fitzgerald's real purpose in writing the story, therefore, is to catch the mood of an actual and memorable day, a day of joy over the end of a terrible war and of the traditional May Day celebration. One can easily conjure the festive scene in one's mind, but the juxtaposition of the arches, flowers, and music with the grave faces looking from the windows suggests something grim behind the glittering façade. With a touch of delight as well as irony, Fitzgerald uses New York City as a microcosm to portray the mood of the entire nation.

"Never had there been such splendor in the great city,"[26] Fitzgerald exclaims in "May Day." In real life, Fitzgerald had exclaimed with the same excitement years before he started writing short stories. He recalled in "My Lost City" in 1932 that on his first visit to New York, he was aghast at its glamour and felt like a "youth of the Midi dazzled by the Boulevards of Paris."[27] Later, he repeatedly exploited the memory of his first impression of New York in portraying his characters. First, in *This Side of Paradise*, Amory is equally fascinated by the resplendence symbolized by the "tall white buildings seen from a Hudson River Steamboat in the early morning" when he pays his first visit to New York as a schoolboy. Although at the time his mind was too "crowded with dreams of athletic prowess at school" to satiate the glamour of the city (*TSP*, 23). The imagery of "whiteness" embodies the newness and innocence of the city, the White City, as Ezra Pound later called it in his poem "N.Y.,"[28] that had just sprung up since the turn of the century. In his description of Amory's another visit to the city, Fitzgerald Amory's memory of the city "as a vivid whiteness against a deep blue sky," whose "splendor" can be rivaled only by the dream cities in the Arabian Nights (*TSP*, 29). What helps this imagery to assume the dimension of illusion, ethereal and suggestive, is the "doubling" strategy Fitzgerald adopted in his description. The white image of the city during daytime is contrasted to the city's glittering vision under the electric lights; the glamorous scenes that fall into his eyes correspond to the romantic sentiments in his mind. Amory is in no hurry this time. He is here to see and partake of the city's wonders. Instinctively, Amory turns to his youthful imagination to savor all the things that "burst" upon him. He can almost feel the "romance" gleam from the chariot-race sign on Broadway and from the "women's eyes at the Astor" (*TSP*, 30). He is in such a "sphere of epicurean delight" because everything, from the night lights to the dinner, the theater, the show, and the fragrance of women's powder, "enchanted him." (*TSP*, 30). After Amory and his friend Paskert watched the play in the theater, they came out into the streets, wandering, "mixing in the Broadway crowd," and "dreaming on the music that eddied out of the cafes" (*TSP*, 31). Amory is completely intoxicated by the exuberant performance in the theater and sprightly night atmosphere in the city. He could not help watching in fascination the faces that "flashed on and off like myriad lights" (*TSP*, 31). All of a sudden, it occurs to him that this night is the kind of the night he wants to enjoy all year round, and this city is the land of glamour he has dreamed of. All of a sudden, all the entangled fantasies and wishes in his mind have been distilled into this clear decision. "He was planning his life. He was going to live in New York" (*TSP*, 31). He is so elated that he seriously confesses to his friend Paskert that he would marry that glamorous girl who plays the leading lady in the show that they have just watched. Here, it is clear that the young actress is romanticized by Amory as a "dream girl," the embodiment of the divinest beauty and the greatest happiness in a man's life. The Amory who is entertaining the dream of this feminine beauty as chaste as that which haunts numerous romantic souls has a perfect resemblance to the young, love-sick, and "way-worn wanderer" in Edgar Allan Poe's famous poem "To Helen," who is brought to "his own native shore" and "brought to home / To the glory that was Greece, / And the grandeur that was Rome."[29] The image of this "dream girl," will take on more significance if one knows that this scene is truthfully contrived based on Fitzgerald's own fantasy. He tells in *The Crack-Up* that after watching Ina Claire in *The Quaker Girl* and Gertrude Bryan in *Little Boy Blue,* he was confused by his "hopeless, melancholy for them both," unable to chose between them. In his mind, "they blurred into one lovely entity, the girl," his "symbol of New York" (*CU*, 23). The image of this "dream girl," which Bryan R. Washington calls "the transmutation of all women into one symbol of grace,"[30] is later reincarnated in many heroines of Fitzgerald's novels and short stories.

Also, it is interesting and important to note that Amory's exclamation at the glamour of New York is soon echoed in Fitzgerald's next novel, *The Beautiful and Damned*. Relatively, the glamour of New York that has bewitched Amory remains stronger than ever in this novel. Its effect on Fitzgerald's characters is again evinced in an episode that parallels, in many ways, that of Amory's night in New York. Like Amory, Anthony starts his joyful night by having a dinner together with his friends. Then they go to a musical comedy with two tickets bought from "the ticket speculator." While waiting in the foyer of the theater, Anthony looks around as the crowd pours in, observing the glamour put on by all kinds of New Yorkers. As he inhales hungrily the air of romance and "the sensuous fragrance of the paint and powder," Anthony's eyes ravenously followed the many-colored opera cloaks, fancy jewels, innumerable silk hats, and shoes of shining colors in the moving crowd. Then, he notices, "there were the high-piled, tight-packed coiffures of many women and the slick, watered hair of well-kept men—most of all there was the ebbing, flowing, chattering, chucking, foaming, slow-rolling wave effect of this cheerful sea of people as to-night it poured its glittering torrent into the artificial lake of laughter" (*BD*, 24). What this well-balanced and beautifully written passage projects is a vivid picture of the people living in this city. By describing what they look like from their heads to their toes, Fitzgerald is actually drawing a symbolic image of New York City. To New York, just as any city in the world, its citizens are certainly its most important component. In a figurative sense, therefore, the dress these people wear and the jewels they put on are nothing but indicators of the glamourous style and luxurious quality in the life of New York. As the well-contrived metaphor at the end of this passage implies, Anthony has caught a glimpse of the "glittering" side of New York's human landscape.

Like Amory, Anthony discovers more glamour and charm of the city as he walks out of the theater into the streets. While Amory is "mixing" among the Broadway crowd, Anthony is "jostling" through the evening masses of Times Square. Both scenes are almost set in the same district of New York and are larded with the same details that would enhance the glamorous atmosphere in the streets of New York. Amory finds "romance gleamed from the Chariot-race sign on Broadway" (*TSP*, 30); it also gleams "from the women's eyes," Anthony notices that Times Square is "made rarely beautiful and bright and intimate with carnival" (*BD*, 25) and that the faces swirling around him, a kaleidoscope of girls, are "faintly and subtly mysterious" (*BD*, 25). Amory ends his night with a mind filled with a new plan to live in New York and a wish to marry that showgirl, his "dream girl." Similarly, by the time Anthony leaves the streets for home, "for the first time in over a year he found himself thoroughly enjoying New York" (*BD*, 26). One chapter later, Anthony encounters his "dream girl," Gloria, who also happens to be a showgirl by profession.

By contrast, however, the glamour of the New York in *The Great Gatsby* is tainted with shallowness and deceptiveness right from the outset. The way Nick sees New York differs sharply from the way Amory and Anthony observe and react to what they encounter in the New York streets. Most likely, having gone through college as well as the war, Nick is older and much more experienced than Amory and Anthony. He comes to New York with a preconceived professional goal. He has begun to like New York, especially "the racy, adventurous feel of it at night" (*GG*, 73), but he is often bothered by "a sinking" in his heart; he has a strong impulse to look beyond the surface glamour. His observation of New York during a trip to the city with Gatsby is a case in point. For some reason, Nick is totally captivated by the image of the city seen from the Queensboro Bridge. What further baffles him is the "wild promise of the mystery and the beauty in the world" (*GG*, 87). Even though this episode is not elaborately described, one cannot miss Fitzgerald's precise realism in portraying the changing scene of New York during Nick's trip. Unlike other novelists, who tend to insert laborious descriptions, Fitzgerald takes his reader directly to the different parts of the city by naming actual streets and bridges. Anyone who knows New York can easily follow Nick on his way into the city. The point being made in this scene is the incomprehensibility, or unpredictability, of what the city stands for. The key word is "wild," which seems to be too paradoxical to be clearly defined. An optimistic reader may take it to mean "great" or "profound," whereas a pessimistic reader may believe it to imply "insecure" or "unwarranted." Nick's reference to a hearse passing Gatsby and himself immediately after this passage strongly suggests his mixed feelings toward New York, toward its beauty as a glamourous city and its chaos as a modern vision of hell. His lament in this episode that "anything can happen now that we've slid over this bridge" (*GG*, 73) evidently seems to be a constant warning to Fitzgerald's characters, underscoring the wide gap between what the city or, rather, America promises and what it can ultimately delivers.

Fitzgerald does not resort exclusively to subtle enigmas like this to let the reader guess his characters', or his own, ominous reflections on the unprecedented glamour New York possesses. In other words, to accentuate newcomer's astonishing reaction to and hence admiration for the magnificent metropolitan physicality is not Fitzgerald's only way to display the glamour of New York; he also does it, with equal effect, by dramatizing the rich and privileged world of New York's elite class, such as Anson Hunter in "The Rich Boy," who claims New York as his city and regards glamour as just one of the things he needs in order to go about his daily life there. In his portrayal of Anson, Fitzgerald does not specifically use the term "glamorous" to describe his life or the life of those in his circle; instead, Fitzgerald relies on some minute but well-selected details to highlight the kind of glamour and luxury that only people like Anson can afford. Anson's father belongs to the class that "composed New York society."[31] Anson himself is entitled to a share of his family's wealth, worth $15 million. Thanks to the help of his English governess, he speaks English "clearly and crisply," with "an accent that is peculiar to fashionable people in the city of New York."[32] Just as most of the privileged young men did at the time, Anson shifts the center of his life to New York long before his studies at Yale are over, because other than providing his education, New Haven is not the right place for him to live with his society standards. Fitzgerald's description of Anson's move to New York is a vivid sketch of a young and aristocratic New Yorker with the forceful tone of a satirist. "He was at home in New York," Fitzgerald claims. The phrase "at home" has to be understood as a pun, suggesting that he is not only the "center" in his family, "with the kind of servants you can't get any more," he is also fitting in comfortably in his world, with "the debutante parties," "the men's clubs," and "the wild spree with gallant girls."[33] With everything that he needs to survive, to enjoy, to succeed, and to shine in this world well provided, it is not surprising that Anson does not have to struggle with any "idealism" or "illusion" as do Gordon, Amory, Anthony, and Nick. There is no need for him to work hard for anything. What he is supposed to do is to accept his place in "the world of high finance and high extravagance."[34] Soon, with a bit of irony and cynicism in his tone, Fitzgerald meticulously illuminates how Anson "plunged vigorously" into the "torrent" of the glamorous New York. We see Anson juggling his profitable brokerage business, his prestigious social clubs, and his wild fun and "moving in three worlds—his own world, the world of young Yale graduates, and that section of the half-world which rests one end on Broadway."[35]

The glamour of New York is also limpidly evoked in Fitzgerald's description of the lavish lifestyle of the city's wealthy residents, such as Gatsby and the Buchanans, who live in grand mansions (fictionalized as the West Egg and East Egg in *The Great Gatsby*). But a typical and equally suggestive example can be drawn from Fitzgerald's description of a wedding ceremony in his short story "Majesty." Like Anson, the heroine of the story, Emily Castleton, also comes from the upper class of New York. "She was one of the most popular, most beautiful girls of her generation with charm, money and a sort of fame" (*TAR*, 276). Yet her personal life is a mess. After "engagements, semi-engagements, short passionate attractions and then a big affair" (*TAR*, 276), she finally comes home, "with marriage in her head if not in her heart" (*TAR*, 276). Her wedding ceremony becomes "the most-talked-of leisure-class event of October" in the city. Fitzgerald's description of the ceremony aims to offer an insight into the monetary and political nature of "splendor." The purpose in setting up those 5,000 pavilions, throwing those huge receptions and balls, and inviting 1,000 prominent guests is more than marking "society nuptials" (*TAR*, 276); it makes more sense to see it as a trade fair for favor, fame, and power. Here is one more example of Fitzgerald's perfect descriptive technique at work. The description is economical, but it is graphic enough for readers to visualize a grad wedding ceremony. Although the word "splendor" accurately conveys the atmosphere of the event, all these well-chosen details about the setting, the wedding arrangements, the stunning costs, and, particularly, the number and composition of the guests create a microcosm of the entire world of the rich and powerful. Besides detailing this lavish preparation for the event, Fitzgerald carries his sarcastic rendition of this wedding to a farcical level by giving the story a silly twist. Emily is nowhere to be found at the wedding. Emily's unexpected disappearance from the wedding adds another irony to the story and completely nullifies the majestic "splendor" the Castleton family gas tried to achieve. Like Anson, Emily has every means available to her whenever she wants to do anything at her will. In a much broader sense, therefore, the symbolic significance of this wedding scandal goes beyond providing a glimpse of the leisure-class life in the city; it also serves to prove that the lifestyle of the city's elite circle has displayed the true nature of New York's glamour as expressively as the city's physical outlook: exuberant and romantic in appearance, but hypocritical and corruptive in essence.

In his article "The Writer and the City," Alfred Kazin called Fitzgerald "the only poet of New York's luxurious upper-class landmarks."[36] What has been discussed so far offers ample evidence to justify Alfred Kazin's comment. True, the theme of New York's glamour always attracts serious treatment in any piece of literature about New York. Nonetheless, Fitzgerald's treatment of this theme is unrivaled among New York writers before and even after him. He set up an abundance of scenes in which glamour seemingly transform New York into a symbol of the American dream, a romantic dreamland where young people could have innumerable opportunities and reckless freedom to fulfill all their wishes and ideals or indulge themselves in all the excitements of American life. Thus, in the eyes of those who come to the city in search for a new, exciting life, New York is not the absolutely puzzling and frightening place it is; it becomes a fantasy utopia for romantically ambitious but socially alienated souls like Amory, Anthony, and Nick.

While still a student at Princeton, Amory tries to visit New York at every opportunity because he sees New York as the city of his dreams, a place full of romance and joy, a place where all kinds of good things happen. He believes that New York is the only place where he can have the opportunity to be what he wants to be and to do what he wants to do. It is only after his tormenting experience there that New York starts to lose its glamour in his eyes. In many respects, Amory is much like Anthony, who is cajoled by the overpowering charm in the life of New York City despite his early recognition of the artificiality and unpredictability in its glamour. Minutes before he learns about his future wife, Gloria, for the first time, Anthony says to his friend, Dick, "Oh, God! One minute it's my world, and the next I'm the world's fool. To-day it's my world and everything's easy, easy. Even nothing is easy!" (*BD*, 34). But once he gets involved with Gloria, whom upon first sight he deems his "dream girl," his doubts are totally gone. To him, New York becomes as ideal and sweet as "home"; it is "the city of luxury and mystery," of preposterous hopes and exotic dreams" (*BD*, 282). Anthony is a man who usually defines reality in terms of what he wants and what privilege he has and will have. He believes that he belongs here, and that with some help from his family, he has every opportunity to be happy and successful in this city. Supported by a handsome allowance from his wealthy grandfather, Anthony indulges himself in all the pleasures New York can offer, satisfying his hunger for the glamorous and the spectacular until he literally exhausts the last penny in his pocket and the last bit of energy in his body. What leads to Anthony's ultimate degradation is his ignorance of the hideous nature of the city. Charles Abrams has argued in *The City Is the Frontier* that a city "is composite of trials and defeats."[37] It seems particularly so in New York City. The sad thing is that Anthony is never aware of the entrapment in the city.

The glamour of New York and the potential it signifies are much more bewitching to innocent but ambitious adolescents like Basil, the protagonist in Fitzgerald's Basil series. Explicit description of New York as a dreamland occurs repeatedly. Like Amory, Basil always looks forward to a visit to New York during his years at St. Regis because each visit gives him "surcease from the misery of his daily life as well as a glimpse into the long-awaited heaven of romance" (*TAR*, 34). In his eyes, everything in New York has a romantic touch and amazes him like a spell. One visit that Fitzgerald depicts in "The Freshest Boy" might be mentioned as a memorable instance. First, we see Basil eating lunch at a table in Manhattan Hotel. While eating his sandwich, he cannot help looking at "the nonchalant, debonair, blasé New Yorkers at neighboring tables, investing them with a romance" (*TAR*, 43). The purpose of such a peep is not merely to satisfy his curiosity at these local residents. The peep gives him such a sensational feeling that his "school had fallen from him like burden" and "he even delayed to open the letter from the morning mail" (*TAR*, 43). The point underscored here is not so much Basil's admiration for their status in this land of glamour and opportunity as his own burning desire to be one of them someday.

The same desire is reaffirmed by Fitzgerald in "The Perfect Life," in which Fitzgerald compares Basil's excitement about visiting his girlfriend's house to "the same longing for a new experience that his previous glimpses of New York had aroused" (*TAR*, 112). When the reader meets him again in "Forging Ahead," Basil's wild passion for New York is still strong, and he is no longer bewildered by what he encounters there. The reason is simple: "He was attuned to the vast, breathless bustle of New York, to the metropolitan days and nights that were tense as singing wires. Nothing needed to be imagined there, for it was all the very stuff of romance—life was as vivid and satisfactory as in books and dreams" (*AA*, 34). Although still of prep-school age, Basil strongly feels that he knows New York well enough to tie his future to it. Just like Gwen, the school girl in "The Pearl and the Fur" who believes that if anything exciting were going to happen to her, it would surely be in New York City, Basil knows that he is ready and that he has become too cosmopolitan and too restless to wait any longer for the start of his adventure in New York.

An even more elaborate, but not obtrusive description of New York as a city of glamour and opportunity shows the city not merely as attractive and baffling to the youth coming of age, or the dandy boys like Amory and Anthony; it is equally so to men like Nick, who has been somewhat weathered in life and is about to set out on a quest with an ambitious long-term plan for his own career. The first thing we should note about Nick is that he is nothing like a Horatio Alger, a young man deprived of any opportunity or resources to establish his own career. He is from a well-to-do and prominent family established in a mid-western city for three generations. Besides, he got a college degree from Yale. Like thousands of young men of his generation, he participated in the "Great War." On his return, he became "restless," but his "restlessness" carries a totally different meaning when we compare it to that of other war veterans, such as Carrol Key and Gus Rose in "May Day," who "were lately vermin-ridden, cold, and hungry in a dirty town of strange land; they were poor, friendless; tossed as driftwood from their birth, they would be tossed as driftwood to their deaths."[38] What makes Nick "restless" is his own revelation that life in the East is becoming more and more ebullient, whereas his own hometown has turned into "the ragged edge of the universe" (*GG*, 6). Naturally, the temptation of New York's glamour and potential career opportunities seems to be too great for Nick to resist. In other words, his decision to move East "permanently" accounts for his anxiety and confidence to brave and ultimately conquer the world in New York. To Nick, however, New York has another newly acquired charm; that is the prospect of getting the most coveted job in the profession that gives New York an additional vital role in postwar American life. With Wall Street becoming the monopolistic center of the American economy, the bond business suddenly turned into the most lucrative and, therefore, most popular vocation among young professionals. Nick says at the beginning of *The Great Gatsby*, "Everybody I knew was in the bond business" (*GG*, 6). A few pages into the novel, Fitzgerald seems to have fully convinced us that Nick is different from other young men. He is a man of vision and quick action. Shortly after his arrival in the city, he bought "a dozen volumes on banking and credit and investment securities." Watching them standing on his shelf "in red and gold like new money from the mint," Nick is lost in deep thought, musing over these money-making and fame-creating secrets, only Midas and Morgan and Maecenas knew" (*GG*, 7). Fitzgerald's colorful and subtle description of Nick's "bonds" furnishes a quite believable prediction of what Nick will accomplish in this land of glamour and opportunity. At this point of his quest, Nick must believe that his dream, like the dream of his neighbor, Gatsby, seems "so close that he could hardly fail to grasp it" (*GG*, 228). The last thing he could imagine is that eventually he would turn his back on New York and return to that "ragged-edge of Universe" in the Midwest. Unfortunately, that is what is going to happen at the end. Being a midwestern man and an Ivy Leaguer himself, Fitzgerald instilled many of his own convictions and experiences into the character of Nick. Like Nick, Fitzgerald launched his quest in New York with great ambition in mind. Wherever he went, everything seemed to be gilded in glamour and romance and, therefore, sufficed to be an auspicious omen for the success of his quest. He was immersed in the pride and excitement of his initial success until a series of setbacks knocked him out of the euphoria. Only then did Fitzgerald start to doubt his deeply rooted conceptions of the false promises in urban life, such as glamour, romance, wealth, and fame, and to discover the forces of evil embedded in the structure of New York, underlying beneath its bewitching aura.

NEW YORK: A CITY OF DEGENERATION AND DESPAIR

One can imagine how painful it must have been for Fitzgerald to comprehend that what he discovered was a hard fact. His disaffection with the city intensified over a long period. For a time, he was not ready to let the romantic phantom of New York, which had for years dominated his thinking and his vision, give way to a gloomy and at times horrifying revelation of this mysterious city. As his old illusion and the newly found revelation prevailed alternately in his mind, New York sometimes still shined like a beacon showing the way to the ephemeral ladder of success, but sometimes it seemed to be a grating force undermining his endeavor for triumph, even though, ironically, it may have promoted and encouraged him in the first place. Such an ambivalent attitude toward New York became not only the most salient and essential feature but also a sustaining theme in Fitzgerald's fiction. As the most recurrent setting in Fitzgerald's fiction, the splendid image of New York Fitzgerald portrayed in *This Side of Paradise* is already shrouded in a mist of doubt toward the end of the novel; it is severely blemished in *The Beautiful and Damned*; but it appears to be most desolate in *The Great Gatsby*.

Undoubtedly, one must trace with care Fitzgerald's painstaking representation of New York's glittering and seamy sides to understand and appreciate his sensibilities and craftsmanship as a city novelist. Given the intricate and dubious nature of urban life, an attempt to present an artistic rendition of a city like New York in a way that neither obsessively celebrates its ostensible appeals nor simply repudiates its hidden eerie evils but, instead, truthfully reveals the subjectivity of consciousness toward the city's appeals and evils would be a great challenge to any artist. In *The Image of the City*, Kevin Lynch discusses the complexity of the city by making an analogy between a city and a text. He suggests that the city has "legibility"; and like the printed page, which can be "visually grasped as a related pattern of recognizable symbols," "a legible city" has "districts or landmarks, or pathways" that "are easily identifiable" and "grouped into an over-all pattern."[39] By pure coincidence, Joyce Carol Oates once asked, "If the city is a text, how do we read it?"[40] To read this "text," I think, would require the artist to have a lined experience in the city, a sharp perception of the physical, human, and social landscape in the city, and a creative imagination that projects oscillating waves of observations and vision. Fitzgerald seems to have them all, and he knows how to use them to their fullest effect. Now the matured New Yorker and writer, Fitzgerald believes that no modern city is free from the innate flaws of urban life. New York is no exception. Traditionally, it was like all the big cities in America, always associated with selfishness, hypocrisy, insensitivity, indifference, and greed and hence with money. Since the Jazz Age, when its mode of life was drastically changed, New York was imbued with the interrelated problems of metropolitan politics, finance, culture, and psychology. When New York bid farewell to the hilarious Jazz Age and entered the Great Depression, its problems remained and worsened. "Like the rest of the Nation," as Robert A. Gates pointed out, "it was afflicted by the economic hard times, but, unlike the rest of the Nation, these hard times had a more searing and lasting effect. New York had been preeminently the epitome of the ebullience and the gaiety that had characterized the 1920s. The Depression ended all this."[41] By Fitzgerald's time, New York appeared in more and more negative images in literature, portrayed as a city of degeneration and despair more often than as a city of glamour and opportunity. In many novels, New York is depicted as a perpetually strange and disturbing city in which there is no hope for an outside young man of moral and aesthetic sensibility to survive in the pleasure-fevered life, just as there is no guarantee for its residents to maintain their ideals, values, integrity, and human dignity.

In Fitzgerald's fiction, the most common and perhaps most effective way to expose the real nature of the city is to draw a panoramic view of its society by making contrasts of wealth and poverty, virtue and vice, glamour and despair. But it is by no means an original invention of Fitzgerald's. According to Raymond Williams, "Satire of corrupt city life, assuming the innocence of moral experience, goes back at least as far as Juvenal."[42] Dickens had also done that in describing the city setting of *Master Humphrey's Clock*:

The day begins to break, and soon there is the hum and noise of life. Those who have spent the night in doorsteps and cold stones crawl off to beg; they who have slept in beds come forth to their occupation, too. . . . The streets are filled with carriages. . . . The jails are full, too, to the throat. . . . So, each of these thousand worlds goes on, intent upon itself, until night comes again—first with its lights and pleasures, and its cheerful streets; then with its guilt and darkness.[43]

In this passage, Dickens reveals the glory and the degeneration of the city by detailed description of the streets. Such description was popular in his time, and in fact was the favored device among the nineteenth-century realistic and naturalistic novelists, including Balzac, Dostoevsky, Zola, and Arthur Monison. Even though cities in the twentieth-century American novel became even worse places filled with the grotesque horrors of a world plagued by war, corruption, crime, poverty, and disintegration, drawing a full view of the city by contrasting the good and evil in its streets was still a common device to be found in many American city novels.

In *Manhattan Transfer*, Dos Passos does not write exclusively about one neighborhood in New York; the real subject of the novel is nothing less than the whole of Manhattan itself, and hence the city of New York. Even the structure of the novel bears a considerable resemblance to the streets of New York, long and diverse, fragmented and disjointed. Although Dos Passos still presents New York as a glamorous and opulent city, what he tries to suggest is the horrible consequence of being trapped in all the flaws in New York society, of being seduced by the city's wealth and glamour. Many of his characters seem to be burned out by life in this great city, unable to bear the strain, isolation, and disillusionment. His emphasis on New York's complexity and degeneration is too obvious to be overlooked.

Incidentally, exactly ten years later Thomas Wolfe tries to make the same point in the "Proteus" section of *Of Time and the River*. Apart from the similarity in length, form, and the presentation of city streets, Wolfe also draws a grim view of New York during the Depression through the eyes of the principal character, Eugene Gant. Like Dos Passos, Wolfe elaborates his protagonist's view of New York by describing Gant's gradual discovery and disappointment with the city's brutality, ugliness, and indifference while Gant is walking the streets between his hotel room and his teaching job at the university. The reversal in Gant's perception of New York first as fascinating and then as suffocating is rendered with subtlety and persuasiveness.

Judging from their concentration on the gloomy cityscape of New York and the depleted life of its residents, it seems safe to say that both Dos Passos and Wolfe treated the city as a "physical locale." By contrast, however, writers like Nathanael West adopted the other approach, that is, to treat the city as a "psychological emblem." The perception of New York presented in West's *Miss Lonelyhearts* is sharply different from what we see in *Manhattan Transfer* or *Of Time and the River*. Even the form and structure are not the same. First, *Miss Lonelyhearts* is much shorter, and its plot does not evolve in a usual realistic framework. Besides, West does not actually describe many street scenes, let alone draw a panoramic view of New York. Conversely, he concentrates on the erratic interaction among a group of strange, insane, and debased characters. What he wants to expose is not merely a dark picture of New York burdened with various social issues but an almost surrealistic landscape of New York as a place of false dreams and an unreal city that reminds one of T. S. Eliot's wasteland, in which its denizens struggle to survive in a dissociated and enervated life.

In Fitzgerald's portrayal of New York as a city of degeneration and despair, the two above-mentioned approaches come to an organic combination. Intermittently and, sometimes, simultaneously, Fitzgerald utilizes New York as a "physical locale" and "psychological emblem" in his fiction. Unlike those writers who first celebrated the glamour of the 1920s in their novels written during the Jazz Age and then deplored the despair of the 1930s in their novels written after the Depression hit the city, Fitzgerald had a much deeper sense of New York's deceptive magic and destructive force hidden behind its seductive glamour, and it is a primary subject in all the major novels he wrote during the 1920s. Whereas *This Side of Paradise* seems to be an example of Fitzgerald's treatment of New York as a "psychological emblem" for his characters, *The Beautiful and Damned* and *The Great Gatsby* portray New York at once as both a "physical locale" and a "psychological emblem." On the one hand, Fitzgerald addresses the real problems that prevail in all urban cities by describing some sporadic, but artfully designed, scenes of the city's life, all of which combine to present the physical cityscape of a degrading New York City, displaying all the negative qualities that characterized life in New York and in the whole nation as well, including gross materialism, greed, vanity, tastelessness, false optimism, vulgarity, corruption, and crime. On the other hand, Fitzgerald uses these syndromes of urban degeneration to define and describe the moral and psychological condition of his characters. In his comparison of Dostoevsky and Dreiser, Frederick Hoffman concludes that "one of the major contributions of nineteenth-century realism and naturalism has been the growing importance of *scene* as a literary focus of what an artist wishes us to accept as a *state of mind*."[44] Fitzgerald tries to present not just the "state of mind" of his characters but, more importantly, the spiritual landscape of the modern city and to show how its shaping influence impinged on his characters' consciousness. In other words, he wants to convince the reader that the city is "a moral landscape, a place for posing serious questions, a space either inner or outer, depending on the author's perspective, a view of life within the walls as everything from a landscape of desire to a landscape of death."[45] Nevertheless, why New York in Fitzgerald's writings is a city that promises hope but never delivers is not an easy question to answer. This is exactly the same question that Fitzgerald persistently attempts to answer in all his fiction.

Where Theodore Dreiser, Upton Sinclair, and Sinclair Lewis had exposed the dismal realities in the city, Fitzgerald proceeded on a different and much more metaphysical hypothesis. He does not have much in common with these three writers, but his writing does suggest that he has a strong social awareness. It might not necessarily be his primary interest to dig out the social evils as the "Muckrakers" did, or to take on these evils as targets for satire as Dreiser and Lewis did; it is certainly true that he depicts numerous scenes when they are necessary for characterization or thematic development. Each of these scenes contains a vivid and poignant image, reflecting one façade of New York's decaying physical entity. Put together, they could assemble an extraordinary showcase of the city's physical decay and more decline. The issue of gross materialism evoked a lot of his criticism. He understood clearly that gross materialism in city life was intrinsically related to the economics of modern industrialism and the mentality of society. As hedonism was the mode of life in the 1920s, New York turned into a pleasure-fevered world and fortune-coveted. The proverb "Money makes the mare go" was the new principle of life at the time, shaping people's minds and conduct. People sincerely believed that and eventually fell under the sway of mammonism because they needed money to maintain their economic and emotional security in an increasingly insecure world. Those who did not have any money dreamed of making a fortune to achieve some sense of identity and value through conspicuous consumption. Those who did have money wanted more to possess a greater share of power and luxury in a competitive society. Thus, greed became the origin of social evils. It was often the motivation behind corruption, indifference, crime, and violence.

In *The Beautiful and Damned*, Anthony's whole life is a battle with and for money; a futile one, to be exact. The prospect of inheriting a big fortune from his family actually plays a big part in ruining his life. Whenever he thinks of the millions, he becomes too eager to wait and too complacent to make career plans. In his belief, money is much more important than anything, even his grandfather, the person who is going to leave the money to him. Upon his return from Rome, Anthony is shocked to find that his grandfather has recovered from a near death illness and become "comparatively well again." The next day, as Fitzgerald describes, Anthony "concealed his disappointment" (*BD*, 13). Such a small detail is not only a suspenseful move in plot development, setting up an ominous sign for Anthony's lifelong battle to dispute his grandfather's will; it is also significant in conveying the piercing irony of Anthony's moral depravity and of the corrosive influence of mammonism.

Fitzgerald's attack on mammonism appears to escalate to a higher level in *The Great Gatsby*. To say that everything in the novel is tied up with greed and manipulated by the desire of possession is no exaggeration. To some extent, the novel is a serious contemplation of the power of money. First, Fitzgerald resorts to his descriptive landscape to define different kinds of wealth in the city. His scrutiny of money-making business encompasses all the channels one can imagine, from the bond transaction on Wall Street to the deals of the underworld hinted by the mysterious phones during the parties at Gatsby's house and by his meeting with that shadow figure, Wolfshiem, in the restaurant. The contrast between the two Eggs is also essential in Fitzgerald's interpretation of what wealth means in city life, not merely because the general setting of the novel divides between the Eggs and New York but also because there is always the inherent contrast between the East Coast and the West Coast. Each of the three major characters, Gatsby, Tom, and Nick, has a designated role in this contrast. Gatsby lives in West Egg and Tom in East Egg. Both Eggs are inhabited by wealthy people. Although located within the sight of each other, each has its distinct character. East Egg is a village for the families that have firmly established respectability; West Egg is a village that is viewed as "the less fashionable of the two" (*GG*, 8), a place for the *nouveau riche* and the hustlers. Clearly, the two Eggs represent different kinds of wealth. To be more accurate, Fitzgerald uses the two Eggs, as Barry Gross has pointed out, "not so much as places but as times, not so much as geographic locales but as states of mind at a specific historical moment."[46] Both Gatsby and Tom belong to the well-to-do class in New York society, representing the glamour, sophistication, and power of the East Coast.

In a sense, Nick is the only person who is in an odd position. Having just arrived in New York from the Midwest, he is completely an outsider to the New York establishment. Even though he finds a place to live in the West Egg, it is only an "all for eighty dollars a month" house and in his words, "a small eyesore" (*GG*, 9) among the big mansions like Gatsby's. Disappointed with "the bored, sprawling, swollen towns" in the Midwest, Nick admires the superiority of the East Coast and sees it as wonderland, a place where one can feel integrated with the world, meet more challenges, and have more opportunities to succeed. To him, the East is the best place to take his chances in life. He hopes he may someday become a real respectable resident in one of the Eggs. After witnessing Gatsby, the star of the East Egg, perish with his romantic dreams, however, Nick reassesses his quest in the East. He looks into other aspects of life in the East, especially things other than its superior qualities. What he discovers is that despite its ostensible splendor, the East is in decline; its moral standards are low; its dreams have been tarnished by gross materialism. Shocked and disheartened by his discovery, Nick promptly and resolutely decides to leave the East. He refuses to identify himself with the East at the expense of his own midwestern moral values.

Fitzgerald's East-West antithesis has been a subject of controversy over the years. It does not make much sense to argue over which coast Fitzgerald speaks for in *The Great Gatsby*. It is more important to realize that by making an issue of the East-West antithesis, Fitzgerald was trying to draw people's attention to the corrosive influence of gross materialism upon the whole nation. According to his disillusioning experiences and keen observations, Fitzgerald overtly anticipated that the city and hence the nation could no longer maintain what they stand for. He was worried about the way America was going, and he was sad to see traditional values being swept away by the nationwide craving for dollars. As he saw in it an imminent threat to the integrity of the American way of life, Fitzgerald recreated a much darker view of New York in *The Great Gatsby* in an attempt to show American society in separate spheres and to test his characters in their dilemma between the restrain of values and the temptation of greed. He did so by situating his characters in various inescapable entrapments and revealing their futile attempts to run away from them. For example, Nick's return to the West at the end of the novel strongly symbolizes historical disillusionment with what New York and the East had promised; Gatsby's failure to lure back his "dream girl," Daisy, despite all the means his money made available to him gives a satiric exposition of money's raw power and its deadly destructive potential; the disappearance of Tom and Daisy after the car accident draws a scathing profile of those who are financially commensurate but morally depraved.

The degeneration of New York was not merely moral; it was also social. Fitzgerald discerned a clear pattern of degeneration in city life. The steadily increasing prosperity of the 1920s gave quick rise to gross materialism, which soon captivated people's minds. To obtain the raw power of money, people would do anything to achieve their purpose. The hedonistic impulse of the whole society changed the mode of life in New York and every other city and threw people into incessant and very amusing self-indulgence. One popular form was the cocktail party, where people gathered for drinking, dancing, gossiping, and flirting. Being an ingenious party host and guest himself, Fitzgerald showed his unusual talent in describing various party scenes. He constantly used the party scene to portray characters and turn them into microcosms within the macrocosms of the city. Thus, the function of each party scene is always determined by the need of characterization and thematic development. Each party is given a particular atmosphere, which in turn reflects the mentality of the host as well as his guests. For example, the party scene is a major means used by Fitzgerald to demonstrate Anthony's degeneration from a designated heir to a big fortune to a penniless drunk, a man who loses his sanity even before he gets his millions. In contrast, the, parties thrown by Gatsby are staged for a different purpose. Despite the magnificence and size of attendance, they are neither socializing nor entertaining occasions to Gatsby; they are only part of his hopeless scheme to attract the attention of his "dream girl," who happens to live in a mansion across the bay. Tom's parties are always characterized by excessive drinking, dirty jokes, and obscene conversations, reflecting the elements of vulgarity and coarseness in his personality. Although different in mood and tone, every party scene in Fitzgerald's fiction evokes the typical New York atmosphere of the time with its sense of hedonistic euphoria. Symbolically, as Fitzgerald hints in his "Echoes of the Jazz Age," every party in his fiction resembles the decade-long party of America, which started fabulously, but gradually got out of hand and ended in chaos and disaster.

One particularly striking thing in his use of the party scene is that Fitzgerald quite frequently, if not always, chose to show the corruption and vulgarity in society through the character's irresponsible behavior at these parties. True, being portrayed either as dreamers or losers, men get the lion's share of Fitzgerald's ridicule; but that does not mean that Fitzgerald did not blame the women for their part in the social degeneration and let them get off the hook so easily. In fact, he used an indirect, but subtler, way to accentuate their looming presence and strong influence upon their men, and he never hesitates to expose their exercise of corruption, such as vanity and tastelessness. In each of his novels, we find at least one corrupted woman in the life of the leading man.

Rosalind, the postwar debutante-flapper, embodies the impact of the city's degenerating forces, such as vanity and greed. She breaks her engagement with Anthony simply because she doubts that Anthony's meager job in an advertising agency can support her in any style. "Marrying you would be a failure" (*TSP*, 194), she tells him. The selfishness and materialism in her character are distinctly manifested in the following dialogue:

Amory: (Wildly) I don't care! You're spoiling our lives!
Rosalind: I'm doing the wise thing, the only thing.
Amory: Are you going to marry Dawson Ryder?
Rosalind: Oh, don't ask me. You know I'm old in some ways—in others—well, I'm just a little girl. I like sunshine and pretty things and cheerfulness—and I dread responsibility. I don't want to think about pots and kitchens and brooms. I want to worry whether my legs will get slick and brown when I swim in the summer. (*TSP*, 196)

What the reader is offered here is a penetrating illustration of what prompts Rosalind to reflect Amory. Rosalind's rejection comes to him as a big surprise; but his loss of Rosalind, and particularly the humiliation he has suffered because of that, also makes him aware of this hard, mammonistic trend among people and turn his anger on the whole social system.

In *The Beautiful and Damned*, Fitzgerald never makes it a secret that Gloria is the object of his ridicule and satire. Even before her first appearance in the story, Fitzgerald gives her a vivid image of a dance girl in a night club when he describes a conversation between her mother, her cousin Dick, and her future husband, Anthony. "She is dancing somewhere," as her mother tells the two gentlemen callers, "Gloria goes, goes, goes. . . . She dances all afternoon and all night" (*BD*, 39). But Gloria knows how to put on a glamorous outlook, even though she herself admits to Anthony, "I've got a streak of what you'd call cheapness" (*BD*, 73). She drinks with Anthony and his friends at parties; side by side, she and Anthony fight fiercely to regain the millions disavowed by the will of Anthony's grandfather. The only thing that concerns her is the preservation of her youth and beauty. "She wanted to exist only as a conscious flower, prolonging and preserving herself" (*BD*, 393). The instant she reads the rejection letter from the movie test, she becomes hysterical, staring at her own thin cheeks and wrinkled eyes. In Fitzgerald's description, every word and gesture seem to be designed to show her vanity, tastelessness, and insensitivity.

The same Gloria-like figure reappears in *The Great Gatsby*, not in one character but in two, Daisy and Myrtle. The image of Daisy Fitzgerald projects is essentially a mockery, insinuating the evil and destructiveness of selfishness. Daisy's personality as a "material girl" is thoroughly brought to light by her breathless exclamation for Gatsby's mansion and the numerous shirts he displays in front of her. It is further accentuated by the disparity that Fitzgerald deliberately sets up between the Daisy of Gatsby's dreams and the Daisy who is Tom's wife. Just as Rosalind's and Gloria's behavior contributed in ruining their men's ideals and lives, Daisy's carelessness and irresponsibility causes, at least partly, the tragic death of Gatsby. Fitzgerald's portrayal of Tom's mistress, Myrtle, who happens to be the innocent victim of Daisy's carelessness, attempts to show how a low-class woman falls under the sway of mammonism. The way she becomes involved with Tom is depicted with a touch of indecency. She is picked up by Tom on a train between West Egg and New York; the reason for her acquiescence in becoming Tom's mistress is nothing but her attraction to his wealth. She sees her relationship with Tom as the only chance to escape the dreariness of her low-class life. As compared to Daisy, Myrtle's artificial glamour cannot cover up the inner coarseness in her character. But she is as vain as Daisy. Here and there, Fitzgerald shows his unique talent in highlighting Myrtle's painful effort at pretension, from the purchase of a dog on the street to the display of cheesy books and magazines in her love nest. The best effect occurs when Fitzgerald describes Myrtle's putting on her "elaborate afternoon dress of creamy colored chiffon" (*GG*, 39) shortly after entering her apartment. An observant reader can tell that Fitzgerald is being sarcastic when he refers to Myrtle's change of clothes as a change of "her costume" (*GG*, 39). The subtle implication is that she is a woman who dresses purely for the attention of others. Then Fitzgerald's focus moves from the change of Myrtle's clothes to the change in her personality. Again Fitzgerald relies on another meaningful word, "*hauteur*," which seems to characterize perfectly the hypocritical trace in "her laughter, her gestures, her assertions" (*GG*, 39). It is obvious that Myrtle desperately wants to pass as an elegant lady of upper-class society. She measures people by their money and their status, but, ironically, she herself is measured by and used because of her inferior background and values. In fact, as Fitzgerald tries to suggest, that was exactly the way people treated each other at that time. Like Rosalind, Gloria, and Daisy, Myrtle is only one of thousands of young women caught in the nationwide corruption rampant in the 1920s. However, if Amory, Anthony, and Gatsby are the innocent Adams, they are disavowed by these savage Eves,[47] for these women have accompanied their men every step of the way in their degeneration.

The corruption pervading the money-worshipping and pleasure-fevered decade not only left its mark on people's thinking but also affected their behavior, giving rise to violence in the city. Unlike Dreiser or Dos Passos, in his fiction Fitzgerald was not interested in making any direct and harsh indictment of social evils; violence or crime is usually seen through the eyes of his characters or depicted as part of their experience, especially when they are in a dejected mood or on a unlucky course in their life. That all his heroes are victims of violence might not be pure coincidence; each of them at least gets a beating. While still deep in the despair of his disillusion, Amory takes a severe beating in a brawl; Anthony is beaten on a street; in *Tender Is the Night*, Abe is beaten to death in a New York speakeasy shortly after his return from Europe; Gatsby is shot to death by Wilson, who mistakes him for the driver who has killed his wife. For Fitzgerald, the beatings and killings are not random incidents of violence; he regarded them as inevitable consequences of the moral depravity in society.

What Fitzgerald considered worse is the rise of gangsters and racketeers after Prohibition. His portrayal of the underworld in New York deserves a special recognition What makes the portrayal remarkable is not a well knit inside story about its cryptic operation. In fact, Fitzgerald never places the underworld as a front scene in the novel; it always has a looming presence in the plot development. Nick's two brief meetings with Wolfshiem, Gatsby's boss and the man "who fixed the World's Series back in 1919," and a few phone calls to Gatsby during his party are the only details that tell us everything about the underworld's powerful influence and Gatsby's association with it. Wolfshiem is obviously Cody's successor, the second father figure to Gatsby, who has helped Gatsby to the fortune he needs to fulfill his dream. The fortune comes from his bootlegging, gambling, and bucket shops, all of which were notorious ways of money gathering during the 1920s. If a man can fix a World Series and create someone else's career, then he must have a lot of influence in this city's life as well. With details as suggestive as these, there is no need for Fitzgerald to give any more descriptions than he has. His impressionistic and evocative method is plain but effective in creating a mysterious atmosphere about the story. Although the figure of Wolfshiem is apparently based on Arnold Rothstein, a well-publicized gangster in New York during the 1920s, Fitzgerald knew him only by gossip and rumor. Besides, the underworld was a new topic for novel writing during his time. Fitzgerald was one of the first writers who incorporated this crime issue into fiction, drawing people's attention to this unprecedented form of crime in the modern city.

Fitzgerald's greatest success by far in portraying New York is to verify forcefully how the city's infinitely seductive and deceptive charm can also spontaneously become an unparalleled source of disasters for anyone who falls under its sway unguardedly, and how it can strip of people's beliefs and values and confine its victims in the abyss of despair. Since Fitzgerald's portrayal of the glamorous New York is always anchored on the city's paradoxical nature, he usually starts with a quite positive and charming image. Some critics have even praised him for featuring New York as if it were the protagonist in his story—a partly true evaluation, because the first half of his novel is usually imbued with romantic and even idealistic descriptions of the city, celebrating its glamour and glorifying its potential for opportunity and success. However, once the young and innocent protagonist encounters setbacks, drifts away, or is driven away from the course of his quest, the story instantly shifts its tone, mood, and imagery in an entirely different direction. The city is no longer a place of splendor, charm, or joy, but a hell-like wasteland, full of misery, menace, and aberration. And the protagonist will have to turn his quest for a wonderful future into a fierce struggle for survival, self-identity, and self-dignity.

Such a drastic reversal is depicted quite suggestively through metaphors and symbols in *This Side of Paradise*. When Amory has a frightening hallucination of a ghostly creature, for the first time he has a sense of guilt-ridden conscience. Feeling nausea inside him, Amory runs out of his apartment into an alley, which is "narrow and dark and smelling of old rottenness" (*TSP*, 115). Such a distressing experience makes him suddenly realize that all the good feelings he used to have about New York are gone. Now, in his eyes, Broadway is "filthy"; even "the babel of noise and the painted faces" (*TSP*, 117) on Fifth Avenue make him sick. Such a feeling of disgust and resentment carries a dual implication: it verifies Amory's agony over his disillusionment and paints a dismal and even coercive picture of New York as well.

Toward the end of the novel, Fitzgerald once again uses the gloomy cityscape of New York to reflect Amory's state of mind. Within a short period of time, Amory is struck by a series of disasters, including the notice in the newspaper of Rosalind's engagement to Dawson, the announcement of his scandalous night with a lady in Atlantic City, the bad news from Chicago, and the sudden death of his mentor, Monsignor Darcy. As a result, he is not merely bothered by a distress. It is much worse than that now: He is in total despair. Walking in the "unwelcome November rain" at night, which looks like the "ancient fence" (*GG*, 254), he finds that "the air became gray and opalescent"; he then notices that lights "danced and glimmered into vision," one after another, especially the "glistening sheens along the already black pavement"; but what saddens him the most is the night's reign over "the day's last hour" (*TSP*, 254). On this dark night of New York, everything that comes into Amory's sight appears in a horrible shape and evokes repugnance. He dislikes the "wet street"; he hates the "dismal sky"; he detests the subway with that "ghastly, stinking crush" (*TSP*, 255). The reference to the "black pavement" seems to educe our memory of that famous conversion about New York's street pavement among Pierre and his two ladies in Herman Melville's *Pierre*. Upon their first sight of the city, Pierre fears that "the buried hearts of some dead citizens have perhaps come to the surface" of the pavement, which makes him "feel both bitter and sad."[48] His ladies find that "these silent side glooms [street] are horrible," and "this silence is fearful."[49] Although nearly seventy years apart, the same fear and resentment toward the city seem to have been shared by Pierre's party and by Amory. Amory is even annoyed by the crowd of men and women who smell of tobacco and stale powder. Here, the day and night, or light and dark, imagery symbolizes New York's paradoxical nature. New York has become for Amory a place depleted of light, color, and life. Even the strolling mass of pedestrians in the streets gives no sign of life; the passers-by are so indifferent and so insensitive, dehumanized to the point of resembling a living corpse, or a ghost, walking around in an urban graveyard.

Balzac said, "Paris is a living being."[50] Other writers also insisted that every city had a "body" and a "character" of its own. But in Amory's eyes, New York City has turned into the "Stone Colossus" the soulless material of this demonic stone-heart."[51] In a similar manner, what Spengler called the "death-symbolism" is frequently exploited in Fitzgerald's other novels. Impressive death imagery in

The Beautiful and Damned is used to set up an illusive scene, in which Anthony is looking out from his apartment window, imagining warfare in cities: "Washington Square had declared war on Central Park and . . . this was a north-bound menace loaded with battle and sudden death (*BD*, 27). Although, as Fitzgerald further explains after this passage, the whole thing is an illusion that fades away in a moment; it is highly symbolic of the fear of death that lingers in Anthony's mind, and more importantly, it is prophetic in the sense that Anthony is extremely paranoid, especially when he steps out of his apartment, that something disastrous may happen to him. That he becomes an invalid at the end of the novel tells us that his fear at this point is not untrue.

By comparison, death imagery is executed much more often in *The Great Gatsby*, but not in a consistent pattern. The first death imagery is created immediately after Nick praises the view of New York from the Queensboro Bridge for its promise of mystery and beauty. Then, the tone of the narrative changes abruptly. Nick sees a hearse passing him, but he looks more closely at the "more cheerful carriages" behind the hearse. He sneers at these passengers for having a "sombre holiday," hoping that "the sight of Gatsby's splendid car" will make them feel a little better at the end of this day (*GG*, 87). Apparently, the imagery unfolds with a humorous touch; what is marvelous about it is the seemingly incompatible juxtaposition of two widely diverse images: the image of the mysterious and beautiful New York, and the image of horrible death. The quick switch between the two images clearly indicates the unpredictability of life and death. Though presented without fancy elaboration, the functional significance of this death imagery is much greater than the next two, namely, the assassination of Rosy by the mob and the death of Myrtle in a car accident. Their lives are "violently extinguished" for nothing (*GG*, 173). Rosy's death has become only an interesting story to be told over the restaurant table, whereas Tom, Myrtle's lover, disappears shortly after the incident in order to avoid any possible liability to himself. Before long, Rosy and Myrtle will be totally forgotten, for their deaths will not leave any mark in the world from which they have just departed.

Of course, the most significant death imagery is the double-death tragedy near Gatsby's pool. If Mr. Wilson dies for what he believed to be dignity and revenge, Gatsby dies virtually for someone else's mistake. In a symbolic sense, though, he dies for his romantic dream. It is more than just a dream; it is a life long goal for Gatsby. He never had any doubts about the dream until minutes before his death. Gatsby's decision to go to the pool, which has not been used for a long time, instead of waiting for the call from Daisy, implies his painful realization that the call, just like the fulfillment of his dream, would never come. Nick's speculation with hindsight conveys this point persuasively. "Gatsby himself didn't believe it would come," Nick tells us, "and perhaps he no longer cared" (*GG*, 203). Nick is quite certain that Gatsby knew before his death that "he had lost the old warm world, paid a high price for living too long with a single dream" (*GG*, 203). That Gatsby's dream has to end in his death is made quite clear long before the tragedy actually takes place. Gatsby is obsessed with his romantic past, and he tries to recapture and hence relive the best moment of his life. Unfortunately, however, the girl in his dream no longer exists; Daisy Buchanan is not the same Daisy whom Gatsby loves so dearly. As Dexter, the hero in Fitzgerald's "Winter Dreams," laments at the end of the story: "Long ago, there was something in me, but now that thing is gone. Now that thing is gone, that thing is gone. I cannot cry. I cannot care. That thing will come back no more."[52] No matter how long Gatsby cherishes his dream or how hard he tries to translate it into reality, there is no chance that his dream will come true. Time has changed, and so have New York and America. Gatsby's tragic death is Fitzgerald's warning, implicit and yet strong, that a man's obsessive yearning can be disastrous.

That New York has deteriorated from a city of glamour to a desolate wasteland is an overriding theme in Fitzgerald's fiction. His consistent and well-articulated strategy in rendering this theme is to draw a parallel, or a comparison, between the "waste of land" and the "waste of man." By using death imagery, Fitzgerald reaches profundity in handling the latter with clarity and insight. As for the former, Fitzgerald explores a set of symbols to describe a "certain desolate area of land" between West Egg and New York, near the Wilson garage (*GG*, 30), as a mirror reflection of the whole city. This scene is the valley of Ashes, a weird and discernible landscape complete with tentacular images of surroundings and human inhabitants. Nothing in it suggests that this is a healthy and fun place to live.

The image of the valley is similar to that of Nathanael West's unnamed park in *Miss Lonelyhearts*. Like the "valley," the park has no sign of spring. Like Amory, Miss Lonelyhearts is distressed easily by the sky and the skyscrapers. To understand what Fitzgerald is trying to convey through this image, one must look at the place carefully and analyze its meaning on different levels. On a simple level, the Valley of Ashes may be equated to the dreary and dismal environment of the Wilsons, who are living only a short distance away. The Wilsons' property is gradually being converted to a part of the ashen valley, as the wind blows the ashen dust, day and night, all over their land. Thus, the life condition of the Wilsons and of the class they represent is brought to light. Nonetheless, the Valley of Ashes is not used to characterize its inhabitants only. It also has a broad symbolic connotation. By emphasizing that the place is "grotesque" and the people "move dimly and already crumbling through the powdery air" (*GG*, 30), the scene is meant to present an oscillating perception of New York, a city in disarray, and its denizen struggling in anguish. Fitzgerald repeatedly returns to the scene to evoke a diverse response from his characters. As the valley is by no means a "physical locale" for any real action in the novel, it is primarily functioning as a "psychological emblem" and thus takes on far greater significance in revealing the psychological landscape in the city. Fitzgerald's reference to the valley as the "waste land" brings to mind T. S. Eliot's *The Waste Land*. Obviously, Fitzgerald's aim is to define his Valley of

Ashes, as James E. Miller, Jr., suggests, "as a symbol for the spiritual aridity of the civilization about which he writes—the kind of barren and waterless land that T. S. Eliot had conceived in his poem of that name."[53]

Also, Fitzgerald's Valley of Ashes is similar to what Dickens described in *Our Mutual Friend*, a "suburban Sahara," where tiles and bricks are burnt, bones are boiled, carpets are beat, rubbish is shot, dogs are fought, and dust is heaped by contractors.[54] A piece of city land becomes a dump site. In a sense, it poses a paradoxical issue: on the one hand, a wasteland like this testifies to the progress of the city; on the other hand, the waste that the progress of the city has produced creates a new problem for the city, a problem to which no proper solution can be found easily. Metaphorically, such a paradox resembles the dilemma of Fitzgerald's young and romantic heroes, who were amazed and excited by the rapid expansion and prosperity of American cities during the postwar era. They regarded New York as a place of glamour, joy, hope and opportunity, where they can have all the inspirations and opportunities they need to fulfill their dreams. Nevertheless, the good time did not last long, as America reached the final stage of its decade-long party. The whole society stumbled on a chaotic, dismal, and at times violent course of decline. New York was no exception. All of a sudden, the city lost its glamour, its vitality, and its values. What the city had promised to these young people was never delivered. They felt betrayed, forgotten, and deserted. What Fitzgerald laments in "My Lost City" may as well be regarded as the concluding remarks for the Jazz Age:

Full of vaunting pride the New Yorker had climbed here and seen with dismay what he had never suspected, that the city was not the endless succession of canyons that he had supposed that *it had limits*—from the tallest structure he saw for the first time that it faded out into the country on all sides, into an expanse of green and blue that was alone limitless. And with the awful realization that New York was a city after all and not a universe, the whole shining edifice he had reared in his imagination came crashing to the ground.[55]

Like Fitzgerald, all the heroes in his fiction have to readapt themselves to the harsh realities in society: gross materialism, selfishness, alienation, poverty, vulgarity, corruption, violence, crime, etc. The sad thing is that very few of them are able to take control of their own life. Being unable to recover from their disillusionment and despair, most of them end up in total failure, or even worse. Amory lost his youth; Anthony lost his sanity; Gatsby lost his life; Dick and his like ran away to Europe but later came back. None of them realizes that, as Ronald Berman has argued, "dreams are bounded by rules."[56] Since Nick lost only his hope for the East, he is the only one who might have a second chance in the future.

In one of the asides for his political comedy *The Vegetable*, Fitzgerald presents a long list of "social evils" in America. At the end, he adds one more sentence as an apology: "I hate to mention these things, but they are part of the plot" (*V*, 5). Fitzgerald might use this good excuse again for representing such a gloomy picture of American city life during the Jazz Age: "I hate to mention these things, but they are part of our city life."

NOTES

1. Blanche H. Gelfant, *The American City Novel* (Norman: University of Oklahoma Press, 1954), 3.

2. Ben Hecht, *A Thousand and One Afternoons in Chicago* (New York: Covici-Friede, 1922), 286.

3. Ann Ronald, *Functions of Setting in the Novel: From Mrs. Radcliffe to Charles Dickens* (New York: Arno Press, 1980), 221.

4. Burton Pike, "Preface." In *The Image of the City in Modern Literature* (Princeton, N.J.: Princeton University Press, 1981), ix.

5. Hana Wirth-Nesher, "The Modern Jewish Novel and the City: Franz Kafka, Henry Roth, and Amos Oz," *Modern Fiction Studies* 24, no. 1 (1978): 91.

6. John Raleigh, "The Novel and the City: England and America in the Nineteenth Century," *Victorian Studies* 11, no. 3 (March 1968): 312.

7. Diana Festa-McCormick, *The City as Catalyst: A Study of Ten Novels* (London: Associated University Press, 1979), 143.

8. Susan M. Squier, *Women Writers and the City: Essays on Feminist Literary Criticism* (Knoxville: University of Tennessee Press, 1984), 3.

9. For details about this notion, please see Robert Park, "The City: Suggestions for the Investigation of Human Behavior in the City Environment," *American Journal of Society* 20 (March 1915): 577-612. In this article, Robert Park, a well-known sociologist, suggests that the city should be understood not merely as a "physical entity" but also as a "psychophysical mechanism."

10. Charles Dickens, *Sketches of Boz* (London: New Oxford Illustrated Dickens, 1947-1958), 138.

11. George Eliot, "The Natural History of German Life," in *The Essays of George Eliot*, ed. Thomas Pinney (London: Routledge and Kegan Paul, 1963), 271.

12. James Joyce, *A Portrait of the Artist as a Young Man* (New York: Bedford Books of St. Martin's Press, 1993), 67-68.

13. Stuart Gilbert, *James Joyce's Ulysses: A Study* (New York: Vintage Books, 1952), 19-20.

14. William Cowper, *The Task*, book 1, *The Works of William Cowper*, vol. 9, ed. Robert Southey (London: Baldwin and Cradock, 1836), 92

15. O. Henry, "The Defeat of the City," in *The Voice of the City* (Garden City, N.Y.: Doubleday, Page and Co., 1919), 85.

16. Eugene Arden, *The New York Novel: A Study in Urban Fiction* (Ann Arbor, Mich.: University Microfilms, 1974), 4.

17. Quoted from *New York: An Anthology*, compiled by Mike Margusee and Bill Harris (Boston: Little, Brown, 1985), 3.

18. Ibid., 4.

19. Susan Edmiston and Linda D. Cirino, eds., *Literary New York: A History and Guide* (Boston: Houghton Mifflin, 1976), 252.

20. Alfred Kazin, "The Writer and the City," *Harper's Magazine* 237, (December, 1968): 122.

21. John Dos Passos, "What Makes a Novelist," *National Review*, January 16, 1968, 31.

22. Donald Barthelme, *City Life* (New York: Farrar, Straus and Giroux, 1970), 166.

23. Quoted from *New York: An Anthology*, compiled by Mike Margusee and Bill Harris (Boston: Little, Brown, 1985), 5.

24. Irving Howe, "The City in Literature," *Commentary* 51, no. 5 (May 1971): 64.

25. Matthew J. Bruccoli, *The Short Stories of F. Scott Fitzgerald: A New Collection* (New York: Charles Scribner's Sons, 1989), 97.

26. Ibid., 18.

27. Fitzgerald, *The Crack-Up*, 24.

28. Ezra Pound, *Selected Poems* (London: Faber and Faber, 1968), 21.

29. Edgar Allan Poe, *The Tell-Tale Heart and Other Writings* (New York: Bantam Books, 1982), 386.

30. Bryan R. Washington, *The Politics of Exile: Ideology in Henry James, F. Scott Fitzgerald, and James Baldwin* (Boston: Northeastern University Press, 1995), 12.

31. Bruccoli, *The Short Stories of F. Scott Fitzgerald*, 318.

32. Ibid.

33. Ibid., 319.

34. Ibid., 320.

35. Ibid., 325.

36. Alfred Kazin, "The Writer and the City," 122.

37. Charles Abrams, *The City Is the Frontier* (New York: Harper and Row, 1965), 16.

38. Bruccoli, *The Short Stories of F. Scott Fitzgerald*, 106.

39. Kevin Lynch, *The Image of the City* (Cambridge, Mass.: MIT Press, 1960), 3.

40. Joyce Carol Oates, "Imaginary Cities: America," in *Literature and the Urban Experience: Essays on the City and Literature*, eds. Michael C. Jaye and Ann Watts (New Brunswick, N.J.: Rutgers University Press, 1981), 11.

41. Robert A. Gates, *The New York Vision: Interpretation of New York City in the American Novel* (Lanham, Md.: University Press of America, 1987), 91.

42. Raymond Williams, *The Country and the City* (London: Chatto and Windus, 1973), 47.

43. Charles Dickens, *Master Humphrey's Clock* (London: Oxford Illustrated Dickens, 1947-1958), 108-109.

44. Frederick Hoffman, "The Scene of Violence: Dostoevsky and Dreiser," *Modern Fiction Studies* 6, no. 2 (summer 1960): 92-93.

45. Jane Marcus, "A Wildness of One's Own: Feminist Fantasy Novels of the Twenties," in *Women Writers and the City: Essays on Feminist Literary Criticism*, ed. Susan M. Squier (Knoxville: University of Tennessee Press, 1984), 135.

46. Barry Gross, "Back West: Time and Place in *The Great Gatsby*," *Western American Literature* 8 (1973): 4.

47. Sy Kahn, "*This Side of Paradise*: The Pageantry of Disillusion," in *F. Scott Fitzgerald: Critical Assessments*, vol. 2, ed. Henry Claridge (Mountfield, East Sussex [England], Helm Information, 1991), 57.

48. Herman Melville, *Pierre, or, The Ambiguities* (New York: Penguin Books, 1996), 230.

49. Ibid., 231.

50. See Donald Fanger, *Dostoevsky and Romantic Realism: A Study of Dostoevsky in Relation to Balzac, Dickens and Gogol* (Chicago: University of Chicago Press, 1965), 26.

51. Oswald Spengler, *The Decline of the West* (New York: Knopf, 1962), 248.

52. Bruccoli, *The Short Stories of F. Scott Fitzgerald*, 236.

53. James E. Miller, Jr., *F. Scott Fitzgerald: His Art and His Technique* (New York: New York University Press, 1964), 124.

54. Charles Dickens, *Our Mutual Friend* (London: New Oxford Illustrated Dickens, 1947-1958), 33.

55. Malcolm Cowley, ed., *The Bodley Head Scott Fitzgerald*, vol. 3 (Oxford: The Bodley Head, 1960), 348-349.

56. Ronald Berman, *The Great Gatsby and Modern Times* (Urbana, Ill.: University of Illinois Press, 1994), 97.

6

HOLLYWOOD: A WORLD OF ART, BUSINESS, AND RIVALRY

When the Jazz Age ended with the crash of the stock market, New York, once the city of all cities and the symbol of the American dream, instantly lost its glamour and charm. Disillusioned young "flappers" and "romantic egotists" either deserted the city, searching for a new frontier for their quest, or stayed behind to ponder what was left of their shattered dreams. Nick and his like went back to where they had started their quest; Dick and his like crossed the Atlantic, taking refuge in Europe, especially on the French Riviera; Anthony and his like lost their wits and senses along with their fantasies; Amory and his like wandered the streets of New York, trying to figure out what had taken away their youth and their romantic ideals. For a time, America did not have a spokesperson to advocate its values and ideals. John W. Aldridge observed: "There was no dream now. There was only horror and sickness."[1] Soon, however, a new enchanted city emerged and boomed on the West Coast. With its own glamour and wealth and the charm of a new art form, Hollywood easily replaced New York as the city of hope in America. In an era of crisis when millions of people were caught in the harsh time of the Great Depression, and when more and more people believed that success came more likely from one's luck rather than one's performance, Hollywood was viewed as a dreamland of quick opportunities and lavish awards. As Leo C. Rosten said, Hollywood became "a giant magnet."[2] It attracted a stream of artists and movie makers, and a swarm of adventurers from all over the country and the world as well.

FITZGERALD GOES TO HOLLYWOOD

Among these faces was Fitzgerald's. Although he wrote only one novel in almost ten years after *The Great Gatsby* (because of some well-documented personal reasons), Fitzgerald had never given up his search for new frontiers for his literary imagination. The "old ambitious and unrealized dreams" (*TSP*, 282), which had been left cold in his heart, were stirred and, ultimately, rekindled by the enticement of Hollywood. Contrary to what Nick did at the beginning of *The Great Gatsby,* Fitzgerald decided to turn his back on the East and to resume his quest in Hollywood on the West Coast, the new and, perhaps, the last frontier of illusions and ideals in America. As he admitted in letters to his daughter and friends, he felt himself drawn to this dazzling empire, which appeared to be even more magnificent and powerful than the one Amory, Anthony, Nick, and Gatsby envisioned. He had such a feeling not merely because he was fascinated by the art of filmmaking—the movie surfacing as the latest popular mode of entertainment—or because he was tempted by the lucrative profit of working there. He sensed that Hollywood, the new, enchanted city taking over the role of the spokesperson for the American dream, could be the best place to jump-start his lagging writing career while he continued to express his concern with and vision of the American way of life.

The use of Hollywood as setting marked a daring change in Fitzgerald's writing. Having been preoccupied with "flappers" and "romantic egotists" and the high-living in cities like New York, Fitzgerald found himself facing a new challenge in dramatizing this tremendously enthralling but somewhat anomalous world of Hollywood. Also, it is vital to note that this would be the first time in his writing career that he would deal with a specific industry in America. If we look at Hollywood against the larger context of the time when Fitzgerald was writing *The Last Tycoon*, if we compare the movie industry in Hollywood to other industries in America, if we compare the way of life in the society of Hollywood to that in metropolitan cities at the time, we discover numerous striking parallels between Hollywood and New York in their glamour, charm, and complexity. To use Hollywood as setting, or to write about it, is not an easy task by any means. "Hollywood, the subject of *The Last Tycoon,*" as Dos Passos once said, "is probably the most important and the most difficult subject for our time to deal with."[3] It was a new industry to the country, a new literary frontier to writers, and a new fictional world to readers. By the time Fitzgerald's writing of the novel was underway, Hollywood had already reached into every corner of the country through the movies. Nonetheless, for quite some time Hollywood remained a mystery to most Americans. What it really meant to them and how it operated could be understood "only dimly and in flashes," as Cecilia Brady, the narrator of *The Last Tycoon*, claims on the first page of the novel (*LT*, 3).

Although a detailed account of Hollywood's history seems unnecessary for this study, a knowledge about its growth in California is imperative in defining its magnetic charm to people in all walks of life and its sweeping influence upon American culture. If we consider the film production in the greater New York City area around 1894 as the beginning of the American movie industry, Hollywood was already more than forty years old when *The Last Tycoon* was conceived. Thanks to its move from New York to Southern California and the standstill of its European counterparts in the wake of World War I, Hollywood was able to expand rapidly into a major industry with a powerful studio system, forge close bonds to banking resources, and retain tight control over theater chains, turning the movies into a national art form.[4] Some statistics may provide a general picture of Hollywood's magnitude and power in 1939: It had a capital investment in America alone of approximately $2 billion, including movie production, theater, and distribution; the total box-office income was well over $.5 billion, which represented 67.4 percent of the total volume of business done in all the commercial places of entertainment in America. Nearly 55 million people went to the movies every week; indeed, there were more movie theaters than banks and department stores in America; and Hollywood produced about 90 percent of all the films made in America.[5] Hollywood was geared not only to the mass market at home but also to mass markets all over the world. Thus, Hollywood's significance at that time could easily be measured by the number of movies it manufactured and the number of viewers it reached. With movie production as the new medium of entertainment, Hollywood took away a large share of the patronage of theatergoers and established a movie star system fostered by the new popularity of the new industry, reinforced by the profit-oriented manipulation of the studios and validated by the increasing fandom nationwide.

Apart from the lavish lifestyle Hollywood displayed on and off the movie screen, few people really knew what it was. The comprehensive nature of Hollywood as an industry in need of the support from various popular arts and professions further complicated its connotations. Commenting on the difficulty in defining Hollywood's significance, Hortense Powdermaker, the well-known anthropologist, insists:

[Hollywood] means many things to many people. For the majority it is the house of the favored, godlike creatures. For others it is a "den of iniquity"—or it may be considered a hotbed of Communism or the seat of conservative reaction; a center for creative genius, or a place where mediocrity flourishes and able men sell their creative souls for gold; an important industry with world-wide significance, or an environment of trivialities characterized by aimlessness; a Mecca where everyone is happy, or a place where cynical disillusionment prevails.[6]

What Powdermaker has summarized here is just a short list of all the definitions and stereotypes Hollywood had acquired; others might easily be added. Even though it was hardly possible to draw a distinction between a commonly acceptable definition and a biased stereotype of Hollywood, no one doubted or took lightly the magnitude of Hollywood's impact upon the life and imagination of American society. In the eyes of most Americans, Hollywood was a perfect replacement for New York, once a symbol of the American dream. With his discerning eye, Fitzgerald saw something more in Hollywood; that is, with its tremendous social, political, economic, moral, and artistic influence, Hollywood would hold a unique place in American life. Like New York before it, Hollywood would come to symbolize and constantly set new standards for the glamour, luxury, success, wealth, and fame that everyone pines for, defining and shaping the desires and fantasies in American society. Hollywood would do something that New York had not been able to: Hollywood would not only speak for America's dreams; it would create them. Thus, to some extent Hollywood would become more than a new symbol of American dreams; it would become a factory for them. For apparently all the movies from Hollywood, though different in quality and form, provide the movie fans with a source of inspiration for their own life. As Robert Sklar points out, "If the movies made the dreams America dreamed, then they were more than just an art form, they were a focal point of national culture, a molder of the nation's destiny."[7]

In reality, its molding influence always came to the masses in a combination of different elements, which suggested both hope and despair. On the one hand, Hollywood exhibited the promise of American life by making the road to success seem so bright and so smooth. It defined success entirely in terms of money. And money, of course, meant easy access to luxury, romance, and fame. Movie stars and executives earned millions of dollars a year; their high-spending life was even more astounding than that of the barons in New York. And they never hesitated to display through their movies all the luxuries and comforts in their life. In a fan's mind, Hollywood was always associated with sexy men, dazzling girls, lavish parties, magnificent palaces, and Cadillacs. On the other hand, as Hollywood embodied and, in a certain sense, created the substance of the American dream, it also inevitably revealed the symptoms of degradation in American society. Hollywood's movies as well as its scandals, manifested certain corruptive and destructive tendencies in American business and hence in the whole society. In the late 1930s the rags-to-riches story was already out of date; it had become part of the folklore of American capitalism. More and more glimpses were allowed into the system of American business, a system that consisted of ambition and competition, and more of greed, deceit, betrayal, fear, corruption, and despair.

When seen as both a creative center of art and a social complex, Hollywood indeed became an outlandish phenomenon in American life. For writers, frantically searching for something exotic and more provoking, such a phenomenon automatically became a magnet. Since its days of expansion under the Southern California palm trees, Hollywood attracted many writers to its studios. Among them were some of the greatest writers the time; these men and women spent considerable periods of their life working as contract writers in Hollywood, though with different degrees of involvement. William Faulkner spent twenty-odd years in Hollywood; Fitzgerald went to work for Hollywood on several occasions and finally died there; Nathanael West took his quest to Hollywood, turning himself from a roughneck, like the characters we see in *The Day of the Locust,* to a revered figure in literary Hollywood. As Tom Dardis noted, however, some critics believed these writers demeaned themselves by going to Hollywood and writing "quickly and /or carelessly 'just' for the money in it."[8] "Selling out to Hollywood" was a common label in reference to these writers. Money was not necessarily the only motivation behind their stint in

Hollywood, however. Faulkner, who had a large family to support, always felt himself prompted by his immediate financial burdens while working in Hollywood. He did not have much confidence in himself as a screenwriter and he managed to make sure that the work he did in Hollywood would leave no apparent marks or traces on his writing career as a novelist. In contrast, on several occasions Fitzgerald openly expressed his strong interest in the movie industry. Financial need was part of the reason he decided to go to Hollywood, but it was definitely not the decisive one. Only his first visit to Hollywood was primarily more money motivated. Early in 1935 Fitzgerald refused an offer from Hollywood to write a screenplay of *Tender Is the Night*. He explained in a letter to Harold Ober, "I hate the place like poison with a sincere hatred"; he would consider going to Hollywood "only as an emergency measure."[9] At the end of that same year, Fitzgerald turned down another offer from Hollywood. This time Fitzgerald gave his agent a much more frank answer, insisting that he would go to Hollywood only when there was no alternative. Having worked on other people's stories before, Fitzgerald knew how boring and frustrating that job could be, especially when someone else, not the writer, decided what to add or cut. What seems to have annoyed Fitzgerald most is that Hollywood refused to use the "qualities" he had.[10] These two rejections tell us two things: First, Fitzgerald did not jump at every money-making opportunity in Hollywood, as some people said in the past; second, money was not his first and only concern even if he did go to work in Hollywood. He wanted to give his own creativity a chance, but he was never willing to be used as a tool. He might have despised the movie industry, yet ample evidence shows that he loved movies all his life and that he had a lifelong fascination with Hollywood. The strongest evidence may be found in a letter he wrote to his daughter in the winter of 1939: "Sorry you got the impression that I'm quitting the movies—they are always there."[11]

Even if we do not count what he had said about movies and Hollywood in his early years, Fitzgerald's interest in Hollywood could be traced to the beginning of his career, when he wrote a number of rejected scripts, and to his later indirect involvement with Hollywood through selling the movie rights of or rewriting his novels and stories for movie production. In fact, some of the themes that he dealt with in his later Hollywood fiction are anticipated in his earlier writings. Apart from his dramatic experience in college, Fitzgerald turned his eyes toward script writing the Broadway theater as early as 1921 when he was conceiving his play *The Vegetable*. He told his agent that he was writing "a play which is to make my fortune," and later he told his editor that he was at work on "an awfully funny play that is going to make me rich forever."[12] He really saw the play as something to guarantee his fortune, if not fame only. He used movie techniques in his fiction; he used movie people as characters; he used Hollywood as literary material and setting; he used movies to point up the distinction between illusion and reality in American life.

Fitzgerald made his first reference to the movie industry as early as "The Diamond as Big as the Ritz," in which Percy Washington tells John Unger that the spectacular Washington estate has been designed by a "motion-picture fella." "He was the only man we found who was used to playing with an unlimited amount of money."[13] In *The Beautiful and Damned,* Fitzgerald describes the movies as a source of quick wealth and celebrity, a means of achieving characteristically American success. Toward the end of the novel, Fitzgerald devotes a long episode to describing how Gloria, who is running out of money while doing nothing but waiting for the result of the legal case, jumps at a chance to do an audition for a movie in the hope that a movie career would change her stagnant life and help her to preserve her youth and beauty on film. In the meantime, the man who tempts Gloria to become a movie star, Joseph Bloeckman, is portrayed as a sinister character, who through the business opportunities the movies industry has provided rises from immigrant peanut vendor to movie magnate with wealth and power.

After he experienced Hollywood firsthand in 1927, Fitzgerald wrote two stories, "Jacob's Ladder" and "Magnetism." Both stories contain many of Fitzgerald's first impressions of Hollywood. The former is set in New York and Hollywood; the latter is set entirely in Hollywood. In terms of setting exploitation and thematic development, these two stories give us the first indications that Fitzgerald began to take Hollywood seriously as setting and subject simultaneously. The immediate result of his second trip to Hollywood is "Crazy Sunday," one of his finest stories, in which Fitzgerald creates his alter ego in the character of Joel Coles, an observer and participant in the story based on an actual figure in Hollywood, Irving Thalberg. Two years later Fitzgerald opens *Tender Is the Night* by introducing the character of Rosemary, the young and beautiful new star from Hollywood, and by describing other Americans' curious and envious reactions to her. When he got another invitation from Hollywood in 1937, Fitzgerald gave a hard thought to the lagging condition of his writing career, as his "next novel" was still far from being accomplished. He realized that what he needed most at that point was fresh material set in a new locale; this would rejuvenate his career instantly. It was under such circumstances that Fitzgerald decided to return to Hollywood for the third time. That Fitzgerald himself was extremely excited about this upcoming challenge is fully indicated in his letter to Mr. and Mrs. Eben Finney: "A writer not writing is practically a maniac within himself. Because of this—I mean too many anxieties and too much introspection—I'm going to Hollywood next month and extrovert a while."[14]

This time, of course, he was motivated neither by a desire to make money nor by a wish to escape from his setbacks and dissatisfaction. As a new symbol of success and failure in America, Hollywood epitomized all kinds of complexities in American life. Like many Hollywood fans, Fitzgerald was obviously not content with any of the publicized connotations that Hollywood had acquired. His decision to go to Hollywood, therefore, was largely prompted by this intriguing ambiguity in Hollywood's mystery. Given his long-cherished interest in Hollywood, it is safe to assume that Fitzgerald knew well about what had been written in the literature of Hollywood. Novels about the movie industry, such as Victor Appleton's *Tom Swift and His Wizard Camera* (1912), were published in the early teens. After the publication of B. M. Bower's *The Phantom Herd* in 1916, writing about Hollywood became a new fashion in American literature. This new fiction genre developed along with the widespread popularity of Hollywood.[15]

Among the large number of novels about Hollywood, however, few are as serious and valuable as John O'Hara's *Hope of Heaven* (1938), Nathanael West's *The Day of the Locust* (1939), and Budd Schulberg's *What Makes Sammy Run* (1941), whose draft Fitzgerald read but did not praise enthusiastically. In his belief, these novels are inadequate in their representation of Hollywood's real nature and its relationship to American society. He realized that he should meet the challenge himself because Hollywood could be a wonderful setting and subject for his "next novel"; it could even be better than Princeton, New York, and Paris. For the last three years of his life, Hollywood was the center of his world. Fitzgerald did what he considered necessary to carry out this self-imposed mission: He worked hard on various film scripts; he abstained from alcohol and social life. Despite all the quarrels and disappointments, Fitzgerald maintained a steady income and a love affair, which in turn enabled him to write his most ambitious novel, *The Last Tycoon,* and later to devote his weekends to writing the Pat Hobby series. He had the kind of passionate interest in Hollywood that he had in Princeton and New York; more importantly, he had confidence that he was talented enough to handle Hollywood well and to bring his writing to a higher level. The creative forces inside him seemed to be reactivated, and the perspective and descriptive gift we have seen in his early novels seems to have been sharpened again. Unfortunately, what he had predicted did not happen. But he never had a doubt about the novel he had planned to write about Hollywood. He wanted to be the first American artist who took Hollywood seriously and wrote something deeper and more enduring about it. From his arrival in Hollywood in 1937 to his death in 1940, Fitzgerald devoted three years to the project and put in his observations and reflections, as well as all the information he could get from Sheilah Graham, his lover and a Hollywood reporter, and from Budd Schulberg, a Hollywood insider. He worked fervently on the novel. In his letters to Zelda, Fitzgerald described how his room in Hollywood was littered with notes and charts for the novel, and he expressed his excitement about the writing, telling her, "I am deep in the novel, living in it, and it makes me happy."[16] Besides, as is indicated in his letter to Edmund Wilson, he felt confident about *The Last Tycoon* and believed that his novel was "good" because "it is first hand," and he was "trying a little hard" in order to be "exact and honest emotionally" (*CU,* 285). Once again, the combination of his talent and effort triumphed. Despite the fact that he wrote very few film scripts during his years in Hollywood and none of them made any vigorous impact at the time and have long since been forgotten,

Fitzgerald's name shines to this day in the literature of Hollywood thanks to the Pat Hobby series and the unfinished novel he left us, *The Last Tycoon*.

For years critics have discarded the seventeen Pat Hobby stories Fitzgerald wrote for the monthly publication *Esquire*, claiming that they are "bread and butter" writing, "bordering on sketches," and therefore do not deserve to be regarded as serious literature about Hollywood. Such an assessment might have been based too much on the comedic caricaturelike portrayal of the central figure, Pat Hobby, in these stories. It is true that after his contract in Hollywood expired Fitzgerald was freelancing, and the monthly publication of the Pat Hobby stories helped him pay the bills that were piling up; it is also true that Fitzgerald himself did not have much enthusiasm about the series at first. Nevertheless, as soon as he finished the first three stories, Fitzgerald became more and more excited about the stories' potential in representing the whole of Hollywood. To achieve a greater cumulative significance for the series in terms of thematic development and structural coherence, he worked diligently on the conception, the order of appearance, and the revision of these stories. Even though one cannot say that the Pat Hobby stories are sophisticated and elegant enough to embody the best of Fitzgerald's fiction, they were—perhaps still are—excellent stories, offering a comic and insightful view of Hollywood's follies and cruelties.

The best quality in Fitzgerald's fiction is not just reinstated but greatly refined in *The Last Tycoon*. To fulfill his dream of writing the Hollywood novel, he devoted all the time and talent he could muster to the project until his untimely death. Even though there has been much speculation about how Fitzgerald would end the novel had he gotten the chance, one thing beyond doubt is that even with the present form of the novel, Fitzgerald already succeeded in giving us a picture of the glamorous and yet complex world of Hollywood. It has been the most widely read and most frequently discussed novel about Hollywood. As Edmund Wilson wrote in the foreword to the first edition of the novel published the year after Fitzgerald's sudden death, "*The Last Tycoon* is far and away the best novel we have had about Hollywood, and it is the only one which takes us inside."[17] Although Fitzgerald did not actually have a chance to urge us to read both *The Pat Hobby Stories* and *The Last Tycoon*, we should do just that if we really want to know how he felt about Hollywood. As Walter Wells has pointed out, "Together, the two works . . . form a complementary pair of Hollywood perspectives, one comic, one tragic."[18]

THE CONFRONTATION BETWEEN ART AND BUSINESS

As Henry Dan Piper has correctly observed, "In Hollywood Fitzgerald, at any rate, had found his greatest theme."[19] Although the material and people he deals with in *The Last Tycoon* were totally new to him, Fitzgerald still had a decent command of the perplexing social, creative, and business life in Hollywood. People have credited much of the novel's success to its tightly knit structure, poetic prose, and delicate characterization, but the functional significance of Hollywood as the setting of the novel is indisputably imperative. Throughout the novel, Hollywood has an overwhelming presence, just like the major settings in the novels of Cooper, Melville, and Twain. Nevertheless, what distinguishes Fitzgerald's Hollywood from those classic settings in American fiction is not only Hollywood's conglomerate nature as a social, political, economic, and artistic entity but also its double function as the setting and the subject of the novel. As is demonstrated in *The Great Gatsby*, Fitzgerald used the same strategy in his depiction of New York, but it seems to have operated with greater effect in his description of Hollywood as a microcosm of the entire American society in the 1930s. Unlike writers like Dos Passos who tended to focus their attention on attacking the sinful side of Hollywood, caricaturing their characters without tracing Hollywood's corrupting and molding influence on them, Fitzgerald treated Hollywood as an equivocal milieu. He re-created that seemingly enchanting but actually cruel world of film industry by detailing its essence and its mechanism. Within that framework, Fitzgerald represented an inside view of Hollywood, a view that had never been exposed to the public before. Furthermore, he openly took on what he perceived to be the two most intricate and most crucial issues about Hollywood, issues that had not been thoroughly addressed by any writers before him: One, the tension between the newly invented art form and the increasingly monopolized industry; the other, the rivalry between the idealistic artist and the materialistic Hollywood.

For the general public in Fitzgerald's time, Hollywood was both a magnet and a puzzle; it was intriguing. As documented in his letters to friends, Fitzgerald had this notion in mind when he started the Pat Hobby series and *The Last Tycoon*. He knew that people would respond to Hollywood according to their own belief, and tastes: Some worshipped it whole-heartedly; some despised it out of jealousy; some even hated it perhaps for moral reasons, just like Cecilia's English teachers, "who pretended an indifference to Hollywood or its products, really *hated* it. Hated it way down deep as a threat to their existence" (*LT*, 3). For a careful reader, it is not difficult to discern a touch of exaggeration in what Cecilia said about her English teachers. But such a passing reference honestly conveys the widespread feeling of resentment toward Hollywood among the intellectuals during the 1930s. Some people, like the sweet little nun in Cecilia's convent, were completely perplexed by what Hollywood flashed at them. On the opening page of the novel, Cecilia warns us that understanding Hollywood is not going to be easy. We will not have much choice in dealing with Hollywood; we either "take Hollywood for granted" (*LT*, 3) or brush it off as something we do not care about.

What then is Hollywood? Or, to be specific, what is the Hollywood Fitzgerald presented in his fiction? At the beginning of the novel, Cecilia implicitly relates it to a "haunted house" when she compares herself to "a ghost" (*LT*, 3). But a few pages into the second chapter, Fitzgerald presents a more graphic picture of what Hollywood is like in his description of the back lot behind Monroe Stahr's studio. He calls this thirty-acre lot a "fairyland." He then clarifies that it is so, "not because the locations really looked like African jungles and French chateaux and schooners at anchor and Broadway by night, but because they look like the torn picture books of childhood, like fragments of stories dancing in an open fire" (*LT*, 25). Fitzgerald's description is succinct and luminous, as usual. Unlike Dickens or Dos Passos, he is not interested in making direct or explicit representations of his setting. Instead, he prefers a much more implicit and subtler approach. As is shown in his exploitation of bar setting, Fitzgerald avoids offering any lengthy description of the physical aspects of his setting. Whatever the reader learns about the setting always comes from some simple but highly symbolic details, scattered here and there in dialogues and introductions of characters. From his home setting to Hollywood in *The Pat Hobby Stories* and *The Last Tycoon,* this strategy of selective description has evolved into a consistent pattern operating with a kind of poetic implicitness and subtleness.

In effect, his description of this back lot behind Stahr's studio is the only relatively long description about the physical setting in the novel. The only slight difference one may detect here is that Fitzgerald gave a touch of parable to the scene of this back lot. Although the back lot behind Stahr's studio is but a tiny part of the whole setting in the novel, it presents a microcosmic picture of Hollywood. Its feature as a "fairyland" is sufficiently symbolized by the names of famous places because each of them creates an image in the reader's mind, signifying the special meaning, with which it is associated. The African jungle may suggest the exotic, wild, and potentially dangerous nature of Hollywood; the French chateaux instantly allude to grandeur and magnificence; Broadway suggests artistic glamour and success. With the schooner as a reminder of the luxury and comfort in Hollywood life, we have a panoramic picture of Hollywood right in front of our eyes. It is crucial, however, to notice the turning point in the second half of Fitzgerald's description, for his comparison of this "fairyland" image to the "torn picture books of childhood" reveals regret and sadness on the part of the author, who apparently believed that all these wonderful things about Hollywood had already turned into fragments of memory, that could be recalled only in illusion.

There is no doubt that in the 1930s Hollywood comes alive in this emblematic description of the back lot, but the description also honestly presents Fitzgerald's own view of Hollywood. In this passage, as well as in other parts of the novel, one may constantly feel a blended sense of fascination and repugnance, which is so characteristic of Fitzgerald's ambivalent attitude evidenced in his descriptions of Princeton and New York. Brian Way accurately observed, "Fitzgerald's fascination with Hollywood—like his fascination with the rich—was balanced by an equally strong sense of disapproval."[20] This is what has always made Fitzgerald's use of settings so objective and so effective. As the first writer who was determined to anatomize Hollywood, the mystified body of modern American culture, and define it in all its functions and motivations, Fitzgerald scrutinized everything in Hollywood through his own keen observation. Hollywood, in his eyes, was not just a place or a small city of movie studios; it was a frontier where various art forms converged into a new medium, various social institutions competed, and various ideas and values clashed. The emergence of the movie industry marked the end of an era in which art always shut itself inside the kingdom and had nothing to do with the mundane world of business. Entering a new epoch of its development, art started to cultivate new domains and assimilate new inspirations in business, whereas business wanted to discover and develop new profitable markets in art. It was such a strange and unprecedented phenomenon in modern life that no consensus could be reached on how art and business could exist and expand on a reciprocal basis. Under such circumstances, tensions between art and business were inevitable.

In general, film is art. Every movie is a work of artistic creation. The only thing that differentiates film from other art forms is its dependence upon the service of many other popular arts as well as the financial support from the banking industry. Because of its heavy dependence on other arts and industries, moving production is also a business, an industry that involves huge expenses, elaborate technologies, and complicated collaborations between the artists who create the movies and the administrators who manage the creating process. Just like any business in America, the movie industry depends for its survival on profit. As Max Lerner has indicated, "The qualities of the industrial process in Hollywood are the qualities of any big American industry: machine-tool technology, division of labor, mass production, bureaucracy, hierarchy."[21] Fitzgerald made this point clear in Cecilia's introduction of her father, Brady: "My father was in the picture business as another man might be in cotton or steel" (*LT*, 3). The same point is further confirmed through Pat Hobby's remark about Hollywood to his colleague in "Boil Some Water—Lots of It": "This is no art, . . . this is an industry" (*PHS*, 22). Hollywood, where the movies were made and distributed and shipped all over the world, was a fast-expanding business. It employed more than 30,000 persons a month; it spent nearly $186 million in producing movies in 1939; its annual payroll reached almost $145 million.[22] It also had close ties with banking and manufacturing businesses. To build more and larger studios, and to make ambitious movies, Hollywood needed funds from bankers and investment groups. As a result, the financial powerhouses on Wall Street became more influential and took greater control in Hollywood's movie production.

In a world such as Hollywood, where money was the law, whoever controlled the financial source controlled the whole kingdom. Before the movie companies changed themselves from private empires into bureaucratic corporations around 1937, the producer was supposed to oversee all the business operations his company, from management and finance to movie production and technical assistance. The control of the investors and the authority of their agent, the producer, are realistically dramatized in Fitzgerald's description of a business meeting between Monroe Stahr and his investors, whom Fitzgerald called "the moneymen" and "the rulers": "Stahr was the youngest of the group—not by many years at this date, though he had first sat with most of these men when he was a boy wonder of twenty-two. Then, more than now, he had been a money man among money men. Then he had been able to figure costs in his head with a speed and accuracy that dazzled them" (*LT*, 45). Although depicted in a sarcastic tone, the meeting presents an insight of the hierarchy inside the Hollywood empire. With the costs of making movies soaring and the trend of extravagance in movie production growing in the 1930s, these "money men" began to tighten their control over Hollywood through their producers. The direct consequence of such a situation, as Fitzgerald brilliantly exposed in the novel, not only escalated the already fierce tension between the art of movie making and the business of movie promotion but also created a dilemma for the producers and the artists working under their command.

Producers in Hollywood were often perceived as "dictators," indulging in the expression of their own tastes, vanities, and impractical impulses. Facing cruel competition from their colleagues, they tended to make decisions on big money movies purely based on their personal egos, rather than their business judgment. Even though the producer in Fitzgerald's novel, Stahr, is modeled after a legendary figure in Hollywood, Irving Thalberg, and is portrayed as one of the new producers who could manage to ease the tension between art and business and to produce movies that could score commercial success while maintaining some artistic values he is still deeply caught up in a dilemma: On the one hand he has to satisfy his financial backers by playing the role for which they hired him; on the other hand, he must inevitably clash with his artists over how much artistic merit they should create in their movies. He has to ask these questions: "How will this movie perform at the box office?" and "Will this movie reach out to a large audience?" He has to make decisions to ensure the profit of his movies without worrying about the artists' concern about their creation. To do his job, Stahr has to enforce his unchallengeable authority. A look at one scene in which Stahr is asking a movie director and his writers about a movie production will explain the point adequately. Obviously, Stahr is not content with the structure of the movie. He even threatens to "put it away" because he does not see "why it should be produced at all" (*LT*, 38). While the director and writers are listening in fear and uncertainty, Stahr gives his instructions in an authoritative voice: "I've told you many times that the first thing I decide is the *kind* of story I want. . . . This is not the kind of a story I want" (*LT*, 39). The message Stahr wants to give to his men is quite clear: The movie is his, and he is the man who decides what kind of movie it should be. Whenever he wants to make a certain kind of movie, he will choose one, or as he says, "When I want to do a Eugene O'Neill play, I'll buy one" (*LT*, 39). To further stress his point, Stahr turns to his writer, Reinmund, and issues a final warning: " Remember this in the future—if I order a limousine, I want that kind of car. And the fastest midget racer you ever saw couldn't do" (*LT*, 39). Thanks to Fitzgerald's perceptive and subtle skill in description, this conversation gives us a clear sense of a producer's typical day on the job as well as his frequent clash with the artists under his command. Written in simple words, some minute details, such as Stahr's short nod of impatience and his resolute order, "That's not under discussion" (*LT*, 39); the changing expressions on his men's faces, from fear and confusion to relief; and their eagerness to apologize to Stahr combine perfectly to delineate the overpowering image of the producer in Hollywood.

The hierarchical system in Hollywood is not merely confined to its studios; instead it is the social structure in that movie city. A series of scenes at the "Big Table" in "Boil Some Water—Lots of It" verifies that one's status and connection in society are basically the determining factors of one's social image and success. When he was young and highly in demand in Hollywood, Pat Hobby used to be a "familiar figure" at this restaurant frequented by many movie stars and executives in Hollywood. But now, people "looked at him with the universal Hollywood suspicion" (*PHS*, 23). The only thing he can do for self-consolation is to try and impress a young and naive nurse by telling her how he usually sits with the "big shots" at the Big Table, the men "representing a thousand dollars an hour in salaries" (*PHS*, 27).

Sensing that downward "fluctuations" of Pat Hobby's fortune and status would not be enough to reveal the money-based and influence-driven hierarchy in Hollywood, Fitzgerald tries to reinforce his point by inserting a dramatic incident at the Big Table. A Russian Cossack, who is identified as an "extra," is first denied service and then severely beaten simply because the big shots mistake him for a lower-class stranger, judging by his dress and his thick Central European accent. The outrageous irony is that Pat Hobby is the one who goes over and crushes the tray on the head of the "extra," even though he himself has been pushed farther down the ladder of the hierarchy in Hollywood.

One might wonder why Pat Hobby would do a thing like that. Is it to please big shots, or give himself the satisfaction that he still belongs to the powerful circle in Hollywood? But one will not miss Fitzgerald's intended message that Pat Hobby's behavior before and after the "blow" embodies the dilemma with which Hollywood writers struggled every day. It is a dilemma between their need to remain inside the Hollywood establishment in order to survive and their inability to do just that; it is a dilemma between wasting their creative talent and pursuing their dreams of materialistic success. Like Pat Hobby and Reinmund, artists in Hollywood were trapped in this dilemma. Lured by Hollywood's charm as both a center of artistic creation and a lucrative business, artists came to the "fairyland" with great expectations. Most of them had neither envisioned tough problems like this nor thought about losing their sacred status as artists. Among all the artists, the writers were caught by the biggest surprise. Before coming to Hollywood, they had enjoyed absolute authority over what and how they wrote, with all their characters, events, and words at their own disposal. They were the only ones, they felt, who had the right to make decisions in the world of their own imagination. Once they landed behind a desk in Hollywood, all their previous privileges and dignities suddenly vanished. In most cases, they would be forced to adapt a novel no matter how inferior it was. They were shocked to realize that they would have no chance to convey their views and visions of life in writing or to move and influence the audience through their creative talent. What their producers demanded from them was something that would entertain the audience and hence make a profit. In Hollywood, a writer was nothing but an employee; he or she was just like an ordinary worker on a production line. Writing or revising a movie script is a menial means of making a living. Newcomers dreamed of making a fortune, but they soon realized that they had to be concerned with daily survival first. Even if they were lucky to get some well-paid offers while young, they knew that they could not continue the high living for long. This is one of the recurrent themes in *The Pat Hobby Stories*. "Pat," as Fitzgerald describes him, "a man in the way," "had been in the money . . . with three cars and a chicken over every garage. Now his clothes looked as if he'd been standing at Hollywood and Vine for three years" (*PHS*, 14). But now he is penniless; even his two ex-wives have "given up asking for alimony" (*PHS*, 23). For many Hollywood writers like Pat Hobby, who had been lured by the great prospect of fame and fortune, life became a daily struggle for survival. They hustled around for writing contracts, not so much to satisfy intense inner compulsion for artistic expression as to make ends meet. Artistic hunger had to be placed second to daily needs. After more than twenty years in the business, Pat Hobby is still trying to sell his ideas for any price. "For years," Pat Hobby tells the young nurse, "it was a dog's life" (*PHS*, 24). In spite of its farcical touch and satirical intention in plot and characterization, Fitzgerald's Pat Hobby stories contain the gloomy miseries of the average writers, dreamers, and fortune seekers who struggle desperately in hardship.

For artists who were lucky to find working opportunities, Fitzgerald reminds us in "Pat Hobby's Secret," their "Distress in Hollywood is endemic and always acute" (*PHS*, 52). Although free from worries of food and rent, they were mostly, if not completely, deprived of any right to their artistic aspirations. To quit for the sake of integrity as artists or to remain on the job for the money, this was the hard choice artists had to make everyday. Speaking of the conflict between integrity and desire, Robert E. Sherwood offered a perceptive comment, "Every writer or actor or artist of any kind who journeys there, however high his hopes or firm his integrity, is bound eventually to arrive at the point where he must utter the same unanswerable question: 'What is the use?' And having done so, he must either depart at once, before the California climate dissolves the tissues of his conscience, or he must abandon his idealistic pretensions, settle down to a monotonous diet of the succulent fruits of the lotus, and live out his days, in sun-kissed contentment, accomplishing nothing of any enduring importance, taking the immediate cash and letting the eternal credit go."[23] Other than this, there was not much choice available to writers to maintain their impulse and dignity as artists. Since writers were smart enough to know that they were only writing "trash," and that they were well paid to produce it, they had no one to blame for bringing them into this dilemma.

According to Jonas Spatz, there might be some hard choices: "The serious artist can survive only by denying his conscience and joining his enemies, by withholding a part of himself to create in his spare time, or by fighting to revolutionize the motion picture industry."[24] The sad thing, however, is that the last two options never appeared feasible. Ever since the time Fitzgerald wrote *The Last Tycoon*, there has been no one who has simultaneously maintained an artistic conscience and succeeded in bringing some fundamental reforms to the movie industry; for anyone who dared to challenge the authority of his employer in Hollywood would immediately be dismissed and replaced, as is suggested by Stahr's threatening question to his men, "Do you writers think you can get hot on it again? . . . Or shall I try somebody fresh?" (*LT*, 40). Hollywood remains the same colony, where money rules and profit is the life of the industry. As to the writers who managed to carry on their own writing career while working for Hollywood, this divided and contradictory effort, as Budd Schulberg once implied, would only produce mediocre screenplays and poor novels. Even a writer as talented and committed as Fitzgerald was hardly able to handle this dual creation perfectly. On the one hand, none of the scripts he worked on became successful; on the other hand, despite three years of hard work, he was never able to devote as much energy and time as he wanted to *The Last Tycoon,* and it is quite possible that his dual creation accelerated the deterioration of his health and prompted his early death. By comparison, the first choice worked relatively well for many artists, but the price they paid was staggeringly high. In other words, they traded their artistic integrity for their desire for money and comfort. A representative figure among them is portrayed in Fitzgerald's characterization of one of Stahr's men, Reinmund. Fitzgerald's description is brief, but it has a flawless visual effect. The simple and smooth choice of diction and the seemingly trivial details about Reinmund enable us to have a face-to-face look at the man. Within a few years, Fitzgerald states, Reinmund has undergone a fundamental transformation from "a handsome young opportunist, with a fairly good education" and "some character," to a thirty-year-old "bad man," who has "none of the virtues." How could this happen? Fitzgerald's answer to this question cannot be simpler: because Reinmund has been "daily forced by his anomalous position into devious ways of acting and thinking" (*LT*, 37). But he knows how to please Stahr. In fact, Stahr likes him and sees him as "a good all-around man" (*LT*, 37). He does not mind betraying and demeaning himself if that is what it takes to gain a share of Hollywood's glamour and luxury. In a broad sense, what we see in the portrayal of Reinmund is not just an ugly picture of an individual's degeneration; we see, more importantly, the grim consequences of the endless tension between art and business in Hollywood. With business always winning the upper hand, the choice for the artist is only between surrender and defeat, nothing else. The tragedy is that in either way, the artists can do nothing but watch their talent wasted, their ideas trashed, their pride violated, and their hopes buried.

Undoubtedly this was the truth as Fitzgerald saw and experienced it. As Gene D. Phillips suggests, it is based on such conclusions Fitzgerald created in *The Last Tycoon* "a dark fable about Hollywood as a land of unfulfilled ambitions and broken dreams."[25] Fitzgerald says repeatedly in his letters that Hollywood really disappointed him. He claims that his dreams about Hollywood are shattered because "everywhere there is, after a moment, either corruption or indifference" (*CU*, 282). His intention to write about Hollywood is not really to take revenge on it, as some critics have misjudged, but, rather, to represent Hollywood to its fans and critics as he personally saw it and experienced it. The claim that *The Last Tycoon* is Fitzgerald's revenge on Hollywood for the unfair treatment he received there seems too simplified; we can hardly discern any obvious sign of anger or complaint on the part of the author. Throughout the novel, Fitzgerald's chief concern is to define accurately the tensions between art and business and to expose their destructive impact upon the disillusionment of American artists.

In contrast to Fitzgerald's primary concern with the dilemma of the American artist, Dos Passos expressed his harsh criticism of the evils of capitalism in Hollywood. In *The Big Money,* which apparently draws a picture of Hollywood in its early years, Dos Passos tries to convince the reader that Hollywood not only has served as a tool for capitalistic propaganda but also has turned into a corrupted place, where "the big money" has eroded the morality of American society. To accentuate his argument, Dos Passos portrays a group of degenerate characters, from a former prostrate, dumb, and insensitive actor to a sexually perverted tycoon. His purpose in creating these characters is to satirize the false values embodied by Hollywood. But Dos Passos's novel seems more like an angry and liberal denunciation of Hollywood's part in the decline of American society than an articulate study on what has caused the nationwide corruption in the first place.

The issue of false dreams, a topic Dos Passos touched upon but failed to elaborate in great depth in his novel, is given a much more poignant and concentrated analysis in Nathanael West's novel *The Day of the Locust.* The novel, published before Fitzgerald's death, is also a notable book about Hollywood. Actually, Fitzgerald made a complementary remark about the novel, saying that it "certainly has scenes of extraordinary power."[26] Even though Fitzgerald and West were never close friends, West was grateful to Fitzgerald. The day after Fitzgerald's death, West and his young wife were killed in a car accident as they were hurrying back to Los Angeles from their weekend in Mexico after hearing about Fitzgerald. Both writers wrote important novels about Hollywood, and both died young. Further, there are some similarities in their portrayal of Hollywood. However, West's primary concern was the exploration of the American myth, tracing a futile quest for a belief and dramatizing humanity's hopeless confrontation with a hostile and meaningless world. Most of West's characters belong to the "other Hollywood" —an underclass of grotesques, wanderers, and failures who invariably vent their frustration toward the social establishment through physical violence. His novel has the kind of sarcastic and angry tone similar to that of Dos Passos's work.

Although Fitzgerald and West shared the view of Hollywood as the embodiment of the failure of American dream, there is certainly a striking difference in their approach to this crucial issue. Contrary to the jaundiced eye with which West saw Hollywood and the harsh tone in which he attacked American society, Fitzgerald scrutinized Hollywood and its connection to the country with discerning eyes and presented a sharp conception of Hollywood as a land of hopeless illusions. Whereas West stressed the abnormality in Hollywood by turning his characters into a group of grotesque misfits, Fitzgerald focused on the portrayal of a few representative figures, including heroes and villains, each of whom is designated a specific role in revealing what Fitzgerald perceived to be the symptoms of corruption in a degenerate society.

To Fitzgerald, Hollywood is not just a symbol of glamour, success, and utopia; it is also a synonym of sin and corruption. Since money is the law there, the obsession with gross materialism bewitches both men and women there and leads them to total moral bankruptcy. Although Fitzgerald does not present many graphic scenes of vulgarity and violence, or paint any awesome-looking grotesques in *The Last Tycoon* or his other Hollywood stories, there are still enough details and sketches to constitute a multidimensional picture of Hollywood, rotted by snobbery, hypocrisy, deceit, and insensitivity. Of special notice is that such degeneration does not involve individuals only; it also involves organizations and institutions. On more than one occasion, for instance, Fitzgerald describes the growing power of the union organization in Hollywood studios. Besides, as we can see in the outline of the unfinished portion of *The Last Tycoon,* Fitzgerald actually intended to exploit the issue of racketeering and gangsterism within Hollywood. Primarily, however, Fitzgerald's concern in the completed portion of the novel is more focused on personal rather than sociological facets of his subject.

One way, sometimes a very effective one, in which Fitzgerald exposes the corruption in Hollywood is his close examination of the merciless competition among Hollywood dreamers. As Wylie says in *The Last Tycoon,* "It's a mining town in lotus land. Who said that? I did. It's a good place for toughies" (*LT*, 11). The popular catchwords "social Darwinism," "struggle for existence," and "survival of the fittest" became the most important principles of the life-and-death competition in Hollywood. Everyone is possessed of both ambition and fear; everyone has a price; everyone belongs to a network of relationships. There is nothing they would not do if their job, or their money, is at stake. The relationship between coworkers is completely dehumanized. People value their relationship with others based exclusively on what and how much they can potentially benefit from it. It is a common belief that in a ruthless world of business such as Hollywood, an individual rises and falls often because of politics and personal networking, nepotism and favoritism, rather than hard work and intelligence. An old-timer like Pat Hobby knows well that "what people you sat with at lunch was more important in getting along than what you dictate in your office" (*PHS*, 22). As early as in his story "Dalyrimple Goes Wrong," about a veteran's struggle for survival in the business community, Fitzgerald already recognized such an obstinate practice in the business world. But he showed a much deeper understanding of this issue in his later works, especially *The Last Tycoon*. In addition revealing this type of networking, Fitzgerald exposed many dirty tricks widely applied in Hollywood, tricks even a smart and powerful man like Stahr is not able to avoid nor defeat. Stahr is always bothered by "the spying that went around him—not just for inside information or patented process secrets—but spying on his scent for a trend in taste, his guess as to how things were going to be. Too much of his vitality was taken by the mere parrying of these attempts" (*LT*, 28). It is all part of the business strategy, for information is the key to success. It gives you an edge in competition and a bargaining chip at the negotiation table.

Brady, Stahr's antagonist in *The Last Tycoon,* is a master of playing dirty tricks. He is, as Fitzgerald defines him in his notes for later chapters, "a shrewd man, a gentile, and a scoundrel of the lowest variety" (*LT*, 138). Here, what Fitzgerald presents is a portrait of a complex character. He is smart, he has decent manners, but he can be as mean as one can imagine. He is so equivocal that his own daughter asks the question, "What did Father look like?" (*LT*, 22) because she does not know how to describe him. But when Cecilia has anything to say about her father, she always says it with a touch of irony or contempt. First of all, she tells us that "there were a lot of strange things about Father's office" (*LT*, 21); then her describes his father's secretaries as "poker-faced" women who sat in the outer part of her father's office "like witches." Up to this point, Cecilia has not said much about what her father looks like or what kind of person he is, but the tone in Cecilia's voice and the detail about where and with whom her father is working are suggestive enough for the reader to realize what kind of man Brady is.

In terms of the tension between art and business in Hollywood, Brady is the man who represents the business end of the conflict. He has all the instincts for business and money matters, he is good at using all sorts of tricks whenever necessary, but he knows nothing about the art of movie making. Again, as his daughter Cecilia tells us, her father does not "know the ABC's of dubbing or even cutting." Brady does not have much "feel [for] America," nor any "sense of a story" (*LT*, 28). Evidently, a typical and mean merchant like Brady is only interested in making money. He claims to be Stahr's friend because it is what Stahr has accomplished that made it possible for Brady to climb to the position he holds. To a large degree, his success or failure depends on the movies Stahr produces for him. But since his every motivation is dictated by the will of the money rulers on Wall Street, Brady has to keep absolutely tight control over all money matters. Similarly, when he finds out that Stahr has artistic and idealistic sides to his character and that he is considerate to his employees, Brady instantly regards Stahr as his enemy, an imminent threat to his own power and interest. Thus, "the struggle between them for the control of the company is rapidly coming to a climax" (*LT*, 129).

It is a great pity that Fitzgerald's manuscript stops at this point. The synopsis of the later part of the novel shows a consistent pattern of the rivalry between Brady and Stahr that goes on for the rest of the story. To defeat Stahr, Brady resorts to every trick he can think of within that mundane world of Hollywood. Alternately, Brady appears in front of us as an exploiter, a manipulator, and a schemer. First, during Stahr's absence, Brady cuts the workers' pay by double-crossing the union and Stahr; then as soon as he learns from his daughter Cecilia about Stahr's involvement with Kathleen, a woman who resembles Stahr's dead wife, and especially Stahr's affair with this woman after she is married, Brady attempts to blackmail Stahr by telling the woman's husband who happens to be the leader of the union; finally, when Brady realizes that nothing can stop Stahr from taking over his own territory, Brady desperately arranges a plot to get Stahr out of the company. "He has even actually and factually considered having him murdered" (*LT*, 140). Like any vicious monger of corporations, banks, or Wall Street, Brady will stop at nothing to get what he wants. This is the basic ethic in the business world of Hollywood, and Brady is the epitome of all the rules and evils in that world.

THE TENSION BETWEEN ARTIST AND HOLLYWOOD

In *American Social Fiction: James to Cozzens*, Michael Millgate claims, "This conflict between the individual and the institution is the central theme explored in the best of the Hollywood novels."[27] It is undeniable that Fitzgerald shows a considerable social interest in his treatment of the tension between art and business. To look at *The Last Tycoon* as a whole, however, Fitzgerald's primary interest is still in Stahr, "the last tycoon," or the last believer of individualism in Hollywood. As the title suggests, his interest in Stahr's rise and fall is the starting point of the novel and he never deviates from it throughout the story. Of course, Fitzgerald's treatment of the tension between art and business has its own functional significance; it helps to set up a logical background for Fitzgerald's treatment of the real central theme of the novel: the tension between romantic individualism and mundane materialism in the final frontier of American values and dreams. Some critics have suggested that Fitzgerald's notes for the continuation and conclusion of the novel indicate a plan to shift his primary interest from characters to events. Probably events would have taken control had Fitzgerald gotten the chance to finish his project. So far as the finished portion stands, however, Fitzgerald's interest in Stahr and his clash with the Hollywood establishment is still the dominant theme of the novel.

Unlike West, who saw Hollywood as a wasteland and portrayed all his characters in Hollywood as a bunch of grotesque creatures wandering around aimlessly, Fitzgerald viewed a dismal picture like this as an oversimplified solution to the problem. As he once complained to Edmund Wilson that no writer would attempt to solve the puzzle of Hollywood by writing a serious novel about it, Fitzgerald seemed to feel obligated to take on this Hollywood issue himself. He did, and did it well. By depicting Stahr's conflict with the monster of greed in Hollywood, Fitzgerald succeeded in presenting Hollywood in all its stark essence. He evidently tried to suggest that the conflict is by no means an isolated "Stahr vs. Hollywood" struggle; each side of the conflict symbolically represents a set of beliefs, values, and ideals. Stahr, a strong believer in individualism and an opponent of all the degenerate evils in society, strives unyieldingly for a perfect balance between artistic integrity and industrial enterprise; whereas Hollywood, the capital of both the newly emerged movie industry and the newly revived American dream, falls under the sway of gross materialism and soon becomes a destructive force, snatching away from its inhabitants all their values, beliefs, ideals, and dreams. Hollywoodians like Stahr fall because they cannot sustain the destructive force of the social establishment. Hollywood falls because it is not able to protect itself from the corruptive symptoms that accompany gross materialism. It is a double tragedy. In a certain sense, the tragedy of Stahr and the tragedy of Hollywood are inseparable just as they are inevitable, for the conflict between them is not merely economic; it is also social, moral, psychological, and spiritual. It is an aspect of the conflict of American society as a whole.

The addition of Stahr to Fitzgerald's fictional heroes is not purely incidental. The way Fitzgerald idealized him apparently reflects his conception of, and perhaps his own wish to be a really strong hero. As Richard D. Lehan has pointed out, "Fitzgerald could write with such conviction in *The Last Tycoon* because he himself had experienced so many of the emotions that he gave to Monroe Stahr."[28] Besides, the portrayal of Stahr is a remarkable achievement in Fitzgerald's fiction because it marked a departure from the stereotype of an emotionally bankrupt character, which dominated all his previous novels, and because it displayed Fitzgerald's new skills in characterization. For example, the use of names, among others things, helps to emphasize a crucial element in Stahr's personality. By calling Stahr a "tycoon," Fitzgerald bestowed on him the quality of a powerful and resolute leader; again, by calling him "Stahr," which sounds exactly like "Star," Fitzgerald gave him the glow of celebrity, even though Fitzgerald may have intended on the pronunciation with a strange spelling, either implying a possible foreign background in Stahr's upbringing or a potential alienation from other people in the future.

Like Gatsby, Stahr is a staunch romantic dreamer for whom the spirit of individualism is a principle of life. As a man who has everything he needs, Gatsby is free from any direct interference or challenge from the forces of materialism; but Stahr has to struggle against the material temptations and manipulations all the time. To maintain his spirit of individualism and his belief in artistic integrity, Stahr must resist the repressive pressure from all facets of the Hollywood power struggle. As a producer working on the frontier between individualism and materialism, every day on the job means a raging battle for Stahr. To win, or even to survive the battle, Stahr needs more than courage and tenacity; he has to find out whom he is fighting and discover what tactics he should use in defeating them. Therefore, by contrast to Fitzgerald's other heroes, such as Amory, Anthony, Dick, and even Gatsby, Stahr is a much more admirable character, one equipped with intelligence, ideas, visions, and leadership quality. As Joan M. Allen points out, "Stahr is a protean mythic figure. He can assume at will various roles: —'one of the boys,' director, cameraman, businessman, lover, father, and miraculous healer."[29] But one of his most important roles is not mentioned here: Stahr is also an artist with great aesthetic sensitivity.

Fitzgerald's success in portraying Stahr as such a captivating character owes much to the fact that he modeled the character of Stahr after Irving Thalberg, the Hollywood legend, known as "a boy wonder," as Fitzgerald called his Stahr in *The Last Tycoon.* Fitzgerald admitted on several occasions that he was "powerfully, hypnotically fascinated by Thalberg. He was a man who was everything the writer wanted to be: young, attractive, glamorous, commercially successful without loss of artistry—and at the same time tragic."[30] Fitzgerald deeply respected Thalberg as one of the few who were really "built on a grand scale."[31] Using Thalberg as the prototype does not mean that Fitzgerald followed Thalberg's life and career closely in depicting Stahr. In actuality, as Mark Royden Winchell has suggested, "Fitzgerald was inspired more by a fictive image of Thalberg than by the producer himself."[32] In his letter to Kenneth Litfauer, his editor at *Collier's,* Fitzgerald explains, "The events I have built around him are fiction, but all of them are things which might very well have happened, and I am pretty sure that I saw deep enough into the character of the man so that his reactions are authentically what they would have been in life."[33] Fitzgerald presented Stahr as a great hero of unparalleled charm and power. Stahr is also the first near-perfect hero in Fitzgerald's fiction with a professional commitment. Amory is only a wandering romantic egotist who never makes any serious commitments; Anthony is a dandy dreamer who finally loses his wits and senses in booze; Gatsby's occupation is a mystery, but he buries himself too much in his dreams anyway; Dick is a quitter who has no courage to meet the tough challenges in life. Only Stahr is engaged in a responsible job.

If we look at the various aspects of Stahr's personality, we see a consistent pattern in Fitzgerald's characterization. Implication, rather than explication, is the distinctive trait of Fitzgerald's art. We are never told directly what Stahr really looks like or what kind of person he is, but there are scattered details in the narrative. We watch him speak and we observe his activities, just as other characters do in the novel. We completely place ourselves at the mercy of the narrator because we can see, hear, and finally learn about Stahr only when Cecilia is willing to mention one or two details between the lines, sometimes about Stahr the producer, but sometimes about Stahr the young New Yorker, as is shown in this passage: "His dark eyes took me in, and I wondered what they would look like if he fell in love. They were kind, aloof and, though they often reasoned with you gently, somewhat superior. It was no fault of theirs if they saw so much" (*LT*, 15). What we see above is a typical example of Fitzgerald's finesse in characterization. Fitzgerald does not use separate and lengthy descriptions to introduce his characters as is done in other Hollywood novels. The portrayals of his characters are often split into bits and pieces and presented at certain moments in the chain of events without any special and temporal restraints. Nonetheless, thanks to such a method each piece of the total picture will stick in the reader's mind and disclose one particular facet of Stahr's personality.

The first solidly presented image of Stahr is that of a businessman. In a half-serious argument with Wylie, Stahr declares, "I'm a merchant. I want to buy what's on your mind" (*LT*, 16). Wylie does not agree with Stahr. To a certain extent, Wylie is perfectly right. It will not make much sense if we compare Stahr to other businessmen in American literature. By nature and profession, Stahr is totally different from William Dean Howells's Lapham, Theodore Dreiser's Cooperwood, or Sinclair Lewis's Babbitt. Stahr is a modern American businessman. For one thing, Fitzgerald never intended to be an antibusiness novelist, portraying the old-fashioned businessman in the tradition of Howells and Jack London. On the contrary, he portrayed Stahr as a businessman-hero and treated him with compassion, understanding, and even admiration. In spite of the fact that "Stahr's education was founded on nothing more than a night-school course in stenography" (*LT*, 17), Stahr seems to have the real feel of the business world in Hollywood. By any standard, Stahr exactly fits Henry Nash Smith's definition of an American businessman: "He was acknowledged to be immediately powerful. He controlled the energies of economic, social, and political change; the future belonged to him."[34] Actually, in several conference scenes, Stahr seems to align himself with the great American capitalists. He is confident, he has the mind for figures, and he knows how to deal with his money backers. During a conversation with Kathleen, Stahr says, "The studio is really home." When Kathleen responds with a tilt of criticism, "That's what I've heard about American business men." Stahr explains immediately, "You do what you've been born to do" (*LT*, 82). Stahr himself strongly believes that business is his line and no one can change that. As a prominent film producer in Hollywood controlling millions of dollars in film production, Stahr understands perfectly how Hollywood functions.

His gift for business is best demonstrated in Chapter 4, where Fitzgerald's description of Stahr's day on the job draws a series of realistic sketches of him working in his office, meeting all kinds of people, and making decisions on different matters, just like the kind of CEO one would see in a big corporation. Everything is done with efficiency and resolution. As a producer, he insists upon tight control over every facet of studio operations, from supervising the writing of a script to surveying the flood damage. He is known as a workaholic, "to whom night and day had never mattered. He was sleepless, without a talent for rest or the desire for it" (*LT*, 15). He works on Sundays (*LT*, 75) and "seldom left the studio before eleven" (*LT*, 24). After the death of his wife, Stahr almost regards working long hours as a kind of compensation, frequently driving himself until he is emotionally and physically exhausted. He does not care to have a life outside the film studio. Even when Cecilia tells him that she would like to marry him, Stahr immediately turns her down, insisting that pictures are his "girl." Nevertheless, Stahr is quite compassionate and thoughtful toward his employees. He always tries to maintain friendly terms between the workers and himself. To his surprise, his magnetic power over his employees and his friendly relationships with them drive his arch rival, Brady, crazy and prompt Brady to arrange one scheme after another against him.

Throughout the novel, Stahr's brilliant image as a businessman constitutes a powerful and touching aspect of his character. However, Stahr's genius for business makes up only part of Fitzgerald's grand conception of him. He has the talent and sense of an eminent artist. Certainly, whether Stahr is a real artist cannot be judged in the conventional sense for the same reason movie-making itself cannot be viewed as a conventional art form. A movie production is a cooperative process of artistic creation; it needs a well-coordinated group effort. In other words, it needs what Budd Schulberg called a "guiding genius" to look for and bring together all the necessary ideas, materials, and forms before the whole production process actually starts.[35] Once the production is under way, this "guiding genius" is supposed to oversee every aspect and every stage of the production and to stand by for any possible problems. Stahr is just such a genius, who not only knows everything about the process but also has enough knowledge of art to appreciate, to judge, and even to inspire his artists. One salient example of Stahr's genius as an artist can be cited from Fitzgerald's notes for the unfinished portion of the novel. Once he sees some artistic merit in a movie project, Stahr will not hesitate to protect its integrity, even when he is facing possible interference or even sabotage from his enemy, Brady. Fitzgerald suggests, since Stahr has "a craftsman's interest in the pictures" (*LT*, 131), as an artist-producer his primary concern is to maintain a high quality in his films. Stahr will do everything he can to prevent pure commercialism from controlling his movie-making, but he always knows how to maintain dedicated to his art. His quality as an artist may also be indicated by his respect for the artists working under his command. Once he tells one of his writers, Brimmer, "I'm a production man" and "I like writers—I think I understand them" (*LT*, 125). What is more noble about his artistic quality is that he "never wanted his name on pictures"—because he believes "credit is something that should be given to the others" (*LT*, 146). The implicit message is not just about his willingness to be an unsung hero; it is about his quality of leadership.

Qualities like these make Stahr look like a nobleman. At this point, the appellation "tycoon," given to Stahr by Fitzgerald really carries profound meaning. Stahr has become a symbol of heroic individualism, as well as a symbol of genius and authority. Fitzgerald's identification of Stahr with Abraham Lincoln, as outlined in Fitzgerald's notes for the unwritten part of the novel, seems to be appropriate in further idealizing Stahr's character. Unfortunately, Stahr never has the chance to realize his long cherished-dream, the dream, as defined by John F. Callahan, "to synthesize pragmatism and rationalism as models of action and creation into an organizational leadership which, through films, would elevate and extend American sensibility."[36] On the contrary, he constantly feels the pressures and threats directed at him simply because of his belief in individualism and his resentment of gross materialism. All of a sudden, he finds himself the target of various destructive forces, which desperately attempt to weaken, to disintegrate, and ultimately to crush him and his movie empire. Brady is waging his vicious war on him one attack after another; the union and the communists are stepping up their pressure; his financiers demand more power and more profit. Besides these man-made odds, natural disasters add to Stahr's woe: the flood and earthquake hit Hollywood. Even his personal life becomes a mess. He is in poor health; since the death of his wife Minna, Stahr has never recovered from emotional bankruptcy, and his repeated failures to find a woman who resembles Minna leaves him in complete despair; his affair with Kathleen has been exploited by his enemies to ruin his reputation. Stahr is losing control over his authority and his life as well.

In view of all that has been said, it is no surprise that Stahr's dream ends with his own death in the air—a terrible airplane crash. His tragedy is a manifesto of Fitzgerald's conviction that the reconciliation of the conflict between idealistic individualism and gross materialism is all but an illusion; it might also be seen as Fitzgerald's stern warning that what happens to Stahr could also happen to people like Joel Coles (in "Crazy Sunday"), Pat Hobby, and others in and outside Hollywood.

NOTES

1. John W. Aldridge, *After the Lost Generation* (New York: Nobody Press, 1966), 51.

2. Leo C. Rosten, *Hollywood: The Movie Colony, the Movie Makers* (New York: Arno Press, 1970), 56.

3. John Dos Passos, "A Note on Fitzgerald," in *The Crack-Up*, ed. Edmund Wilson (New York: New Directions, 1956), 343.

4. For a more detailed discussion, see Tino Balio's "Hollywood" in *UNESCO Courier*, July-August 1995, 12-15.

5. All figures are from Leo C. Rosten, *Hollywood: The Movie Colony, the Movie Makers,* 3-4.

6. Hortense Powdermaker, *Hollywood: The Dream Factory* (Boston: Little, Brown, 1950), 16.

7. Robert Sklar, *F. Scott Fitzgerald: The Last Laocoon* (New York: Oxford University Press, 1967), 334.

8. Tom Dardis, *Some Time in the Sun* (New York: Charles Scribner's Sons, 1976), 6.

9. Fitzgerald to Harold Ober, January 16, 1935, in *As Ever, Scott Fitz—*, ed. Matthew J. Bruccoli (London: Woburn Press, 1973), 216.

10. Ibid., 241.

11. F. Scott Fitzgerald, *The Letters of F. Scott Fitzgerald,* ed. Andrew Turnbull (New York: Charles Scribner's Sons, 1963), 48.

12. Quoted from the introduction by Charles Scribner III in F. Scott Fitzgerald's play *The Vegetable* (New York: Charles Scribner's Sons, 1976).

13. Malcolm Cowley, ed., "The Diamond as Big as the Ritz," in *The Bodley Head Scott Fitzgerald,* vol. 5 (London: Bodley Head, 1963), 66-67.

14. Fitzgerald, *The Letters,* ed. Andrew Turnbull, 548.

15. For a more detailed discussion of the history of the Hollywood novel, see Nancy Brooker-Bowers, "Fiction and the Film Industry" *Literature-Film Quarterly* (Salisbury, Md.) 15, no, 4 (1987): 260-67.

16. Fitzgerald, *The Letters*, ed. Andrew Turnbull, 145.

17. Edmund Wilson, foreword in Fitzgerald's *The Last Tycoon* (New York: Charles Scribner's Sons, 1941), x.

18. Walter Wells, *Tycoons and Locusts: A Regional Look at Hollywood Fiction of the 1930s* (Carbondale, Ill.: Southern Illinois University Press, 1973), 103.

19. Henry Dan Piper, *F. Scott Fitzgerald: A Critical Portrait* (New York: Holt, Rinehart and Winston, 1965), 280.

20. Brian Way, *F. Scott Fitzgerald and the Art of Social Fiction* (New York: St. Martin's Press, 1980), 154.

21. Max Lerner, *America as a Civilization: Life and Thoughts in the United States Today* (New York: Simon & Schuster, 1957), 823.

22. All figures are from Leo C. Rosten, *Hollywood: The Movie Colony, the Movie Makers,* 4.

23. Robert E. Sherwood, "The Blessed and the Cursed," in *America as Americans See It,* ed. Fred J. Ringle (New York: Literary Guild, 1932), 72.

24. Jonas Spatz, *Hollywood in Fiction: Some Versions of the American Myth* (Paris: Mouton & Co., Printers, The Hague, 1969), 93.

25. Gene D. Phillips, *Fiction, Film, and F. Scott Fitzgerald* (Chicago: Loyola University Press, 1986), 5.

26. Quoted from the dust jacket of Nathanael West's *The Day of the Locust* (New York: New Directions, 1950).

27. Michael Millgate, *American Social Fiction: James to Cozzens* (London: Oliver and Boyd, 1964), 150.

28. Richard D. Lehan, "The Los Angeles Novel and the Idea of the West," in *Los Angeles in Fiction: A Collection of Essays,* ed. David Fine (Albuquerque: University of New Mexico Press, 1995), 32.

29. Joan M. Allen, *Candles and Carnival Lights: The Catholic Sensibility of F. Scott Fitzgerald* (New York: New York University Press, 1978), 138-39.

30. Roland Flamini, *Thalberg: The Last Tycoon and the World of M-G-M* (New York: Crown Publisher, 1994), 149.

31. Bob Thomas, *Thalberg: Life and Legend* (Gardern City, N.Y.: Doubleday, 1970), 10.

32. Mark Royden Winchell, "Fantasy Seen," in *Los Angeles in Fiction: A Collection of Essays,* ed. David Fine (Albuquerque: University of New Mexico Press, 1995), 169.

33. Matthew J. Bruccoli, ed., *F. Scott Fitzgerald: A Life in Letters* (New York: Charles Scribner's Sons, 1994), 409.

34. Henry Nash Smith, "The Search for a Capitalist Hero: Businessmen in American Fiction," in *The Business Establishment*, ed. Earl F. Cheit (New York: John Wiley and Sons, 1964), 55.

35. Budd Schulberg, *The Disenchanted* (New York: Random House, 1950), 279.

36. John F. Callahan, *The Illusions of a Nation* (Urbana, Ill.: University of Illinois Press, 1972), 201.

SELECTED BIBLIOGRAPHY

Abrams, Charles. *The City Is the Frontier*. New York: Harper and Row, 1965.

Abrams, M. H. *The Mirror and the Lamp*. New York: Norton, 1958.

Adams, Henry. *The Education of Henry Adams*. Boston: Houghton Mifflin, 1973.

Aldridge, John W. *After the Lost Generation*. New York: Nobody Press, 1966.

Allen, Joan M. *Candles and Carnival Lights: The Catholic Sensibility of F. Scott Fitzgerald*. New York: New York University Press, 1978.

Anderson, Sherwood. *Winesburg, Ohio*. New York: Modern Library, 1974.

Arden, Eugene. *The New York Novel: A Study in Urban Fiction*. Ann Arbor, Mich.: University Microfilms, 1974.

Arnold, Aerol. "Picture, Scene, and Social Comment: *The Great Gatsby*." *The University Review* (Kansas City) 30 (1963): 111-17.

Bailey, David W. "A Novel about Flappers for Philosophers." *Harvard Crimson*, May 1, 1920.

Bakhtin, Mikhail. *Problems of Dostoevsky's Poetics*. Trans. R. W. Rotsel. Ann Arbor, Mich.: Ardis, 1973.

———. *Rabelais and His World*. Trans. Helene Iswolsky. Cambridge, Mass.: MIT Press, 1968.

Balio, Tino. "Hollywood." *UNESCO Courier* (July-August 1995): 12-15.

Barthelme, Donald. *City Life*. New York: Farrar, Straus and Giroux, 1970.

Berman, Ronald. *The Great Gatsby and Modern Times*. Urbana, Ill.: University of Illinois Press, 1994.

Bewley, Marius. *The Eccentric Design*. New York: Columbia University Press, 1959.

Bloom, Harold, ed. *F. Scott Fitzgerald*. New York: Chelsea House Publishers, 1985.

Bode, Carl. *The Young Mencken*. New York: Dial Press, 1973.

Brooker-Bowers, Nancy. "Fiction and the Film Industry." *Literature-Film Quarterly*. (Salisbury, Md.) 15, no. 4 (1987): 260-67.

Bruccoli, Matthew J. *The Composition of "Tender Is the Night": A Study of the Manuscripts*. Pittsburgh: University of Pittsburgh Press, 1963.

———. *F. Scott Fitzgerald: A Descriptive Bibliography*. Pittsburgh: University of Pittsburgh Press, 1987.

———. *Some Sort of Epic Grandeur: The Life of F. Scott Fitzgerald*. New York: Harcourt Brace Jovanovich, 1981.

————, ed. *As Ever, Scott Fitz—*. London: Woburn Press, 1973.

————, ed. *F. Scott Fitzgerald: A Life in Letters*. New York: Charles Scribner's Sons, 1994.

————, ed. *F. Scott Fitzgerald's Ledger: A Facsimile*. Washington, D.C.: Bruccoli Clark, 1972.

————, ed. *The Notebook of F. Scott Fitzgerald*. New York: Harcourt Brace Jovanovich / Bruccoli Clark, 1978.

————, ed. *The Price Was High: The Last Uncollected Stories of F. Scott Fitzgerald*. New York: Harcourt Brace Jovanovich, 1979.

————, ed. *The Short Stories of F. Scott Fitzgerald: A New Collection*. New York: Charles Scribner's Sons, 1989.

Bruccoli, Matthew J., and Jackson R. Bryer, eds. *F. Scott Fitzgerald in His Own Time: A Miscellany*. Kent, Ohio: Kent State University Press, 1971.

Bruccoli, Matthew J. and Margaret M. Duggan, eds. *Correspondence of F. Scott Fitzgerald*. New York: Random House, 1980.

Bryer, Jackson R. ed. *F. Scott Fitzgerald: The Critical Reception*. New York: Burt Franklin, 1978.

————, ed. *New Essays on F. Scott Fitzgerald: Neglected Stories*. Columbia, Mo.: University of Missouri Press, 1996.

————, ed. *The Short Stories of F. Scott Fitzgerald: New Approaches in Criticism*. Madison: University of Wisconsin Press, 1982.

Callahan, John F. *The Illusions of a Nation*. Urbana, Ill.: University of Illinois Press, 1972.

Camus, Albert. *A Happy Death*. Trans. Richard Howard. New York: Knopf, 1972.

Carter, John F., Jr. "These Wild Young People." *Atlantic Monthly* 126 (September 1920): 301-4.

Cheit, Earl F., ed. *The Business Establishment*. New York: John Wiley and Sons, 1964.

Claridge, Henry. ed. *F. Scott Fitzgerald: Critical Assessments*. Mountfield, East Sussex [England]: Helm Information, 1991.

Cohen, Richard. "The Inessential Houses of *The Great Gatsby*." *The Hudson Review* 2 (1968): 48-57.

Coleridge, Samuel. *Biographia Literaria,* ed. John Shawcross. London: Oxford University Press, 1907.

Cowley, Malcolm. *Exile's Return: A Literary Odyssey of the 1920s*. New York: Penguin, 1976.

————, ed. *The Bodley Head Scott Fitzgerald,* vols. 5 and 6. London: Bodley Head, 1963.

Cowper, William. *The Works of William Cowper,* vol. 9, book 1. Edited by Robert Southey. London: Baldwin and Cradock, 1836.

Dardis, Tom. *Some Time in the Sun*. New York: Charles Scribner's Sons, 1976.

Davis, Lennard J. *Resisting Novels*. New York: Methuen, 1987.

Deamer, Robert G. *The Importance of Place in the American Literature of Hawthorne, Thoreau, Crane, Adams, and Faulkner*. Lewiston, N.Y.: Edwin Mellen Press, 1990.

Dickens, Charles. *Master Humphrey's Clock*. London: New Oxford Illustrated Dickens, 1947-1958.

————. *Our Mutual Friend*. London: New Oxford Illustrated Dickens, 1947-1958.

————. *Sketches by Boz*. London: New Oxford Illustrated Dickens, 1947-1958.

Donald, Miles. *The American Novel in the Twentieth Century*. New York: Barnes and Noble, 1978.

Donaldson, Scott. *Fool for Love: F. Scott Fitzgerald.* New York: Congdon & Weed, 1983.

Dos Passos, John. *Manhattan Transfer.* Boston: Houghton Mifflin, 1963.

———. "A Note on Fitzgerald." In *The Crack-Up,* ed. Edmund Wilson. New York: New Directions, 1956.

———. "What Makes a Novelist." *National Review* 20 (January 16, 1968): 29-32.

Eble, Kenneth. *F. Scott Fitzgerald.* Boston: Twayne, 1977.

Edel, Leon, ed. *The Spoils of Poynton.* London: W. Heinemann, 1967.

Edmiston, Susan, and Linda D. Cirino, eds. *Literary New York: A History and Guide.* Boston: Houghton Mifflin, 1976.

Eliot, George. "The Natural History of German Life." In *Essays of George Eliot,* ed. Thomas Pinney. London: Routledge and Kegan Paul, 1963.

Eliot, T. S. "Tradition and the Individual Talent." In *Selected Prose of T. S. Eliot,* ed. Frank Kermode. New York: Farrar, Straus and Giroux, 1975.

Emerson, Ralph Waldo. *Emerson: Essays and Lectures,* ed. Joe Porte. New York: Literary Classics of the United States, Viking Press, 1983.

———. "Nature." In *Selections from Ralph Waldo Emerson,* ed. Stephen E. Whicher. Boston: Houghton Mifflin, 1957.

Fanger, Donald. *Dostoevsky and Romantic Realism: A Study of Dostoevsky in Relation to Balzac, Dickens, and Gogol.* Chicago: University of Chicago Press, 1965.

Festa-McCormick, Diana. *The City as Catalyst: A Study of Ten Novels.* London: Associated University Press, 1979.

Fiedler, Leslie A. *Love and Death in the American Novel.* New York: Dell Publishing, 1966.

Fiffer, Sharon, and Steve Fiffer, eds. In *Home: American Writers Remember Rooms of Their Own.* New York: Pantheon Books, 1995.

Fine, David, ed. *Los Angeles in Fiction: A Collection of Essays.* Albuquerque: University of New Mexico Press, 1995.

Fitch, Noel Riley. *Literary Cafés of Paris.* Washington, D.C.: Starrhill Press, 1989.

Fitzgerald, F. Scott. *Afternoon of an Author,* ed. Arthur Mizener. Princeton, N.J.: Princeton University Library, 1957.

———. *The Basil and Josephine Stories,* eds. Jackson R. Bryer and John Kuehl. New York: Popular Library, 1976.

———. *The Beautiful and Damned.* New York: Charles Scribner's Sons, 1950.

———. *The Crack-Up,* ed. Edmund Wilson. New York: New Directions, 1956.

———. *Flappers and Philosophers.* New York: Charles Scribner's Sons, 1920.

———. *The Great Gatsby.* New York: Charles Scribner's Sons, 1961.

———. *The Last Tycoon.* New York: Charles Scribner's Sons, 1941.

———. *The Pat Hobby Stories.* New York: Charles Scribner's Sons, 1962.

———. *Six Tales of the Jazz Age and Other Stories.* New York: Charles Scribner's Sons, 1960.

———. *Tales of the Jazz Age.* New York: Charles Scribner's Sons, 1922.

———. *Taps at Reveille.* New York: Charles Scribner's Sons, 1935.

———. *Tender Is the Night.* New York: Charles Scribner's Sons, 1962.

———. *This Side of Paradise.* New York: Charles Scribner's Sons, 1970.

———. *The Vegetable.* New York: Charles Scribner's Sons, 1976.

Flamini, Roland. *Thalberg: The Last Tycoon and the World of M-G-M.* New York: Crown Publisher, 1994.

Forster, E. M. *Howards End.* New York: Vintage Books, 1921.

Freud, Sigmund. *A General Introduction to Psychoanalysis.* New York: Pocket Books, 1971.

Frost, Robert. *The Poetry of Robert Frost.* New York: Holt, Rinehart and Winston, 1969.

Fryer, Sarah Beebe. *Fitzgerald's New Women: Harbingers of Change.* Ann Arbor, Mich.: UMI Research Press, 1988.

Gallo, Rose A. *F. Scott Fitzgerald.* New York: Frederick Ungar Publishing, 1978.

Gass, William H. *Fiction and the Figures of Life.* Boston: Nonpareil Books, 1989.

Gates, Robert A. *The New York Vision: Interpretation of New York City in the American Novels.* Lanham, Md.: University Press of America, 1987.

Gelfant, Blanche H. *The American City Novel.* Norman: University of Oklahoma Press, 1954.

Gelley, Alexander. "Setting and a Sense of World in the Novel." *Yale Review* 62 (winter 1973): 186-201..

Gilbert, Stuart. *James Joyce's Ulysses: A Study.* New York: Vintage Books, 1952.

Gill, Richard. *Happy Rural Seat.* New Haven, Conn.: Yale University Press, 1972.

Gindin, James. "Gods and Fathers in F. Scott Fitzgerald's Novels." In *F. Scott Fitzgerald,* ed. Harold Bloom. New York: Chelsea House Publishers, 1985.

Goldhurst, William. *F. Scott Fitzgerald and His Contemporaries.* Cleveland: World Publishing, 1963.

Good, Dorothy B. "'Romance and a Reading List': The Literary References in *This Side of Paradise.*" In *Fitzgerald/Hemingway Annual* (1976): 35-64.

Graham, Sheilah. *College One.* New York: Viking Press, 1967.

Gray, Stephen. "Sense of Place in the New Literatures in English, Particularly South Africa." In *A Sense of Place in the New Literatures in English,* ed. Peggy Nightingale. St. Lucia, N.Y.: University of Queensland Press, 1986.

Grenberg, Bruce L. "Fitzgerald's 'Figured Curtain': Personality and History in *Tender Is the Night.*" In *Critical Essays on F. Scott Fitzgerald's Tender Is the Night,* ed. Milton R. Stern. Boston: G. K. Hall, 1986.

Grill, Richard. *Happy Rural Seat.* New Haven, Conn.: Yale University Press, 1972.

Gross, Barry. "Back West: Time and Place in *The Great Gatsby,*" *Western American Literature* 8 (1973): 3-13.

Gross, Seymour L. "Fitzgerald's 'Babylon Revisited.'" *College English* 25 (November, 1963): 128-35.

Hamilton, Mary Agnes. "Where Are You Going My Pretty Maid?" *Atlantic Monthly* 138 (September 1926): 297-302.

Hardy, Thomas. *Jude the Obscure.* New York: Dell Publishing Co., Laurel Edition, 1959.

Hawthorne, Nathaniel. *The House of the Seven Gables.* New York: Bantam Books, 1981.

Hecht, Ben. *A Thousand and One Afternoons in Chicago.* New York: Covici-Friede, 1922.

Hemingway, Ernest. *A Moveable Feast.* New York: Bantam Books, 1970.

Hendriksen, Jack. *This Side of Paradise as a Bildungsroman.* New York: Peter Lang, 1993.

Henry, O. "The Defeat of the City." In *The Voices of the City.* Garden City, N.Y.: Doubleday, Page, 1919.

Higgins, John A. *F. Scott Fitzgerald: A Study of the Stories.* Jamaica, N.Y.: St. Johns University Press, 1971.

Hindus, Milton. *F. Scott Fitzgerald: An Introduction and Interpretation.* New York: Holt, Rinehart and Winston, 1968.

Hoffman, Frederick. "The Scene of Violence: Dostoevsky and Dreiser." *Modern Fiction Studies* 6, no. 2. (summer 1960): 91-105.

———. *The Great Gatsby: A Study*. New York: Charles Scribner's Sons, 1962.

———. *The 20's*. New York: Free Press, 1965.

Howe, Irving. "The City in Literature." *Commentary* 51, no. 5 (May 1971): 61-68.

Huonder, Eugen. *The Functional Significance of Setting in the Novels of Francis Scott Fitzgerald*. Bern: Herbert Lang; Frankfurt/M., Peter Lang, 1974.

James, Henry. *Roderick Hudson*. Boston: Houghton Mifflin, 1917.

Jameson, Frederic. *The Political Unconscious*. Ithaca, N.Y.: Cornell University Press, 1981.

Johnson, Bruce. *The Correspondence: A Phenomenology of Thomas Hardy's Novels*. Tallahassee, Fla.: University Press of Florida, 1983.

Joyce, James. *A Portrait of the Artist as a Young Man*. New York: Bedford Books of St. Martin's Press, 1993.

Kahn, Sy. "This Side of Paradise: The Pageantry of Disillusion." In *F. Scott Fitzgerald: Critical Assessment*, vol. 2. ed. Henry Claridge. Mountfield, East Sussex [England]: Helm Information, 1991.

Kazin, Alfred. *F. Scott Fitzgerald: The Man and His Work*. New York: Collier Books, 1951.

———. "The Writer and the City." *Harper's Magazine* 237 (December 1968): 110-27.

Kellman, Steven G. *The Self-begetting Novel*. London: Macmillan, 1980.

Keyes, Frances P. Foreword to *Home by the River* by Archibald Rutledge. New York: Bobbs-Merrill Company, 1955.

Kriegel, Leonard. "Geography Lessons." *Sewanee Review* 102 (autumn 1994): 604-11.

Kuehl, John. *F. Scott Fitzgerald: A Study of the Short Fiction*. Boston: Twayne, 1991.

———. ed. *The Apprentice Fiction of F. Scott Fitzgerald: 1909-1917*. New Brunswick, N.J.: Rutgers University Press, 1965.

Latham, Aaron. *Crazy Sundays: F. Scott Fitzgerald in Hollywood*. New York: Viking Press, 1971.

Lawrence, D. H. *Phoenix: The Posthumous Papers of D. H. Lawrence,* ed. Edward D. McDonald. London: W. Heinemann, 1961.

Le Vot, Andre. *F. Scott Fitzgerald: A Biography*. Trans. William Byron. Garden City, N.Y.: Doubleday, 1983.

Lee, A. Robert. *Scott Fitzgerald: The Promises of Life*. New York: St. Martin's Press, 1989.

Lehan, Richard D. *The Great Gatsby: The Limits of Wonders*. Boston: Twayne, 1990.

———. "The Los Angeles Novel and the Idea of the West." In *Los Angeles in Fiction: A Collection of Essays*, ed. David Fine. Albuquerque: University of New Mexico Press, 1995.

———. *F. Scott Fitzgerald and the Craft of Fiction*. Carbondale, Ill.: Southern Illinois University Press, 1969.

Lerner, Max. *America as a Civilization: Life and Thought in the United States Today*. New York: Simon & Schuster, 1957.

Lhamon, W. T., Jr., "The Essential Houses of *The Great Gatsby*." *Markham Review* 6 (spring 1977): 56-60.

Long, Robert E. *The Achieving of The Great Gatsby*. Lewisburg, Pa.: Bucknell University Press, 1979.

Lubbock, Percy. *The Craft of Fiction*. London: Jonathan Cape, 1954.

Lutwack, Leonard. *The Role of Place in Literature.* Syracuse, N.Y.: Syracuse University, 1984.

Lynch, Kevin. *The Image of the City.* Cambridge, Mass.: MIT Press, 1960.

Mangum, Bryant. *A Fortune Yet: Money in the Art of F. Scott Fitzgerald's Short Stories.* New York: Garland, 1991.

Marcus, Jane. "A Wildness of One's Own: Feminist Fantasy Novels of the Twenties." In *Women Writers and the City: Essays on Feminist Literary Criticism,* ed. Susan M. Squier. Knoxville: University of Tennessee Press, 1984.

Margusee, Mike, and Bill Harris, eds. *New York: An Anthology.* Boston: Little, Brown, 1985.

Mellard, James M. "Academia and the Wasteland: Bernard Malamud's *A New Life* and His View of the University." In *The American Writer and the University,* ed. Ben Siegel. Newark: University of Delaware Press, 1989.

Mellow, James R. *Invented Lives: F. Scott and Zelda Fitzgerald.* Boston: Houghton Mifflin, 1984.

Melville, Herman. *Pierre, or, The Ambiguities.* New York: Penguin Books, 1996.

Middleton, Catherine A. "Roots and Rootlessness: An Exploration of the Concept in the Life and Novels of George Eliot." In *Humanistic Geography and Literature,* ed. Douglas C. D. Pocock. New York: Barnes and Noble, 1981.

Milford, Nancy. *Zelda: A Biography.* New York: Harper and Row, 1970.

Miller, James E., Jr. *F. Scott Fitzgerald: His Art and His Technique.* New York: New York University Press, 1964.

Millgate, Michael. *American Social Fiction: James to Cozzens* (London: Oliver and Boyd, 1964).

Mizener, Arthur. *The Far Side of Paradise: A Biography of F. Scott Fitzgerald.* Boston: Houghton Mifflin, 1951.

Morace, Robert A., and Kathrya Vanspankeren, eds. *John Gardner: Critical Perspectives.* Carbondale, Ill.: Southern Illinois University Press, 1982.

Nagel, James. "Initiation and Intertextuality in the *Basil and Josephine Stories.*" In *New Essays on F. Scott Fitzgerald's Neglected Stories,* ed. Jackson Bryer. Columbia, M.O.: University of Missouri Press, 1996.

Nightingale, Peggy, ed. *A Sense of Place in the New Literatures in English.* St. Lucia, N.Y.: University of Queensland Press, 1987.

Oates, Joyce Carol. "Imaginary Cities: America." In *Literature and the Urban Experience: Essays on the City and Literature,* eds. Michael C. Jaye and Ann Watts. New Brunswick, N.J.: Rutgers University Press, 1981.

Oldenburg, Ray. *The Great Good Places.* New York: Paragon House, 1989.

Olson, Charles. *Call Me Ishmael.* San Francisco: City Lights Books, 1947.

Orlofsky, Michael. "The Power of Place." *Writer's Digest* 74, no. 10 (October 1994): 37-41.

Park, Robert. "The City: Suggestions for the Investigation of Human Behavior in the City Environment." *American Journal of Society* 20 (March 1915): 577-612.

Perkins, Maxwell. "Letter to Fitzgerald (November 20, 1924)." In *The Great Gatsby: A Study,* ed. Frederick Hoffman. New York: Charles Scribner's Sons, 1962.

Perosa, Sergio. *The Art of F. Scott Fitzgerald.* Trans. Charles Matz and the author. Ann Arbor, Mich.: University of Michigan Press, 1968.

Petry, Alice Hall. *Fitzgerald's Craft of Short Fiction: The Collected Stories—1920-1935.* Ann Arbor, Mich.: UMI Research Press, 1989.

Phillips, Gene D. *Fiction, Film, and F. Scott Fitzgerald.* Chicago: Loyola University Press, 1968.

Pike, Burton. *The Image of the City in Modern Literature.* Princeton, N.J.: Princeton University Press, 1981.

Piper, Henry Dan. *F. Scott Fitzgerald: A Critical Portrait.* New York: Holt, Rinehart and Winston, 1965.

Poe, Edgar Allan. *The Tell-Tale Heart and Other Writings.* New York: Bantam Books, 1982.

Pound, Ezra. *Selected Poems.* London: Faber and Faber, 1968.

Powdermaker, Hortense. *Hollywood: The Dream Factory.* Boston: Little, Brown, 1950.

Price, Martin, ed. *Dickens: A Collection of Critical Essays.* Englewood Cliffs, N.J.: Prentice-Hall, 1967.

Proctor, M. R. *The English University Novel.* Berkeley: University of California Press, 1957.

Raleigh, John. "The Novel and the City: England and America in the Nineteenth Century." *Victorian Studies* 11, no. 3 (March 1968): 291-328.

Ring, Frances Knoll. *Against the Current: As I Remember F. Scott Fitzgerald.* Berkeley, Calif.: Creative Arts, 1985.

Ringle, Fred J. *America As Americans See It.* New York: Literary Guild, 1932.

Ronald, Ann. *Functions of Setting in the Novel: From Mrs. Radcliffe to Charles Dickens.* New York: Arno Press, 1980.

Rosten, Leo C. *Hollywood: The Movie Colony, The Movie Makers.* New York: Arno Press and the New York Times, 1970.

Roulston, Robert, and Helen H. Roulston. *The Winding Road to West Egg: The Artistic Development of F. Scott Fitzgerald.* Lewisburg, Penn.: Bucknell University Press, 1995.

Rovit, Earl H. "The American Concept of Home." *The American Scholar* (autumn 1960): 521-30.

Schlack, Deborah D. *American Dream Visions: Chaucer's Surprising Influence on F. Scott Fitzgerald.* New York: Peter Long, 1994.

Scholes, Robert. *Approaches to the Novel: Materials for a Poetics.* San Francisco: Chandler Publishing, 1966.

Schorer, Mark. "Fitzgerald's Tragic Sense." In *F. Scott Fitzgerald: The Man and His Work,* ed. Alfred Kazin. New York: Collier Books, 1951.

Schulberg, Budd. *The Disenchanted.* New York: Random House, 1950.

Seiters, Dan. *Image Patterns in the Novels of F. Scott Fitzgerald.* Ann Arbor, Mich.: UMI Research Press, 1986.

Sherwood, Robert E. "The Blessed and the Cursed." In *America as Americans See It,* ed. Fred J. Ringle. New York: Literary Guild, 1932.

Shirer, William L. *20th Century Journey.* New York: Simon & Schuster, 1976.

Shorer, Mark. "Fitzgerald's Tragic Sense." In *F. Scott Fitzgerald: The Man and His Work,* ed. Alfred Kazin. New York: Collier Books, 1951.

Siegel, Ben, ed. *The American Writer and the University.* Newark: University of Delaware Press, 1989.

Sinzelle, Claude M. *The Geographical Background of the Early Works of D. H. Lawrence.* Paris: Etudes Anglaises, 1964.

Sklar, Robert. *F. Scott Fitzgerald: The Last Laocoon.* New York: Oxford University Press, 1967.

Smith, Henry Nash. "The Search for a Capitalist Hero: Businessmen in American Fiction." In *The Business Establishment,* ed. Earl F. Cheit. New York: John Wiley and Sons, 1964.

Smith, Scottie Fitzgerald, Matthew J. Bruccoli, and Joan P. Kerr, eds. *The Romantic Egotists: A Pictorial Autobiography from the Scrapbooks and Albums of F. Scott Fitzgerald and Zelda Fitzgerald.* New York: Charles Scribner's Sons, 1974.

Spatz, Jonas. *Hollywood in Fiction: Some Versions of the American Myth.* Paris: Mouton & Co., Printers, The Hague, 1969.

Spencer, Benjamin. "Fitzgerald and the American Ambivalence." *Southern Atlantic Quarterly* 66, no. 3 (summer 1967): 367-81.

Spengler, Oswald. *The Decline of the West.* New York: Knopf, 1962.

Squier, Susan M. *Women Writers and the City: Essays on Feminist Literary Criticism.* Knoxville: University of Tennessee Press, 1984.

Stein, Gertrude. *The Autobiography of Alice B. Toklas.* New York: Harcourt Brace Jovanovich, 1933.

Stern, Milton R. *Tender Is the Night: The Broken Universe.* New York: Twayne, 1994.

———, ed. *Critical Essays on F. Scott Fitzgerald's Tender Is the Night.* Boston: G. K. Hall, 1986.

Stevens, Wallace. *Opus Posthumous,* ed. Samuel French Morse. New York: Knopf, 1957.

Tate, Allen. *On the Limits of Poetry.* New York: Swallow Press, 1948.

Thomas, Bob. *Thalberg: Life and Legend.* Garden City, N.Y.: Doubleday, 1969.

Thorp, William, ed. *The Lives of Eighteen from Princeton.* Princeton, N.J.: Princeton University Press, 1946.

Tristram, Philippa. *Living Space in Fact and Fiction.* London: Routledge, 1989.

Turnbull, Andrew. ed. *The Letters of F. Scott Fitzgerald.* New York: Charles Scribner's Sons, 1963.

———, ed. *Scott Fitzgerald: Letters to His Daughter.* New York: Charles Scribner's Sons, 1965.

Washington, Bryan R. *The Politics of Exile: Ideology in Henry James, F. Scott Fitzgerald, and James Baldwin.* Boston: Northeastern University Press, 1995.

Way, Brian. *F. Scott Fitzgerald and the Art of Social Fiction.* New York: St. Martin's Press, 1980.

Wechsberg, Joseph. "The Viennese Coffee House: A Romantic Institution." *Gourmet* 26 (December 1966): 16, 90-99.

Wells, Walter. *Tycoons and Locusts: A Regional Look at Hollywood Fiction of the 1930s.* Urbana, Ill.: Southern Illinois University Press, 1973.

Welty, Eudora. *The Eye of the Story: Selected Essays and Reviews.* New York: Random House, 1978.

Wescott, Glenway. "The Moral of F. Scott Fitzgerald." In *F. Scott Fitzgerald: The Man and His Work,* ed. Alfred Kazin. New York: Collier Books, 1951.

West, James L. W. III., "Did F. Scott Fitzgerald Have the Right Publisher?" *Sewanee Review* 100, no. 4 (fall 1992): 644-56.

West, Nathanael. *Miss Lonelyhearts & The Day of the Locust.* New York: New Directions, 1969.

West, Suzanne. "Nicole's Gardens." In *Fitzgerald/Hemingway Annual 1978,* eds. Matthew J. Bruccoli, and Richard Layman. Detroit: Gale Research, 1978.

Williams, Raymond. *The Country and the City.* London: Chatto and Windus, 1973.

Wilson, Edmund, ed., *The Last Tycoon.* New York: Charles Scribner's Sons, 1941.

Winchell, Mark Royden. "Fantasy Seen." In *Los Angeles in Fiction: A Collection of Essays*, ed. David Fine. Albuquerque: University of New Mexico Press, 1995.

Wirth-Nesher, Hana. "The Modern Jewish Novel and the City: Franz Kafka, Henry Roth, and Amos Oz." *Modern Fiction Studies* 24, no. 1 (spring 1978): 91-109.

INDEX

Abrams, Charles, 127, 144n.37
Abrams, M. H., 10, 13n.26
"Academia and the Wasteland"
  (Mellard), 109n.27
The Achieving of The Great Gatsby
  (Long), 47n.44
Adams, Henry, 8, 81-82, 87-88,
  109n.13, 109n.16, 115
The Adventures of Huckleberry Finn
  (Twain), 81
After the Lost Generation (Aldridge),
  170n.1
Aldridge, John W., 147, 170n.1
Alger, Horatio, 33
Alice in Wonderland (Carroll), 51
Allen, Joan M., 167, 171n.29
America as Americans See It (Ringle
  editor), 171n.23
America as a Civilization (Lerner),
  171n.21
The American City Novel (Gelfant),
  111, 143n.1
American college novel, 83
"The American Concept of Home"
  (Rovit), 45n.3
The American dream, 39, 119, 148-50
  163, 166
American Dream Visions (Schlack),
  109n.32
American Journal of Society
  (periodical), 143n.9
*The American Novel in the Twentieth
  Century* (Donald), 47n.24

The American Scholar (periodical),
  45n.3
American Social Fiction (Millgate),
  165, 171n.27
*The American Writer and the
  University* (Siegel editor), 109n.27,
  110n.39
Anderson, Hilton, 37, 46n.28
Anderson, Sherwood, 93, 96, 103,
  109n.22, 112; "Departure," 96;
  George Willard, 93, 96, 112
Appleton, Victor, 153
Approaches to the Novel (Scholes),
  46n.32
Arden, Eugene, 118, 143n.16
Arnold, Aerol, 45, 47n.45
The Art of F. Scott Fitzgerald (Perosa),
  47n.42
As Ever, Scott Fitz— (Bruccoli editor),
  171n.9
Atlantic Monthly (periodical), 51,
  76n.4, 76n.6
Austen, Jane, 18
The Autobiography of Alice B. Toklas
  (Stein), 3, 12n.9

"Back West: Time and Place in *The
  Great Gatsby*" (B. Gross), 144n.46
Bailey, David W., 82, 108n.5
Bakhtin, Mikhail, 2, 12n.2, 13n.13
Balio, Tino, 170n.4
Bars, 49-50, 53; Biltmore bar, 50, 59;

Coconut Grove, 56, 59; Dingo Bar, 50; in Fitzgerald's fiction, 49, 54; in the 1920s, 51, 53; Knickerbocker Bar, 56, 58-59; Lethe, 56; Marathon, 63-66, 70-72; Ritz Bar, 54, 63, 70, 71-76; Sammy's, 63, 67-70, 74; Shanley's, 56, 58-59; and writers, 50; Yonkers, 59
Barthelme, Donald, 120, 144n.22
Beckett, Samuel, 84
Bellow, Saul, 84, 108, 118
Berman, Ronald, 145n.56
Bewley, Marius, 46n.25
The Big Money (Dos Passos), 162
Bildungsroman, 79-81, 108n.2, 108n.4
Biltmore Hotel, 17
Biographia Literaria (Coleridge), 13n.20
Bleak House (Dickens), 40
"The Blessed and the Cursed" (Sherwood), 171n.23
Bloom, Harold, 76n.12
Bode, Carl, 76n.3
The Bodley Head Scott Fitzgerald (Cowley editor), 76n.19, 76n.21, 108n.9, 145n.55, 171n.13
The Bostonians (James), 116
Bower, B. M., 153
Brontë, Charlotte, 4
Brooker-Bowers, Nancy, 171n.15
Bruccoli, Matthew J., 9, 13n.23, 46n.35, 47n.36, 76n.7, 76n.14, 76n.22, 77n.29, 77n.32, 108n.2, 109n.10, 109n.14, 109n.20, 109n.21, 144n.25, 144n.31, 144n.38, 145n.52, 171n.9, 172n.33
Bryer, Jackson, 109n.12, 109n.20
The Business Establishment (Cheit editor), 172n.34
Byron, William, 109n.15

Call Me Ishmael (Olson), 13n.18
Callahan, John F., 170, 172n.36
Camus, Albert, 53, 76n.10
Candles and Carnival Lights (Allen), 171n.29
Carter, John F., 51, 76n.6
Chase, Richard, 39
Cheit, Earl F., 172n.34

Cirino, Linda D., 143n.19
City: in America, 112, 115-17, 132-33; in Fitzgerald's fiction, 111, 116-18, 131-33, 139-43; as physical locale, 113, 132; as psychological emblem, 114, 132
The City as Catalyst (Festa-McCormick), 143n.7
"The City in Literature" (Howe), 144n.24
The City Is the Frontier (Abrams), 127, 144n.37
City Life (Barthelme), 144n.22
"The City: Suggestions for the Investigation of Human Behavior in the City Environment" (Park), 143n.9
Claridge, Henry, 144n.47
Cohen, Richard, 37, 46n.29
Coleridge, Samuel, 8, 13n.20
College English (periodical), 77n.31
Commentary (periodical), 144n.24
Confessions (Rousseau), 81
Conrad, Joseph, 6, 8
Cooper, James Fenimore, 6-7, 39, 155; Natty Bumppo, 7, 39
The Correspondence (Johnson), 109n.26
Correspondence of F. Scott Fitzgerald (Bruccoli/Duggan editors), 108n.2
The Country and the City (R. Williams), 144n.42
Cowley, Malcom, 2, 12n.4, , 76n.19, 76n.21, 84, 108n.9, 145n.55, 171n.13
Cowper, William, 116, 143n.14
The Craft of Fiction (Lubbock), 46n.33
Crane, Stephen, 50
Critical Essays on F. Scott Fitzgerald's Tender Is the Night (Stern editor), 77n.27

Dardis, Tom, 150, 171n.8
Darwinism, 163
da Verrazano, Giovanni, 118
David Copperfield (Dickens), 81
Davis, Lennard J., 4, 13n.11
The Day of the Locust (West), 150, 153, 162, 171n.26

Deamer, Robert G., 39, 46n.30
de Balzac, Honoré, 6, 20, 39, 112, 131,
    139; Eugène de Rastignac, 112
The Decline of the West (Spengler),
    145n.51
Defoe, Daniel, 4, 30
Depression, 3, 69, 130-31, 147
de Toqueville, 112
*Dickens: A Collection of Critical
    Essays* (Price editor), 13n.29
Dickens, Charles, 4, 11, 40, 50, 81, 84,
    112-16, 120, 130, 142, 143n.10,
    144n.43, 145n.54, 156
"Did F. Scott Fitzgerald Have the Right
    Publisher?" (J. West), 110n.38
The Disenchanted (Schulberg),
    172n.35
Donald, Miles, 33, 46n.24
Donaldson, Scott, 60, 76n.13, 109n.28,
    109n.31
Dostoevsky, F. M., 131, 132
Dostoevsky and Romantic Realism
    (Fanger), 144n.50
Dos Passos, John, 6, 120, 131, 137,
    144n.21, 148, 155-56, 162-63,
    170n.3
Dreiser, Theodore, 9, 50, 53, 103, 112,
    115-16, 120, 132, 137, 168; Sister
    Carrie, 112
Dublin, 114
The Dubliners (Joyce), 103
Duggan, Margaret M., 108n.2

Eble, Kenneth, 86, 109n.11
The Eccentric Design (Bewley), 46n.25
Eclognes (Virgil), 113
Edel, Leon, 45n.2
Edmiston, Susan, 143n.19
The Education of Henry Adams
    (Adams), 81-82, 87, 109n.13,
    109n.16, 115
Eliot, George, 13n.16, 18, 143n.11
Eliot, T. S., 8, 13n.19, 113, 131, 141
Emerson: Essays and Lectures (Porte
    editor), 13n.14
Emerson, Ralph Waldo, 5-7, 13n.14,
    29, 46n.16; "Character," 5; "Nature,"
    29, 46n.16; "The Young American,"
    7

The English University Novel (Proctor),
    82, 108n.3
Entwicklungsroman, 79, 81, 108
Erziehungsroman, 79
Esquire (periodical), 154
The Essays of George Eliot (Pinney
    editor), 143n.11
"The Essential Houses of *The Great
    Gatsby*" (Lhamon), 46n.27
Exile's Return (Cowley), 12n.4
The Eye of the Story (Welty), 13n.12

F. Scott Fitzgerald (Bloom editor),
    76n.12
F. Scott Fitzgerald (Eble), 109n.11
F. Scott Fitzgerald (Gallo), 46n.11
F. Scott Fitzgerald: A Biography (Le
    Vot), 109n.15, 110n.37
*F. Scott Fitzgerald and the Craft of
    Fiction* (Lehan), 45n.10
F. Scott Fitzgerald: A Critical Portrait
    (Piper), 45n.7, 171n.19
*F. Scott Fitzgerald: Critical
    Assessments* (Claridge editor),
    144n.47
*F. Scott Fitzgerald: His Art and His
    Technique* (Miller), 145n.53
F. Scott Fitzgerald in His Own Time
    (Bruccoli/Bryer editors), 109n.20
F. Scott Fitzgerald: The Last Laocoon
    (Sklar), 170n.7
F. Scott Fitzgerald: A Life in Letters
    (Bruccoli), 9, 13n.23, 172n.33
*F. Scott Fitzgerald: The Man and His
    Work* (Kazin editor), 12n.6
Fanger, Donald, 144n.50
"Fantasy Seen" (Winchell), 171n.32
The Far Side of Paradise (Mizener),
    13n.24, 47n.39, 71n.20
Faulkner, William, 6, 8, 39, 150-51
Festa-McCormick, Diana, 113, 143n.7
Fiction, Film, and F. Scott Fitzgerald
    (Phillips), 171n.25
Fiction and the Figures of Life (Gass),
    46n.23
"Fiction and the Film Industry"
    (Brooker-Bowers), 171n.15
Fielding, Henry, 112; Tom Jones, 112
Fieldler, Leslie A., 44, 47n.43

Fiffer, Sharon and Steve, 45n.4
Fine, David, 171n.28, 171n.32
Finney, Mr. and Mrs., 152
Fitch, Noel R., 53, 76n.11
Fitzgerald, F. Scott: adolescence, 87-
    88; an avid reader, 112; childhood,
    17, 86; critical assessment of, 3;
    death, 153; drinking, 52-54, 62;
    education, 85-88, 94, 101-02; and
    Ginevra King, 21; and Henry
    Adams, 81-82 ; in Hollywood, 17,
    147-49, 151-53; in New York, 17,
    119; parents of, 89; and Princeton,
    101-8; and Sheila Graham, 17; view
    of city life, 113; view of Hollywood,
    148; view of home, 16-18, 39; view
    of New York, 119-120; view of
    setting, 2, 4, 8-9, 11; works, novels:
Afternoon of an Author, 94, 97-98,
    104-5, 108, 109n.19, 109n.35;
The Beautiful and Damned, 6, 10,
    18-29, 52, 63-69, 71, 118, 123-
    24, 127, 132-33, 136, 140, 152;
    Gloria Gilbert, 21-29, 63-67;
    Anthony Patch, 18, 20-30, 63-69,
    123-24, 129; his apartments and
    houses, 20, 23-26; his drinking,
    67;
The Crack-Up, 51-52, 106, 109n.34,
    123, 144n.27, 162, 170n.3;
The Great Gatsby, 4-5, 10-11, 18,
    30-39, 117-19, 124-29, 133-42;
    Tom Buchanan's house, 44-45,
    121; Tom Buchanan and Daisy
    Buchanan, 31-34, 37-39; Tom
    Buchanan and Gatsby, 37-39,
    136-37; Nick Carraway, 32-39,
    128-29; Nick Carraway's house,
    37; Dan Cody, 33-34, 138; "East
    Egg" and "West Egg", 11, 38,
    126, 133-34, 141; Gatsby, 30-39,
    124-25; Gatsby's dream, 34-35,
    39; Gatsby's mansion, 16, 30-32,
    36, 39; Gatsby as a myth, 31, 35;
    Gatsby's party, 36, 39; tragedy,
    39; Myrtle Wilson, 31; Myrtle
    Wilson's apartment, 43-45, 119,
    139; Meyer Wolfshiem, 33, 34,
    71, 138;

The Last Tycoon, 6, 10, 42, 148,
    153-70; Brady, 164; Cecilia,
    148, 164; Kathleen, 168;
    Reinmund, 161; Stahr, 42, 166-
    68; Stahr as an artist, 169;
    Starhr as a businessman, 168;
    Stahr as a dreamer, 166-8;
    Stahr's home, 42;
The Ledger, 52, 76n.7, 85,
    87, 100, 109n.10, 109n.14;
The Pat Hobby Stories, 152-64; Pat
    Hobby, 159-60; Basil Lee Duke,
    85, 87-89, 91-100, 104-8,
    127;
Six Tales of the Jazz Age, 47n.40;
Tales of the Jazz Age, 41, 47n.41,
    121;
Taps at Reveille, 87-89, 92, 96, 97,
    104, 106, 125-27;
Tender Is the Night, 10, 40-41, 69,
    73-74, 137, 151-52; Abe North,
    69, 72-73, 120; Diver, 41-42;
    Nicole's garden, 40;
This Side of Paradise, 2-3, 10, 54-
    60, 63, 79-93, 98-108, 108n.2,
    108n.4, 116, 1218-19, 121-24,
    132, 138-39; Amory, 54-60,
    89-91, 99-108, 122, 126; Amory
    as an egoist, 92; Amory's
    drinking, 56-59; Monsignor
    Darcy, 89-90, 94, 102; Sigourney
    Fay, 8, 82, 89; Rosalind, 54-59;
The Vegetable, 142, 151, 171n.12;
works, stories:
"An Alcoholic Case," 62;
"Babylon Revisited," 53, 62, 69, 74-
    76; Charlie Wales, 74-76;
"Basil and Cleopatra," 99-100, 104;
"Boil Some Water—Lots of It,"
    157-59;
"The Bridal Party," 63, 70-76;
"Crazy Sunday," 152, 170;
"The Curious Case of Benjamin
    Button," 83;
"The Diamond as Big as the Ritz,"
    151, 174n.13;
"Family in the Wind," 62;
"Forging Ahead," 94, 98-99, 127;
"The Freshest Boy," 87, 104, 127

"He Thinks He's Wonderful," 91, 103;
"Jacob's Ladder," 152;
"The Jelly-Bean," 41;
"Jemina," 42;
"The Lees of Happiness," 42;
"Lipstick," 83;
"The Lost Decade," 62;
"Magnetism," 152;
"Majesty," 125;
"May Day," 83, 118, 121-22, 128;
"More than Just a House," 42;
"Mr. Icky," 42;
"My Lost City," 122, 142;
"The Mystery of the Raymond Mortgage," 86;
"A New Leaf," 61;
"A Night at the Fair," 87;
"One Trip Abroad," 60;
"Pat Hobby's Secret," 160;
"The Pearl and the Fur," 128;
"The Perfect Life," 127;
"Princeton," 105;
"Reade: Substitute Right Half," 102;
"The Rich Boy," 83, 118, 127;
"The Scandal Detectives," 95, 103;
"The Sensible Thing," 83;
"What I Think and Feel at 25," 93;
"Who's Who--and Why," 85, 94-95;
"Winter Dreams," 141
Fitzgerald, Zelda Sayre, 17, 21, 119, 153
"Fitzgerald and the American Ambivalence" (Spencer), 12n.7
Fitzgerald and the Art of Social Fiction (Way), 171n.20
Fitzgerald and His Contemporaries (Goldhurst), 109n.29
Fitzgerald/Hemingway Annual (Bruccoli/Layman), 46n.35, 108n.6
"Fitzgerald's 'Babylon Revisited'" (S. Gross), 77n.31
"Fitzgerald's 'Figured Curtain'" (Grenberg), 77n.27
"Fitzgerald's Tragic Sense" (Schorer), 13n.22
Flamini, Roland, 171n.30
Flaubert, Gustave, 39

Fool for Love: F. Scott Fitzgerald (Donaldson), 76n.13, 109n.28, 109n.31
Forster, E. M., 29, 46n.15
French Riviera, 9
Freud, Sigmund, 29, 46n.14
"From the Wasteland to East Egg" (Anderson), 46n.28
Frost, Robert, 16, 45n.5; "Death of the Hired Man", 16
The Functional Significance of Setting in the Novels of Francis Scott Fitzgerald (Huonder), 12, 46n.20
Functions of Setting in the Novel (Ronald), 143n.3

Gallo, Rose A., 45n.11
Gardener, John, 84
Gass, William H., 32, 46n.23
Gates, Robert A., 130, 144n.41
Gelfant, Blanche H., 111, 143n.1
Gelley, Alexander, 1, 12n.1
A General Introduction to Psychoanalysis (Freud), 46n.14
The Geographical Background of the Early Works of D. H. Lawrence (Sinzelle), 45n.8
"Geography Lessons" (Kriegel), 13n.21
Geroud, Gordon H., 101
Gilbert, Stuart, 115, 143n.13
Gill, Richard, 18, 45n.9
Gindin, James, 54, 76n.12
"Gods and Fathers in F. Scott Fitzgerald's Novels" (Gindin), 76n.12
Goethe, J. W., 80-81
Goldhurst, William, 101, 109n.29
Golding, William, 84
Good, Dorothy B., 108n.6
Goodwin, Donald, 52
Gourmet (periodical), 76n.2
Graham, Sheilah, 17, 153
Gray, Stephen, 3, 13n.10
The Great Gatsby: The Limits of Wonders (Lehan), 46n.26
The Great Gatsby and Modern Times (Berman), 145n.56
The Great Gatsby: A Study (Hoffman editor), 46n.17, 46n.19

The Great Good Places (Oldenburg), 76n.1
Grenberg, Bruce L., 73, 77n.27
Gross, Barry, 134, 144n.46
Gross, Seymour L., 75, 77n.31
Gurgannus, Allan, 16, 45n.4

Hamilton, Mary A., 51, 76n.4
A Happy Death (Camus), 76n.10
Happy Rural Seat (Gill), 45n.9
Hardy, Thomas, 96-97, 112; Jude, 96-97, 109n.25, 112
Harper's Magazine (periodical), 143n.20
Harris, Bill, 143n.17, 144n.23
Harvard University, 19, 83, 88, 106
Harvard Crimson (periodical), 82, 108n.5
Hawthorne, Nathaniel, 4, 7, 16, 45n.6; Hester Prynne, 7
Hecht, Ben, 111, 143n.2
Heller, Joseph, 108
Hemingway, Ernest, 39, 50, 53, 69, 76n.9
Hendriksen, Jack, 90, 108n.4, 109n.18
Henry, O., 117, 143n.15; "The Defeat of the City", 117
Hibben, John Grier, 107
Hoffman, Frederick, 30, 46n.17, 46n.19, 76n.5, 132, 144n.44
Hollywood, 10, 147, 149-50, 154-70; as dreamland, 152-63; in fiction, 148; as industry, 157-58, 162; in *The Last Tycoon*, 6, 10
"Hollywood" (Balio), 170n.4
Hollywood: The Dream Factory (Powdermaker), 170n.6
Hollywood: The Movie Colony, the Movie Makers (Rosten), 170n.2, 170n.5, 171n.22
Hollywood in Fiction (Spatz), 171n.24
Home: definition, 15; in literature, 15-16; metaphor, 18; as mirror of the mind, 29-30; as motif of personality, 39-45
Home: American Writers Remember Rooms of their Own (Fiffer eds.), 16, 45n.4

Home by the River (Rutledge), 15, 45n.1
Hope of Heaven (O'Hara), 153
The House of the Seven Gables (Hawthorne), 16, 45n.6
Howard, Richard, 76n.10
Howards End (Forster), 29, 46n.15
Howe, Irving, 121, 144n.24
Howells, William D., 168
Hugo, Victor, 121
Humanistic Geography and Literature (Pocok editor), 13n.16
Huonder, Eugen, 11, 30, 46n.20
The Hudson Review (periodical), 46n.29

The Illusions of a Nation (Callahan), 172n.36
The Image of the City (Lynch), 129, 145n.4, 144n.39
Image Patterns in the Novels of F. Scott Fitzgerald (Seiters), 46n.12
"Imaginary Cities: America" (Oates), 144n.40
The Importance of Place in the American Literature of Hawthorne, Thoreau, Crane, Adams, and Faulkner (Deamer), 46n.30
In the American Grain (Williams), 10
"The Inessential Houses of *The Great Gatsby*" (Cohen), 46n.29
"Initiation and Intertextuality in *The Basil and Josephine Stories*" (Nagel), 109n.12
Iswolsky, Helene, 12n.2
Ivy League, 80, 81, 83-84, 88, 100

James, Henry, 8, 10, 13n.27, 15, 45n.2 50, 116, 121
James Joyce's Ulysses (Gilbert), 143n13
Jameson, Frederic, 6, 13n.17
Jaye, Michael C., 144n.40
The Jazz Age, 3, 29, 50-51, 72-73, 101, 112, 118, 121, 130-31, 142-43,
John Gardner: Critical Perspectives (Morace/Vanspankeren editors), 108n.7
Johnson, Bruce, 97, 109n.26

Jolas, Eugene, 52
Joyce, James, 4, 8, 16, 81, 84, 102, 112, 114-16, 120, 143n.12; Stephen Dedalus, 112; Leopold Bloom, 115
Jude, the Obscure (Hardy), 96, 109n.25

Kahn, Sy, 144n.47
Kazin, Alfred, 52, 119, 126, 143n.20, 144n.36; "The Writer and the City," 126, 143n.20, 144n.36
Keats, John, 21
Kellman, Steven G., 108n.8
Kermonde, Frank, 13n.19
Kerr, Joan P., 109n.21
Keyes, Frances P., 15, 45n.1
King, Ginevra, 21
Kriegel, Leonard, 8, 13n.21

Lawrence, D. H., 10, 13n.25, 17, 81
Leatherstocking Tales (Cooper), 6
Le Père Goriot (Balzac), 20
Le Vot, Andre, 105, 109n.15, 110n.37
Lee, A. Robert, 31, 46n.22
Lehan, Richard D., 19, 33, 45n.10, 46n.26, 166, 171n.28
Lerner, Max, 157, 171n.21
Les Misérables (Hugo), 121
Lessing, Doris, 84
The Letters of F. Scott Fitzgerald (Turnbull editor), 12n.8, 46n.18, 77n.28, 108n.1, 109n.17, 109n.30, 171n.11, 171n.14, 171n.16
Lewis, Sinclair, 132, 168
Lhamon, W. T., Jr., 46n.27
Literary Cafés of Paris (Fitch), 53-54, 76n.11
Literary New York (Edmiston/Cirino editors), 119, 143n.19
Literature and the Urban Experience (Jaye/Watts editors), 144n.40
Literature-Film Quarterly (periodical), 171n.15
Litfauer, Kenneth, 167
Little Boy Blue (theatrical production), 123
The Lives of Eighteen from Princeton (Thorp editor), 12n.5, 110n.36
Living Space in Fact and Fiction (Tristram), 46n.13

London, 11, 112-14
London, Jack, 168
Long Island, 9
Long, Robert E., 45, 47n.44
Los Angeles in Fiction (Fine editor), 171n.28, 171n.32
"The Los Angeles Novel and the Idea of the West" (Lehan), 171n.28
Lost Generation, 3, 73
Love and Death in American Novel (Fiedler), 47n.43
Lowell, James Russell, 112
Lubbock, Percy, 39, 46n.33
Lutwack, Leonard, 39, 46n.34
Lynch, Kevin, 129, 144n.39

McDonald, Edward D., 13n.25
Mackenzie, Compton, 8, 81-82, 90, 103, 108n.4
Malamud, Bernard, 100, 108
Manhattan Transfer (Dos Passos), 119-20, 131-32
Marcus, Jane, 144n.45
Margusee, Mike, 143n.17, 144n.23
The Markham Review (periodical), 46n.27
Master Humphery's Clock (Dickens), 130, 144n.43
Matz, Charles, 47n.42
Maugham, Somerset, 81
Mellard, James M., 100, 109n.27
Melville, Herman, 4, 7, 139, 144n.48, Ishmael, 7
Mencken, H. L., 50
Middleton, Catherine A., 6, 13n.16
Miller, Henry, 84
Miller, James E. Jr., 142, 145n.53
Millgate, Michael, 165, 171n.27
The Mirror and the Lamp (Abrams), 13n.26
Miss Lonelyhearts (West), 131, 141
MIT (Massachusetts Institute of Technology), 83
Mizener, Arthur, 13n.5, 13n.24, 42, 47n.39, 71n.20, 93, 109n.19
Modern Fiction Studies (periodical), 143n.5, 144n.44
"The Modern Jewish Novel and the City" (Wirth-Nesher), 143n.5

Moll Flanders (Defoe), 4
Monison, Arthur, 131
"The Moral of F. Scott Fitzgerald"
    (Wescott), 12n.6
Morace, Robert A., 108n.7
Morse, Samuel F., 13n.15
A Moveable Feast (Hemingway), 53,
    76n.9

Nagle, James, 86, 109n.12
Nassau Literary Magazine (periodical),
    101
National Review (periodical), 144n.21
"The Natural History of German Life"
    (G. Eliot), 143n.11
*New Essays on F. Scott Fitzgerald's
    Neglected Stories*
    (Bryer editor), 109n.12
A New Life (Malamud), 100
New Republic (periodical), 108n.8
New York: An Anthology
    (Margusee/Harris editors), 143n.17,
    144n.23
New York City, 10-11, 19, 111-12,
    117-42, 147; in Fitzgerald's fiction,
    121-32; in literature, 119-21
The New York Novel (Arden), 143n.16
The New York Vision (Gates), 144n.41
"Nicole's Gardens" (S. West), 46n.35
Nightingale, Peggy, 13n.10
"A Note on Fitzgerald" (Dos Passos),
    173n.3
"A Novel about Flappers for
    Philosophers" (Bailey), 108n.5
"The Novel and the City" (Raleigh),
    143n.6

Oates, Joyce Carol, 109, 132, 144n.40
Ober, Harold, 153, 171n.9
Of Human Bondage (Maugham), 81
Of Time and the River (Wolfe), 131
O'Hara, John, 10, 155
Oldenburg, Ray, 50, 76n.1
Olson, Charles, 7, 13n.18
On the Limits of Poetry (Tate), 46n.31
O'Neill, Eugene, 161
Orlofsky, Michael, 11, 13n.28
Opus Posthumous (Stevens), 13n.15

Our Mutual Friend (Dickens), 145,
    145n.54

Parable, 1-3
Paris, 143
Paris Tribune (periodical), 53
Park, Robert, 143n.9
Pater, Walter, 15
Pendennis (Thackeray), 81
Perkins, Maxwell, 30, 82, 46n.17
Perosa, Sergio, 44, 47n.42
The Phantom Herd (Bower), 155
Phillips, Gene D., 164, 171n.25
Phoenix (Lawrence), 13n.25
"Picture, Scene, and Social Comment"
    (Arnold), 47n.45
Pierre (Melville), 142, 144n.48
Pike, Burton, 114, 143n.4
Pinney, Thomas, 143n.11
Piper, Henry Dan, 17, 45n.7, 157,
    171n.19
Pocok, Douglas C. D., 13n.16
Poe, Edgar Allan, 16, 43, 125, 144n.29;
    "The Fall of the House Usher", 16,
    43; "To Helen", 125
"The Poet of Borrowed Time"
    (Mizener), 12n.5
The Poetry of Robert Frost (Frost),
    45n.5
The Political Unconscious (Jameson),
    6, 13n.17
The Politics of Exile (Washington),
    46n.21, 144n,30
Porte, Joe, 13n.14
A Portrait of the Artist as a Young Man
    (Joyce), 81, 114-16, 143n.12
Pound, Ezra, 124, 144n.28
"The Power of Place" (Orlofsky),
    13n.28
Powdermaker, Hortense, 151, 170n.6
The Prelude (Wordsworth), 81
Price, Martin, 11, 13n.29
Princetonian (periodical), 104
Princeton University, 10-11, 52, 80, 82,
    84-86, 94-96, 100-9, 119; Glee Club,
    94, 101; Triangle Club, 94, 103, 106
Problems of Dostoevsky's Poetics
    (Bakhtin), 13n.13
Proctor, M. R., 82, 108n.3

Prohibition, 52, 57
Proust, Marcel, 8

The Quaker Girl (theatrical
    production), 125

Rabelais, 2
Rabelais and His World (Bakhtin),
    12n.2
Radcliffe, Ann, 18
Raleigh, John, 114, 143n.6
Resisting Novels (Davis), 13n.11
Ringle, Fred J., 171n.23
Robinson Crusoe (Defoe), 4
Roderick Hudson (James), 11, 13n.27
The Role of Place in Literature
    (Lutwack), 46n.34
"Romance and a Reading List" (Good),
    108n.6
The Romantic Egotists
    (Smith/Bruccoli/Kerr editors),
    109n.21
Ronald, Ann, 114, 143n.3
"Roots and Rootlessness" (Middleton),
    13n.16
Rosten, Leo C., 149, 170n.2, 170n.5,
    171n.22
Roth, Philip, 109
Rotsel, R. W., 13n.13
Roulston, Helen H., 109n.33
Roulston, Robert, 109n.33
Rousseau, Jean-Jacques, 81
Rovit, Earl H., 15, 45n.3
Rutledge, Archibald, 15, 45n.1

"The Scene of Violence" (Hoffman),
    144n.44
Schlack, Deborah D., 101, 109n.32
Scholes, Robert, 46n.32
School: as the cradle of the elite, 79;
    life in, 80; in literature, 79-81;
    Newman News (periodical), 86;
    Newman School, 84, 87-88, 90-91,
    102, 109, 119; St. Paul Academy,
    84-85, 88, 91, 101; *St. Paul Academy
    Now and Then* (periodical), 86, 102;
    St. Regis, 88-89, 91-95, 98, 127
Schorer, Mark, 9, 13n.22
Schulberg, Budd, 153-54, 169, 172n.35

Scott Fitzgerald: The Promises of Life
    (Lee), 46n.22
Scott, Sir Walter, 4, 6
Scribner, Charles III, 171n.12
"The Search for a Capitalist Hero"
    (Smith), 172n.34
Seiters, Dan, 46n.12
Selected Poems (Pound), 144n.28
Selected Prose of T. S. Eliot
    (Kermonde editor), 13n.19
Selections from Ralph Waldo Emerson
    (Whicher editor), 43n.16
The Self-begetting Novel (Kellman),
    108n.8
*A Sense of Place in the New Literatures
    in English* (Nightingale editor),
    13n.10
"Sense of Place in the New Literatures
    in English, Particularly South
    Africa" (Gray), 13n.10
Setting, 1, 3-6; in American Literature,
    7-8; as a state of mind, 10; as
    symbols, 11
"Setting and a Sense of World in the
    Novel" (Gelley), 12n.1
Sewanee Review (periodical), 13n.21,
    110n.38
Shawcross, John, 13n.20
Sherwood, Robert E., 160, 171n.23
Shirer, William L., 52, 76n.8
*The Short Stories of F. Scott
    Fitzgerald: A New Collection*
    (Bruccoli editor), 48n.36, 76n.14,
    76n.22, 77n.29, 77n.32, 144n.25,
    144n.31, 144n.38, 145n.52
Siegel, Ben, 109n.27, 110n.39
Sinclair, Upton, 132
Sinister Street (Mackenzie), 81-82,
Sinzelle, Claude M., 45n.8
Sister Carrie (Dreiser), 53, 115-16
Sketches of Boz (Dickens), 143n.10
Sklar, Robert, 150, 170n.7
Smith, Henry N., 7, 172n.34
Smith, Scottie Fitzgerald, 100, 109n.21
Some Time in the Sun (Dardis), 171n.8
Sons and Lovers (Lawrence), 81
The South Atlantic Quarterly
    (periodical), 12n.7
Southey, Robert, 143n.14

Spatz, Jonas, 161, 171n.24
Spencer, Benjamin, 2, 12n.7
Spengler, Oswald, 139, 145n.51
The Spoils of Poynton (James), 45n.2
Squier, Susan, 113, 143n.8, 144n.45
Stein, Gertrude, 3, 12n.9, 73
Stern, Milton R., 77n.27
Stevens, Wallace, 5, 13n.15

Tarkington, Booth, 8
Tate, Allen, 39, 46n.31
*The Tell-Tale Heart and Other
    Writings* (Poe), 144n.29
Thackeray, William, 16, 112
Thalberg, Irving, 152, 167
*Thalberg: The Last Tycoon and the
    World of M-G-M* (Flamini), 171n.30
Thalberg: Life and Legend (Thomas),
    171n.31.
"These Wide Young People" (Carter),
    76n.6
"*This Side of Paradise*: The Pageantry
    of Disillusion" (Kahn), 144n.47
*This Side of Paradise as a
    Bildungsroman* (Hendriksen),
    109n.18
Thomas, Bob, 171n.31
Thoreau, Henry David, 39
Thorp, William, 13n.5, 110n.36
*A Thousand and One Afternoons in
    Chicago* (Hecht), 111, 143n.2
Thurber, James, 52
Tom Swift and His Wizard Camera
    (Appleton), 153
Town Tattle (periodical), 44
"Tradition and the Individual Talent"
    (Eliot), 13n.19
Tristram, Philippa, 28, 46n.13
The Tropic of Cancer (Miller), 84
Trotsky, Leon, 118
Turnbull, Andrew, 8, 12n.8, 46n.18,
    77n.28, 108n.1, 109n.17, 109n.30,
    171n.11, 171n.14, 171n.16
Twain, Mark, 4, 39, 81, 93; Huck Finn,
    7, 39, 93
The 20's (Hoffman), 76n.5
20th Century Journey (Shirer), 76n.8
Tycoons and Locusts (W. Wells),
    171n.18

Ulysses (Joyce), 5-6, 114-16
UNESCO Courier (periodical), 170n.4
*The University of Mississippi Studies in
    English* (periodical), 46n.28
The University Review (periodical),
    47n.45
U.S.A. (Dos Passos), 6

Vanity Fair (Thackeray), 16
Vanspankeren, Kathrya, 108n.7
Victorian Studies (periodical), 143n.6
"The Viennese Coffee House"
    (Wechsberg), 76n.2
Virgil, 113
Virgin Land (Smith), 7
The Voice of the City (O. Henry),
    143n.15

Walden (Thoreau), 39
Washington, Bryan R., 31, 46n.21, 123,
    144n.30
The Waste Land (Eliot), 8, 141
Watts, Ann, 144n.40
Watts, Ian, 112
Way, Brian, 156, 171n.20
Wharton, Edith, 8
*Webster's Third International
    Dictionary*, 15
Wechsberg, Joseph, 50, 76n.2
Wells, H. G., 4, 8
Wells, Walter, 171n.18
Welty, Eudora, 4, 13n.12
Wescott, Glenway, 12n.6
West, James L. W. III, 107, 110n.38
West, Nathanael, 131, 141, 150, 153,
    162, 171n.26
West, Suzanne, 46n.35
Western American Literature
    (periodical), 144n.46
"What Makes a Novelist" (Dos
    Passos), 144n.21
What Makes Sammy Run (Schulberg),
    153
"Where Are You Going My Pretty
    Maid?" (Hamilton), 76n.4
Whicher, Stephen E., 46n.16
"A Wildness of One's Own" (Marcus),
    144n.45
Wilhelm Meister (Goethe), 80

Williams, Raymond, 130, 144n.42
Williams, William Carlos, 10
Wilson, Edmund, 3, 106, 153, 170n.3,
171n.17
Winchell, Mark R., 167, 171n.32
The Winding Road to West Egg
(Roulston/Roulston editors), 109n.33
Winesburg, Ohio (Anderson), 103,
109n.22
Wirth-Nesher, Hana, 112, 143n.5
Wolfe, Thomas, 84, 120, 131
Women Writers and the City (Squier),
143n.8, 144n.45

Wordsworth, William, 81
The Works of William Cowper
(Southey editor), 143n.14
World War I, 50, 81
Writer's Digest (periodical), 13n.28

Yale Review (periodical), 12n.1
Yale University, 83, 95, 97-98, 107
Yoknapatawpha County, 6
The Young Mencken (Bode), 76n.3
Youth's Encounter (Mackenzie), 81-82

Zola, Emile, 50, 131

About the Author

AIPING ZHANG is Assistant Professor of English at California State University at Chico. He has published articles on Mark Twain and F. Scott Fitzgerald, and contributed to anthologies and reference books. Zhang currently teaches courses in American literature and multiculturalism.

ISBN 0-313-30238-3

90000>

EAN

9 780313 302381

HARDCOVER BAR CODE